P9-DFB-486

NEW ZEALAND
RUGBY
SKILLS & TACTICS

Produced with the advice and assistance of the New Zealand Rugby
Football Union and its Coaching Committee
Technical Editor: Ivan Vodanovich
Graphics Editor: Peter Coates
Assistant Technical Editor: Hamish Fletcher

Published by Lansdowne Press — a division of Rigby International
Limited
26 Customs Street
Auckland, New Zealand
© Lansdowne Press
First published 1982

Typeset in New Zealand by Linoset Services Limited
Printed in New Zealand by Woolmore Printing Limited
10-12 Charles Street, Auckland
Bound by Trade Ruling and Binding Company (1975) Limited
43A Linwood Avenue, Auckland
ISBN 0 86866 064 7

Design and Art Direction: Leonard Cobb
Graphics Illustrator: Graeme Gash

Acknowledgements

To the many participants in this project who could not be
individually mentioned, a special thanks for their valuable
assistance and encouragement.

The authors and the publisher wish to thank the major
photographic contributors: Peter Bush, *Auckland Star*,
Christchurch Press, Evening Post, NZ Herald & Weekly News.
Our appreciation extends also to Moa Publications for
assistance in compiling biographies.

We are grateful to Mrs R. A. Jarden and to the publisher for
permission to use the material in the chapter, 'Beating the
Man', from the late Ron Jarden's book, *Rugby on Attack*
(Whitcombe & Tombs, 1961).

Editors Note: The Laws of the game of Rugby Football
are revised regularly. It was to be
expected that some new experimental
Laws introduced about this time would
be firmly adopted eventually.
Subsequent reprints of this book would
update these revisions as they become
internationally accepted.

NEW ZEALAND
RUGBY
SKILLS & TACTICS

Ivan Vodanovich
Technical Editor
Peter Coates
Graphics Editor

Lansdowne Press
Auckland Sydney London New York

Foreword

From the rough country paddock with its manuka goal posts to the well-trimmed fields of major playing grounds, rugby football has become the sporting passion of a great many New Zealanders. It is an amateur sport — anyone can play, and does! As a national pastime it has proved to be perhaps the strongest social bond bringing together, in camaraderie and appreciation of skill, all sorts of people in all sorts of places. The rugby ball has even been kicked by New Zealanders at Scott Base in the Antarctic.

A dynamic sport, rugby is constantly undergoing changes as laws are refined, styles streamlined and methods improved. In compiling the material for this book the authors contribute to this development and continue a tradition that has grown with a country. For all concerned with playing rugby and playing it well, *New Zealand Rugby, Skills and Tactics* provides a comprehensive guide to current rugby playing.

The official history of rugby in New Zealand began over 100 years ago when the Nelson Football Club adopted Rugby Football laws in 1870 at the suggestion of Charles Monro who had recently learned the game in England — according to one historian, "an event of much significance and one which was to have a great impact on the lives of future generations of New Zealanders . . ."

The first match was played at Nelson in 1870 between the Nelson Club and Nelson College where Monro had also introduced the game. In enthusiastic succession other rugby football clubs were formed, Wellington being the first to follow Nelson in 1871. By 1890 there were 700 active clubs and 16 major unions, although survival of these clubs was often threatened by a still largely itinerant population. By the turn of the century, however, rugby was firmly established.

Fledgling rugby in New Zealand was rather unorthodox — a curious mix of inconsistent laws, local lore and variation, and arbitrary team numbers and playing times. A 40-a-side team with play lasting two or three hours, if not days, was not uncommon. Colourfully named teams were often born in the lively talk of the public bar. Rugby seemed to suit this sturdy nation characterised by an independent and indomitable spirit; it appealed to the rugged and determined nature of a people looking for an identity. And rugby thrived, despite the occasional protest at the 'rough and tumble'. During these formative years teething troubles were inevitable. Tradition was challenged but the controversies and the new ideas and interpretations all helped to shape the vital game that rugby is today.

In 1882 the first overseas team played in New Zealand — from the Southern Rugby Union of New South Wales. Two years later the visit was returned by the first New Zealand rugby team to play overseas. Internationally New Zealand's reputation began with the successful year-long 1888-89 tour of Britain by the Native Team — a team originally intended to be a Maori one, it did, however, include four European players. In 1910 the New Zealand Maori Team was given official status and over the years the Maori contribution to rugby has been outstanding. As a result Maori identity has been strengthened and national life has been enriched by an interracial contact that had previously not existed. In 1905 the New Zealand team ('The Originals') touring Britain was inadvertently (a printer's error) called the All Blacks, a name that stuck and that has become synonymous with first-class rugby.

The strong appeal that rugby has had for New Zealanders extended even to the war years when it was a welcome diversion, a morale booster and a link with home. Between the battles and the tragedies New Zealand soldiers overseas during both World Wars played rugby. War-time conditions proved no deterrent and matches were as well organised as during peace time.

Russ Thomas has been a member of the Canterbury Rugby Union for twenty-two years and is past president of the same. He is Chairman of the Victory Park (Lancaster Park) Board of Control, and a Director of the NZ Sports Federation. Selected as manager of the 1978 All Blacks against Australia in NZ, and the 1979 team against France in NZ. As honorary manager he toured with the 1978 All Blacks to England and again in 1979 to England, Scotland and Italy. Represented Canterbury in junior and senior reserve representative sides. Played rugby for Christchurch Boys' High OB.

Since the 1950s rugby in New Zealand has been confronted with many crises that have threatened the basic nature of the game. Amongst these was a new gladiatorial determination to win at all costs — an attitude that risked losing the respect and support that rugby had previously enjoyed. Players and coaches no less than the public expressed their distress at the disagreeable aspects of contemporary play. More recently rugby has faced perhaps its greatest difficulties during controversial tours. It may be that especially in such tense and confusing times the major challenge is to hang on to that bold independence that characterised the early New Zealand spirit and epitomises fine rugby.

Rugby today still inspires that earlier hardy spirit. Aspiring eight-year-olds and seasoned players alike experience an exhilaration in pitting their skills against the opposition, in trying their strength and stamina on the field — in battling for mastery in scrum, maul or ruck, watching the ball travel lightning fast along the backline, scoring tries, winning and, sometimes losing. Regardless of adverse weather Saturday after Saturday these dedicated 'indefatigables' run out on to the field.

Considering the extensive club involvement from the pre-season training days of early February through to the final presentation of trophies in October, it is not difficult to see the fervour that rugby engenders in so many for at least nine months of every year, whether at school, club, provincial or international level. Behind these players functions the invaluable support network of team managers, coaches, club administrators and, not least of all, team supporters and club members, including the sometimes unsung heroines and heroes — the mums and dads. Club commitments inevitably increase and that so many local clubs have met these challenges is a tribute both to their administrators and to the participation of club associates. This vast army of voluntary workers is an essential part of modern rugby both in New Zealand and overseas. As with any major business enterprise the success of rugby depends absolutely on promotion and public relations — aspects which are vital in ensuring that rugby continues to motivate enthusiasm and remains an exciting and worthwhile sport.

The Promotions and Public Relations Committee recommends this book as an invaluable text for players, coaches and all lovers of rugby football.

Russ Thomas
Member NZRFU Council
Chairman Promotions and Public Relations Committee NZRFU

Contents

Introduction

Often it has been said that rugby is a simple game, as indeed it is if the players have the basic skills required. Nevertheless, to have knowledge and experience and to be able to pass them on effectively to young people are entirely different matters.

One of the difficulties is that although many books and pamphlets have been written about various aspects of rugby football, there are few authoritative books that cover the whole range of rugby skills.

The need for such a reference book is considerable, if only because many people who would be willing to assist with the coaching of teams — particularly at the school or junior levels — have been reluctant to take up the task because they feel inadequate as regards technical knowledge. As a result of the coaching structure established a few years ago in New Zealand, however, it is hoped that this tentative attitude has been reduced in this country.

NZ Rugby Skills and Tactics seeks to remedy the deficiency in reference books. It has been produced in a format that is both attractive and, more importantly, easily understood.

The contents encompass many areas of rugby, and the authors have been selected because of their personal experience in the subject of their contribution. It could never be contended that the views expressed in this book are the 'only way'. They will, however, repay careful study because they have proved effective and should therefore be regarded as a basis that can be used wholesale, built on, or adapted to meet specific requirements.

Above all it is necessary for players and coaches to think about the game constantly. Although the principles may not have changed, there is always something to be learnt about rugby football and this is particularly true of individuals.

In this regard, *NZ Rugby Skills and Tactics* should be a useful guide to discussions on the technical aspects of the game and an inspiration to implement these ideas on the field.

C. A. BLAZEY

Chairman
N.Z. RUGBY FOOTBALL UNION

Rugby at Eden Park, Auckland

NZURFC 1936 to 1969, Chairman 1945 to 1967, Life Member.
NZRFU Executive since 1957, Chairman since 1977.
International Rugby Football Board Member since 1967,
Chairman 1965 and 1972. International Laws Committee since
1972.
Played senior club rugby for the University Club, Christchurch
1927, 1928, and 1931 to 1934.
OBE.

Bob Stuart on

Coaching in New Zealand

- To maximise his or her effectiveness the coach must keep abreast of current practices in rugby: technique and tactics being the main areas of revision.
- The coach must also pay attention to the innovations in conditioning and sports medicine.
- Changes, however, do not mean the abandonment of basic skills and tactics, rather an augmentation.
- The dictatorial approach to coaching has been replaced by a more positive and constructive interpersonal style of coaching.
- The successful and respected coach will be certain of the team's objectives, be thoroughly conversant with all aspects of rugby, be a sensitive analyst, a competent organiser, and an imaginative teacher.

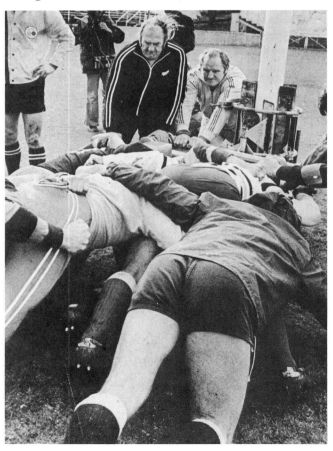

J. J. Stewart (in black) and Wilson Whineray supervise during a coaching session at a scrum machine.
Auckland Star

For many decades New Zealand rugby was condemned for its concentration — indeed, reliance — on coaching. We were accused, incorrectly, of having coaches all from the same mould, and this was reflected in stereotyped play at all levels.

Like most generalisations, there may have been some truth in this criticism, but in no way was it the whole truth. Uniformity if any was confined to a region, and techniques, attitudes and styles varied considerably. Many coaches introduced fresh approaches, displayed initiative, imagination and a flair to produce a brand of rugby — more often than not, winning rugby — attractive to both player and spectator, based on sound fundamentals.

It is ironical to reflect that despite the earlier accusations of 'overcoaching' in New Zealand, organised coaching is now the 'in thing' in those very countries given in the past to criticising the role of a coach in this country.

Paradoxically, when coaching was being accepted overseas as an acceptable component of the game, the New Zealand Rugby Football Union was taking a long, hard look at its own system. And what was seen was not encouraging.

In simple terms, far from being overcoached, New Zealand rugby was suffering from coaching that was not organised at any level, coaching of an indifferent and uneven quality, unco-ordinated, and immune from new ideas, changing trends and needs. What was being done by many enthusiastic and dedicated coaches was by instinct and hearsay — and all credit to them.

By far the most serious symptom was the apparent failure to grasp the significance of change — changes in the laws of the game, in patterns of play, in education and, above all, in the attitudes of the young to learning techniques and the use of leisure.

The associated skills of coaching were handed down on a father-to-son basis. Thus, coaches inherited as gospel an ingrained approach and attitude, and through no fault of their own were insulated from change. The concept of being coached or trained as a coach was foreign — what was good enough in the past was good enough in the present, and in the forseeable future.

The position was developing also where coaches lacked status. Clubs themselves expanded in numbers and affluence, the social base of activities was broadened, but little thought was given to the *selection, training, retention* and *recognition* of coaches — except perhaps the coach of the senior team. It was all very casual, and the conduct of practices was left to the individual coach, who usually adopted a standardised, predictable and, most times, boring format.

The position in the majority of schools had changed dramatically to the extent that these very nurseries of rugby could no longer be taken for granted.

Still, the game flourished, though there were disquieting

A fine loose foward and particularly admired as an outstanding captain. A provincial player with Manawatu 1941 (St. Patrick's OB); Canterbury 1946-53 (University) and captain from 1950; South Island 1948, 49. Played in NZ Trials 1948, 50, 53; NZ Universities 1946, 48, as captain 1949, 51; New Zealand XV 1953; NZ Services 1943; Represented NZ 1949, 53, 54. At 32 he captained the 1953-54 All Blacks on tours to Britain and France. Canterbury selector 1958, 59. Co-opted All Blacks Coach 1956. NZRFU executive member since 1974 and NZ rep on the International Board since 1978. Awarded OBE.

features emerging: the wastage rate in critical age groups was increasing, and 'winds of change' affecting the game were largely ignored. At the same time, an increasing number of coaches, clubs and unions were demanding assistance to cope with changes that were suspected of having a major impact on the game and attitudes of players.

Coaches, and those responsible for ensuring that coaches are kept up to date, must learn to identify changes on a continuing basis and adjust for the ultimate benefit of all concerned. There are three main areas of change: *technical*, *tactical*, and *sociological* — and all have, or can have, a profound influence on the game, and on coaching attitudes and techniques.

Technical and tactical changes

Changes in techniques and tactics have their origins mainly in changes in the laws of the game and imaginative new approaches by leading coaches and players — also in sheer necessity. They include:

- New techniques of scrummaging
- New or amended laws or new interpretations of laws affecting:
   Line-out skills and drills
   The tackled ball and the tackle
   Off-side laws
   Kick into touch
- The vastly improved opportunities for imaginative and effective back play and ploys
- An expanded role for the full-back
- A game that is more free flowing — or should be
- A greater emphasis on the attractive features of the game, and in particular the acquisition of knowledge and technical skills
- The emergence of a more scientific approach to physical conditioning and sports medicine

In many respects, a combination of the above changes in recent years, has opened up literally a 'whole new ball game'. In my opinion, new laws and improved coaching techniques have enhanced — contrary to many others' opinions — the traditional New Zealand driving forward game, and provided back lines with opportunities undreamt of a few years ago.

For some coaches, these changes herald a radical departure from the traditional approach; for others, more prudent in outlook, the development of new skills and ploys are superimposed on traditional, well-tried basic skills and tactics.

Changes do not imply any diminution of the basic individual skills, and it would be fair to claim that in the absence of these skills, present-day rugby can be untidy and scrambling in the extreme. All the law changes imaginable will not counter a negative approach to the game and sloppy techniques.

Nor do new technical and tactical skills in any way eliminate the need for proper physical conditioning and fitness. In fact, this facet of rugby has become more demanding, if for no other reason than because of changes in lifestyles.

Sociological change

Coaching is bound up with human interrelationships, and is an exercise in communication and man-management. The Rev. Brother E. Willets, a former coach at the National School for Promising Players, insisted that there is no infallible way of coaching — no two coaches were the same — but if they were to be successful there were two things they must have in common: 'an understanding of their players and what they are looking for in rugby, and the ability to impart an approach to the game that will satisfy those aspirations.

'This means that the old domineering, dictatorial attitude is outdated. It might bring short-term results, but the primary aim of coaching is not so much to win cups, competitions and matches (though one must play rugby to win) but rather "to enable young men to find rugby a stimulating and satisfying recreation and to foster an abiding affection for the game".'

Thus, coaching must be attractive and fulfilling to each individual; it must be demonstrated that it is a game worth playing — a physical and intellectual challenge.

In the light of the foregoing changes, the New Zealand Rugby Football Union in the early 1970s recognised the increasing responsibilities being imposed on a coach at any level of rugby, and in particular, junior levels. It was recognised too, that coaches were amateurs, volunteers, enthusiastic, busy and operating under a number of limiting factors outside their control.

Before designing, implementing and promoting a long-term remedial programme, the National Coaching Committee looked at the aims and principles of coaching, the application of the principles, and the qualities of a coach.

Aims of coaching

These aims of coaching can be summarised as helping players to:
- obtain maximum satisfaction and enjoyment from the game, in matches, practices and other related training
- thoroughly understand the game
- develop a positive approach, and recognise the need for team work

Principles of coaching

If the coach is conversant with the technical knowledge and skills, he or she must then understand learning procedures and how players — as a team and as individuals — are motivated.

The coach must bring an organised approach to this task, first by identifying clearly its aims and objectives, and then by developing measures to meet these. (The alternative is a disorganised approach — 'playing it by ear'.)

A coach must learn to be an analyst by observing objectively what is happening — he or she must learn to analyse a match, a movement, and identify a player's actions and reactions and be informed as to appropriate remedial measures.

Applying the principles

A major challenge to coaches is in the conduct of practice sessions. In the final analysis, coaches are judged by players not on how much knowledge they possess but on their ability to impart that knowledge. This means the ability to instruct in the technical skills; to translate theory into practice in the tactical area; and to motivate, to relate to players, to be accepted and respected.

Qualities of a coach

Having abandoned any dictatorial approach, a good coach adopts and maintains a set of ethical standards for himself and a set of behavioural standards for his team. He must be professional in his knowledge of and attitude to players, and his own standard of behaviour must be exemplary at all times.

A coach today will not be respected simply because he is a coach — he must *earn* that respect. Thus he must himself be prepared to continue learning, to maintain always a lively curiosity about the game, its changes, challenges and rewards. To achieve the respect his position warrants, he must, among other things:

- Be interesting and informed to the best of his personality and ability
- Satisfy players' desire to analyse, explore and create
- Have an imaginative approach to practice sessions, team talks and discussions
- Permit time for discussion and learn to be a good listener
- Be organised

Coach Bill Freeman with forwards of Christchurch's Albion team — 'an exercise in communication and man-management'.
Christchurch Press

- Be prepared to learn to maintain a high level of competence

This does *not* mean that a coach needs to abdicate either authority or responsibilities — nor does it mean abandonment of the hard repetitive drilling, the need to instil discipline, or the encouragement of the physical fitness so necessary to the acquisition of technical skills.

If a coach can achieve meaningful co-operation, this will then have been made possible because players are enjoying themselves and find all aspects of rugby stimulating. And the people who count most in rugby are the players.

A major aim of coaching is to demonstrate that rugby is a game worth playing: 'a physical and intellectual challenge'. A major challenge for the New Zealand rugby unions each year is who will carry off the Ranfurly Shield, the most-coveted trophy of inter-provincial rugby since the Earl of Ranfurly presented it in 1902.
Peter Bush

All Black Andy Leslie (second from left) was one of the players lending a hand at a coaching school held at Petone in 1976.

Peter Bush

Father John Weir on

Motivation

- **A player should be involved in the game at the appropriate level and should be encouraged to develop skills and proceed further in the game.**
- **Members must be treated as individuals. The coach must take an interest in them, correct any weaknesses they may have and be aware of their playing problems.**
- **Good communication develops the understanding required by all members to produce the maximum team efficiency on the field.**
- **The coach should be flexible and be prepared to accept suggestions that lead to better play and greater enjoyment for the players on the field.**
- **The coach must have the respect of the players and will attain this by free and reasoned discussion on methods and tactics — tactics which, accepted by the team, will lead to concerted and whole-hearted effort during the match.**

England and New Zealand take the field. Only teams that are properly motivated 'are capable of making a supreme effort and playing to the absolute limit of their strength and ability'. All Black Captain Tane Norton, England Captain Fran Cotton, at Eden Park.
Peter Bush

Even if players know and practise all the skills described in this book, they will not achieve the success they are capable of unless they are well motivated. While the ability to motivate others is to some extent a gift, any coach can become a successful motivator if certain important principles are kept in mind.

For example, the coach must allow players to play at an appropriate level; confront them with a challenge they can meet. You can't expect them to be highly motivated when they've been misgraded.

It is important, too, to recognise the particular skills and abilities each player has, to commend them for these and to suggest how they can be further developed. This will promote a high degree of personal motivation. At the same time the coach must be determined enought to prevent anyone's selfishness overriding the good of the team. Out of loyalty, a player must conform to a team's pattern of play, although both coach and team must be aware of and allow scope for the outstanding individual.

Following from this, as coach you should take a personal interest in the special needs of all your players. You should be concerned about their health, for example, and knowledgeable about it, too. Don't insist that they train or play when they are ill, injured or unwilling. Players can scarcely be well motivated if they believe that they shouldn't be playing.

Be realistic in your expectations. You should recognise that rugby is a game, a leisurely activity. Don't make unreasonable demands on your players. Don't make the winning of a game appear to be a matter of life or death. Don't make practices tedious or uninteresting. Don't neglect or overlook any of your players — even difficult ones. Take an interest in them. Don't become highly emotional in your team talks. Don't harangue the players and don't (ever) advocate violence.

It is essential, also, to foster comradeship among the team members. Not only should you take a personal interest in your players, but each of them should take a similar interest in one another. In effect you are building a small, closely knit community. You can encourage this by means of a friendly word or enquiry, by showing interest in their other activities, by arranging celebrations — socials, birthdays and so on. All this will draw the members of a team together and result in much greater on-field dedication and loyalty. Fundamentally, you should make each player feel appreciated and needed.

Sharing decision-making

The degree of motivation of any team depends considerably on clear communication within the team. Team policy can be arrived at through consultation with the players regarding the team's aims for the season, its overall strategy and its particular tactics. Having established these aspects early in the season, and having reviewed their effectiveness from time to time, the players should be highly motivated as a result of helping to formulate the very principles by which their team operates. While it is especially important for the coach to establish an understanding with the captain who is, after all, a key communicator and motivator within the team, it is also worthwhile to involve as many players as possible in

Has taught at college and university levels and has successfully coached secondary school teams, up to and at 1st XV level, as well as club under-age teams. Currently Rector of St Patrick's College, Wellington.

the team's administration — as vice captain, pack leader, members of a social committee — so that everyone develops an extended interest in the affairs of their team.

As coach you must learn also to consider your players' suggestions seriously even though these ideas may not prove practical or profitable. You may find that you are able to provide the players with germinal thoughts which they then develop themselves as recommendations. You must be prepared to learn from your players.

Like any mentor be positive. Emphasise the aspects the team is to concentrate on if it is to succeed. Don't lament the team's weaknesses, or create needless anxiety about the strength of the opposition. Challenge your players to perform their rugby skills to optimum level; make such challenges an essential part of your motivation efforts. Besides being positive, you must be honest. Answer questions; don't sidestep them. Above all, don't be afraid to praise your players individually and those elements of the team's play which deserve praise. After a match, congratulate your players and thank them for their efforts — particularly when they have lost. Keep any negative after-match criticism to yourself, until the next practice when you can express it more calmly, more positively and more constructively.

Love of rugby is a 'natural' inheritance of New Zealanders, and enjoyment of the game through proper motivation is as important to players as it is to these followers whose spirits at least are undampened.
Evening Post

Interpersonal relationships

Keep in mind the diversity amongst individuals and teams. Each player is different and should be treated differently — an approach that will work with one may not be successful with another. You must know your players as persons first, and only then can you motivate them as members of a team. Not only is each player different temperamentally, but each team, too, differs and your coaching should take this into account. As a coach you must be open to diversity and individuality.

This flexibility should also extend to your attitude to the season's draw. If you put the pressure on at some practices and not at others, if you approach some matches more nonchalantly than others, then you should be able to demand from your players concerted effort when the need for it arises. In other words, you will be able to motivate them for the crucial matches.

No one can substitute for the coach as a motivator. He knows his players and their capabilities. If players are confident of the coach's ability as a coach — his knowledge of rugby skills, his ability to plan a game, the effort he makes in preparing his team — and if they trust him and respond to him as a person, then they are capable of making a conscientious effort and of playing at optimum strength and ability. That, after all, is 'providing motivation'.

Barry Hislop on

Training Programmes

- **Regular progressive training enables the body to achieve the optimum fitness level.**
- **Warm-up and stretching exercises must precede any strenuous training; a wind-down after training is also essential – both to prevent excessive strain or injury.**
- **Sensible diet should be an important aspect of any training programme.**
- **Regular fitness testing provides the coach with a basis for individual and team analysis and improvement.**

In any training programme certain principles apply to help you achieve your ultimate aim. To be able to apply the skills under stress — that is, during a match — the following discussion will assist you in training and in achieving maximum efficiency.

Overload

In order to accomplish body conditioning and peak physical fitness, the body must do more work than it does normally. In exercise programmes, overload is accomplished in two principal ways:
- by progressively increasing the total work (for example, you run further)
- by progressively increasing the total work rate (for example, you run faster)

Progression

Adaptation is a function of stress — a certain intensity and duration of stress will produce the corresponding adaptation. This concept is the key to understanding the changes in body function brought on by jogging/running. Too much of this particular stress will produce a breakdown — a natural response to excessive stress and itself a form of adaptation.

The principle of progression is to apply stress to your body gradually and slowly. The body is a wonderful mechanism and given the chance it will adapt.

Regularity

To adapt to stress, the body must have stress placed upon it at regular intervals. Research tells us that a minimum of three sessions a week (with a day's rest in between) is required for adaptation.

Work/rest concept

The body needs to recover from stress before it is ready to readapt. In the early stages, a day in between runs is ideal until you have built up to 5-6 kilometres. Also it is not so time-consuming, and this will help you keep your motivation high. It is a myth that you have to train every day (though maybe if you were training for a marathon you would need to train four or five days a week).

Monitoring the heart

Train, don't strain. Too much stress will cause a breakdown.

Progressive training will lower your pulse rate. Learn to take your pulse — your basal pulse (that is, the resting pulse) should be taken as soon as you wake up — as it can be an accurate guide to the success of your training routine. The carotid artery in the neck is probably the easiest to monitor.

A slower pulse means that your heart is becoming stronger and more powerful. In fact, what is happening then is that your heart is pumping a large volume of blood each beat, thus becoming a more economical pump.

Warm-up and stretching

It is recommended that you set aside some time for a gradual warm-up before any strenuous effort. Stretching exercises are essential to avoid later strains and sprains.

Take every joint through the full range of movement — this will allow connective muscles to stretch to the maximum length.
- The arm joint is a ball and socket joint and to obtain full benefit the arm exercise should include a circled action forwards and backwards, raised outwards upwards and rotated, the arm remaining outstretched and the palm facing down.
- The spine is a little more limited. Movements should be forwards, sideways, backwards — the upper torso rotating in each direction. When leaning forward bend knees slightly to reduce strain on the lower back.
- The hip and upper leg joint is the same structure as the arm joint. To get full benefit it is better to lie on your back and work each leg separately, moving it in a cycling motion.
- Knee and ankle joints are primarily hinge joints and should be flexed and extended through their full range of movement. Although the feet comprise many moveable joints these movements are limited. Nevertheless they need to be extended through their full movement. From a sitting position circle each foot separately, to the left then to the right.
- Statically stretch the hamstring muscle group by sitting on the floor, reaching towards your toes and holding the position.
- Lean against the wall and force back on the calf muscles. Jog out slowly, then go at your training pace.

Don't be overly ambitious — 15 minutes should be sufficient for the average person.

Began playing rugby in Hawke's Bay (Central Hawke's Bay 1st XV, Central Hawke's Bay College 1960-63); senior rugby for Navy, (Auckland) 1964-72. Coached 6th grade. Physical trainer Waitemata Rugby Club 1972-78 and Auckland Representative Squad 1977-80. Consultant Auckland Coaching Scheme. As sports medicine adviser in conditioning, he travels throughout NZ, coaching schools. During the past 10 years has tested over 4000 rugby players from North Auckland to Timaru. Currently he is Physical Director of the Masterton YMCA.

Static stretching exercises before and after jogging

To minimise the chances of injury or soreness, the following exercises should be done before and after running. If you find the exercises difficult to perform, you may want to do them twice when warming up to increase flexibility. Stretch slowly and do not bounce to attain prescribed positions.

Achilles tendon and calf stretcher
Stand facing the wall approximately 70 cm away. Lean forward and place palms of hands flat against wall. Keep back straight, heels firmly on the floor, and slowly bend elbows to hands, and tuck hips toward wall. Hold position for 30 seconds. Repeat exercise with knees slightly flexed.

Thigh stretcher
Stand arms length from wall with left side toward wall. Place left hand on wall for support. Grasp right ankle with right hand and pull foot back and up until heel touches buttocks. Lean forward from waist as you lift. Hold for 30 seconds. Repeat exercise with opposite hand and foot.

Back stretcher
Lie on back with legs straight and arms at side with palms down. Slowly lift legs, hips and lower part of back and attempt to touch toes to floor behind head. Keep legs straight and hold position for 30 seconds.

Hurdler's stretch
Sit on floor with one leg extended straight ahead. Upper part of other leg should be at right angles to the body, with heel close to buttocks. Slowly slide hands down extended leg and touch foot. Hold position for 30 seconds. Keeping legs in same position, slowly lean back and rest elbows on floor. Hold for 30 seconds. Reverse position and repeat both stages of exercise.

On the field

Jog around the field four times. Start at one end of the field and jog up to the 22 metre line then stride out at three-quarter pace, relaxing the arms, and at the other 22 metre line jog down. Turn around and repeat the routine, covering in this way four lengths of the field. Then walk back to the half-way mark. Do a legs-bend at the 10 metre line, then move faster and jog back. Repeat nine times over 10 metres. Lie on your back, do some back-arches, sit-ups, jumping exercises, press-ups and stretches. Now you are ready to play.

Warming up for a trial, 1960's. From left: Graham Williams, Brian Lochore, Colin Meads, Jack Hazlett, Mac Herewini, Ian McRae, Lyn Davis, Alan Sutherland.
Evening Post

Leapfrogging, South Africa 1970. From left: Grahame Thorne, Wayne Cottrell, Buff Milner, Colin Meads, Tom Lister (bending), Bruce McLeod.

Cooling off

If you stop moving after you have completed your run, your blood will pool in the legs and this could make you feel dizzy and nauseated. Therefore keep moving after your run, at least at walking pace. If you are exhausted walk around for five minutes and then lie down with your feet supported about half a metre off the ground.

Your lower leg muscles help pump the blood back to your heart by the squeezing action of muscle contractions. A system of one-way valves normally prevents the return of blood downwards. However, after exercise the valves will be overtaxed and without the squeezing action of the muscles the blood tends to pool in the legs.

Remember that many injuries can occur if players do not have a cool-down period as well as a stretching and warm-up period.

Diet

Don't become obsessed with diet. Be sensible about eating habits: a balanced diet is quite adequate for your purposes. If you want to lose weight, cut down on your overall calorie intake.

Before you run make sure that you have eaten something at least one hour before. Blood sugar levels alter throughout the day and night — after a night's sleep your blood sugar level falls dramatically, logically, because you haven't ingested any food for eight to ten hours. A quick way to boost this low level is to have a hot drink with plenty of sugar.

Testing fitness

There are several tests that can be applied to gain a general team fitness profile. The purpose of these tests is to create a comprehensive statistical picture of the players' physical fitness, which can then be used to measure progress and to adjust the conditioning programme for each individual player. Regular testing should follow in order to study the improvement in the team as the remedial suggestions outlined are carried out. The fitness appraisal should include cardio-vascular function, muscular endurance, muscular strength, and body mobility and skill.

The tests that follow are those undertaken a couple of years ago by 20 members of the senior team of the Cornwall Rugby Club, just before the start of the season. When the results were compared with the standard, they gave the coaches and players a clear picture of their general fitness.

These tests would be more purposeful if done prior to pre-season training and again just before the competition. Then coaches would have a clearer picture of progress. The tests also provide standards of what programme adjustments can be made for each individual during the fitness build-up.

Endurance

Dr K. D. Cooper's 12-minute walk/run test is a measure of general endurance (aerobic capacity). At the starting signal each player runs for 12 minutes at his own pace. The aim is to cover as much distance as possible. This is recorded to the nearest metre. The standards are as follows:

Excellent	3520 m (2.2 miles)
Very good	3040 m (1.8 miles)
Good	2640 m (1.6 miles)
Fair	2200 m (1.4 miles)

Specific conditioning can markedly improve jumping performance in line-outs.
Auckland Star

The average distances covered by members of the Cornwall Rugby senior team were:

Team average	2626 m
Forwards	2607 m
Backs	2655 m

The results showed that many players needed to improve their cardio-vascular capacity and therefore their endurance.

Speed

The YMCA Sports Conditioning Centre 45 metre Sprint Test is a measure of speed over distance. The aim for each player is to run from a standing start and cover the measured distance as fast as possible. The results are recorded to the nearest tenth of a second. The standards are as follows:

Excellent	6.5 sec
Very good	6.9 sec
Average	7.4 sec
Fair	7.8 sec

Cornwall Seniors

Team average	6.9 sec
Forwards	7.0 sec
Backs	6.73 sec

In general the team average was very good. The recommendation was that to enhance this speed each player should adhere to the endurance programme advised.

Explosive strength

Squat, (Sargent), jumps are a test of explosive strength related to backs (for immediate explosiveness from inert standing) and forwards (during line-outs etc). The aim is to jump upwards as high as possible. The standards are as follows:

Excellent	762 mm
Very good	660 mm
Average	558 mm
Fair	482 mm

Cornwall Seniors

Team average	574 mm
Forwards	552 mm
Backs	606 mm

Many players can improve their performance by explosive exercises — either weight training or circuit training.

Grip test

For determining overall body strength. The test instrument is a hand dynamometer which measures the force of the hand's muscular contraction. The instrument is held in one hand, then squeezed as tightly as possible with the hand and arm extended away from the body. The standards are as follows:

Excellent	71
Very good	63
Average	56
Fair	53

Cornwall Seniors

	Right	Left
Team average	59.7	57.7
Forwards	58.3	56.8
Backs	61.8	59.3

In both hands the forwards' average score was below the team average. Many of the forwards needed to concentrate on development of the arm/shoulder — this strength is a major requirement in their game (for example, in mauls and scrums).

In addition, as a test of muscular endurance and strength of the arm and shoulder region, press-ups can be timed over 30 seconds with the following standards:

Excellent	32
Very good	29
Average	25
Fair	21

A player who tends to be a lazy strider has to learn to increase knee lift in front and pushing out through the back. Speed can be increased by improving technique in running.
Rand Daily Mail

Leg and back strength

The test instrument is a leg dynamometer which measures the force of the leg and the strength of the player's back. The subject stands on the dynamometer base with feet apart, head up, back straight, and then bends the knees. The handle is hooked into the chain so that the subject's knees are flexed at an angle of between 115 and 125°. The bar will be on the thigh during the lift, hands placed in the middle or outside of the bar. The subject lifts straight up. At the completion of the lift the knee joints should be almost completely extended to ensure maximum effort. The standards are as follows:

Excellent	280 kg
Very good	240 kg
Average	200 kg
Fair	160 kg

Cornwall Seniors

Team average	199.6
Forwards	197.2
Backs	203.3

As in the grip test, the backs proved stronger — a result quite the reverse of what might have been expected.

Sit-ups

This is a measure of strength and endurance for the abdominal muscles. The standards, timed over 30 seconds, are as follows:

Excellent	30
Very good	26
Average	22
Fair	19

Cornwall Seniors

Team average	22.6
Forwards	21.7
Backs	23.9

The results of these tests provide a general fitness profile for each individual. For individual players in any team the results will vary according to the player's position, the specific job required, and their attitude.

The comparison tests do, however, give an indication of the levels other players have reached. For example, the forwards tend to score better in strength tests, which is a major requirement for their game.

To encourage better fitness in your team, even healthy competition among players, the coach could maintain fitness charts to show week-by-week development of the fitness profiles.

I suggest that at the end of each training session you incorporate interval training by, for example, 200 metre runs at 70 per cent effort with 1-2 minutes' rest between each repetition. At first there will be, say, three repetitions, increasing to eight repetitions.

Remember, *train* don't *strain*.

Power and strength are the two main assets demanded of forwards — the ability to do very heavy work and to do it often. All Blacks v Springboks. All Blacks from left to right Kerry Tanner, Peter Whiting, Ken Lambert.
Peter Bush

Barry Hislop on

Fitness to Play

There are five factors in conditioning a player to play rugby. These are the five S's: stamina, strength, speed, suppleness and skill.

- **Stamina is the ability to persist at a physically tiring task.**
- **Strength is the ability of a muscle to apply force against resistance.**
- **Speed is the ability to increase the rate of movement over distance.**
- **Suppleness is the extent of function permitted by the muscles and surrounding tissues at a movable joint.**
- **Skill is the ability to perform a physical activity with ease and efficiency.**

In pre-season training the main objective is to develop the individual's aerobic fitness — in other words, their ability to utilise oxygen. This largely depends upon one's individual heart and lung capacity. In principle this conditioning needs to be done slowly and steadily at regular intervals, with, for instance, a 3-5 kilometre run at 60 per cent of the player's maximum effort. A typical period of this work would be 8-12 weeks.

To continue towards peak fitness, the next period is for anaerobic conditioning, to enhance the oxygen utilisation and to allow the muscles to withstand oxygen deficiency. A typical training for this would be over 4-6 weeks, depending on the time available. This activity can best be monitored by running 200 or 400 metres at 80 per cent of the player's maximum effort. During the season speed conditioning can be introduced: maximum activity (in other words, 100 per cent) over 30 seconds.

The days when practising for skill was enough to cover basic needs for physical fitness, are over. Often some skills cannot be acquired before a sufficient basis of fitness has been established.

Dressing for training

In general terms, running is itself preventative medicine. The foremost consideration should be the shoes that the player wears. The shoes must have toe room, be flexible on the ball of the foot, be pliable but not overly so, must have a durable sole, and have at least a 15 mm rise from the heel to the ball of the foot. The shoe should also have a firm heel, so that if you put it on the floor you can't pull the shoe sideways, and it must have an arch support. Most importantly the shoes should be comfortable. Don't just buy a popular brand name if the shoes are not suitable for you. Most injuries in pre-season training stem from poor footwear.

The other important point is the maintenance of this footwear. You start jogging and the shoes begin to wear down at the back of the heel. It is important to keep this built up, and for this purpose there are spreading compounds that you can apply.

Footwear has been one of the most neglected items with most rugby players I have known. The simple fact is that if the footwear is not supporting the foot, it should be discarded. After all, you don't run a Mercedes car on four-ply tyres — you run it on radials.

Clothing is also important. Forwards who are heavy in the thighs and tend to suffer friction there, should wear a pair of light trousers without heavy centre seams — normal rugby trousers would only irritate. Socks shouldn't restrict movement in the calves. In the pre-season when it's usually hot, it's better to wear a singlet rather than a football jersey. The old theory that if you wear as much as you can, you lose more weight is erroneous. The fact is that you dehydrate more if you wear clothes that are too heavy, so you become fatigued and distressed and tend to take in more liquid. The solution is to wear light clothes and put on a track suit afterwards.

Warming up

Care of the body is of paramount importance and the main concern is to stretch the muscles, especially in the hamstring and calf area, which tend to shorten in jogging. You have to stretch them statically and this can be done before jogging, by doing mobility exercises that will increase the circulation of the blood around the particular muscle groups you are to work on. There are specific exercises for this. (See p 19.)

Jogging

I would suggest a varied running programme: hill runs to increase the strength of the quadriceps (thigh) muscles, beach runs to improve foot action and cross country runs to improve ankle flexion.

Long, slow, distance running should be tackled at an easy pace, and on return the heart-rate should not exceed probably 60 per cent of the maximum. But as you become fitter you can put in a steady 5-7 kilometre run, which would bring your oxygen intake up to 60 per cent and the heart-rate up to approximately 150. Again, as you become fitter there should be variation in the speed training.

Ideally, about half-way through the 10-15 week pre-season training, train in a bush area where you can run uphill, downhill and around trees, varying your speeds. Uphill work, on a gradient of 1 in 7, provides particularly effective back exercise. Find a stretch about 200 metres long, and bound up the hill lifting your knees up, stretching out — in other words, more like a hop. This is an ideal strength exercise and about 80 per cent anaerobic training. Do that once a week and fartlek once a week, then easy runs on the other days.

For leg speed — getting the legs going as fast as you can — running down slopes is recommended, but on very gentle slopes. It's an excellent exercise. Ideally you should co-ordinate your training with an easy run, then hill training, then jog for half a kilometre, then come back to that same hill and jog half-way down and let yourself go, go as fast as you can, then turn around and do your hill sprints back up again.

Ian Kirkpatrick, supported by Sid Going, beats off an attempted tackle by Mervyn Davies. Second Test, Wales v New Zealand, 1969.
NZ Herald

Fartlek training

Fartlek training, or speed play, originally developed in Sweden, is done in open parks or over the countryside. You never quite exhaust yourself, but on the other hand you never quite regain your breath.

The pattern is varied rather than repetitive. You jog for 800 metres, stride for 50 metres, jog again for 100 metres, increase speed until you are sprinting at the end of 200 metres, then gradually slow down and jog until you nearly regain your breath. After that you run up a hill with knees up high for 30 metres or so, jog another 100 metres, then sprint down the hill, run another 800 metres at better than jogging speed, and jog for another 400 metres. After all this, sit down and rest for a minute or two, then return home, using a different pattern by another route.

A variation of fartlek training is 'circuit' training which comprises a 3 kilometre circuit. Such a circuit would be completed two or three times a session against the clock, with 10 minutes' rest between circuits.

Building stamina with other exercises

Obviously the needs differ between the backs and the forwards. The forwards need to concentrate on the large muscle groups of the upper body — the chest, back and arms — trying to develop as much heavy resistance work as they can. This includes weight training. But resistance training is not just using weights, it is players using their own bodies. Clubs should have equipment for this, although different coaches recommend different equipment. It is better therefore, to strike a happy medium by developing something simple and inexpensive around the grounds: logs are suitable, a sweat course, doing exercises around the perimeter of the field such as press-ups, pull-ups, chin-dips, and so on. Weight training really requires expertise.

Backs, on the other hand, need more reflex work, although they still have to work with heavy weights. Some of the fastest backs are those who can actually work heavier resistances than the forwards. It's an individual matter and depends on experience, whether they've done the activity before.

A typical pre-season weight training programme would start with 40 per cent of the player's body weight, working up to about three sets of ten; and when they manage that, going on to the next phase — 60 per cent of their body weight, then 80 per cent. It is a pyramid system; they increase their resistances, and then they decrease their resistances: you work up to a heavy programme and then come down to a light programme.

Variety in training is also important and, if including other sports, you do have to look closely at the value of the activity. Swimming, for instance, is an excellent aerobic exercise and is ideal for developing the arms and the shoulders. Any other aerobic sport, such as cycling, does add interest to a training regime.

Planning the pre-season training programme

In the first eight weeks the players should do a little, a lot — not a lot, a little. I tend to under-programme rather than over-programme. If we're looking at a time basis per week, I'd suggest players set aside three hours minimum a week.

On a maximum of running, players should do no more than 70 kilometres a week. The target in the aerobic running is that once a week they should do a longer endurance run, increasing that run each week. During the pre-season training period, I schedule this for the day of the week and the time of the day that the team will be playing, in the season itself — to prepare them for the game.

After the first eight weeks unfortunately, many players tend to do less. It is important therefore, that the coach constantly evaluates their fitness, so that a player has a record of his standard of fitness. With such a record the coach can also assess the fitness level of the team overall. On this basis the coach then knows what improvements are necessary and can say to a player, 'Look, this is how you are in relation to the other players in the team, so do this . . .'

At this stage in training most coaches would still be concentrating on running, rather than on trials, to find out the standard of the players' rugby.

Ideally each player should train individually on Monday, Wednesday, Friday and one day at the weekend; on those days he could be doing aerobic running — that is running based on energy derived from oxygen. On Tuesday and Thursday he could begin anaerobic training, such as repetition running, running 400s, lengths of the field, working at 80 per cent of the maximum oxygen intake. Anaerobic training involves working on a different energy output — you're not relying on the oxygen you're taking in, but on the energy source that is in the muscle structure.

As with aerobic training, the purpose is to develop the cardio-vascular system. Anaerobic conditioning contrasts with aerobic training, however, because it aims at increasing the tolerance of work where the oxygen consumption exceeds the intake. It means the ability to work at near maximum effort over a short time.

When the full season is underway and the training sessions are more technical and demanding, the players should be doing specific conditioning on Monday Wednesday and Sunday. Tuesday and Thursday would be used for team training. On Monday they could do some form of aerobic conditioning, such as hill training or fartlek training. On Wednesday they could do an easy run between their two training sessions — this because they will be starting to develop a high waste product within the muscle structure — or start introducing some anaerobic runs, 100 metres, 200 metres, or whatever. And then on Tuesday and Thursday some speed work could follow training.

A high waste product in the muscle means that there is a certain amount of metabolic waste developed after the body has performed a concentrated level of work. The body eliminates this waste through the blood circulating, and the body needs time to recover from each build-up, to get rid of it. The essence of any training programme should be recovery: work and rest, work and rest. If you had a graph showing your running, one day 7 kilometres, the next day 3 kilometres, then 7 again, it would show a flowing curve up and down; the balance, the recovery, is allowed for.

A typical aerobic training programme

A minimum period of 6 weeks (Jan-Feb) is necessary for this training phase.

Monday	Thirty minutes — variation running, cross country, hill running
Tuesday	Forty-five minutes — easy pace
Wednesday	Thirty minutes — variation running, cross country, down hill and up hill running
Thursday	Forty-five minutes — easy pace
Friday	Rest day
Saturday	Build up to jogging continuously for 1½-2 hours at a very easy pace
Sunday	Rest day optional; recovery jog

In the above programme distance has not been mentioned. The object is not to cover a great distance; the purpose of the exercise is to increase each individual's oxygen uptake. The physiological benefits gained in this type of training result from large muscle groups being used continually. Also time is a great leveller for the big person or the person who finds jogging naturally difficult. The programme has a work/rest pattern to allow the body to adapt to the extra work.

A typical anaerobic training programme

Monday	Optional variation run — cross country, hill runs
Tuesday	Anaerobic — 200 metre runs, 400 metre runs, 800 metre runs
Wednesday	Recovery, aerobic run, easy 30 minutes
Thursday	Anaerobic — 200 metre runs, 600 metre runs, 800 metre runs
Friday	Rest day
Saturday	Anaerobic — 1 kilometre timed, 2 kilometres timed, 3 kilometres timed
Sunday	Recovery aerobic run, easy 30 minutes

The easy aerobic running has been included in the programme to help the body recover and prevent the waste product (lactic acid) from building up. The distances have been selected because of the physiological benefits related to the sporting demand.

Recovery between the repetitions is very important. A rule of thumb is for time of work, double the time for the recovery, for example 1 minute anaerobic run — 300 to 400 metres should have 2 minutes recovery. A very easy jog is recommended.

Progress your repetitions slowly:

    Day 1   2 x 200 metres or 1 x 400 metres
    Day 2   3 x 200 metres or 2 x 400 metres

Build up to a total of 10 x 200 metre runs or 6 x 400 metre runs.

Psychologically this form of training is difficult; coaches can assist by recording times over the distance. Players should concentrate on extending stride length during the phase.

All Blacks v France 1981. During a N.Z. drop kick. An unusual shot showing that players sometimes do just stand and watch.
Peter Bush

Developing strength

Strength, as mentioned earlier, is the ability of a muscle to apply force against a resistance. This can be developed properly only by the use of progressive resistance (weight) training. Strength and power is best achieved by low repetition and heavy resistance. While muscular endurance is achieved best by high repetition and light resistance, other forms of exercise include general exercises utilising the body weight, target and circuit training against the clock. Forwards, because of the nature of their work, are required to be robust and strong, and it is recommended that they concentrate on developing the large muscle groups of the torso area. Ideally it would be an excellent target to work up to at least 60 per cent of their body weight in resistances.

Here I refer to the specific strength required of forwards: the ability to push, the ability to rip the ball away from somebody, the ability to pull together to apply weight. Primarily we are after power, strength, in the forwards — the ability to undertake a heavy work load and to do it often — whereas with the backs we are after reaction, explosive reaction, the speed to go from inertia to rapid action in the shortest possible time. For this I would tend to work on more speed explosive strength work around the lower limbs. Speed is often affected when strength is underdeveloped.

Power weight training would be undertaken generally before the pre-season running; then you would begin explosive training — by introducing circuits, targets and so on — during the running training. Then would follow the introduction of exercise with body contact more oriented to the game.

Even during the season you'd want to maintain power weight training at least twice a week. High-level national athletes train every day with weights and resistances. High calibre players train daily on that aspect — possibly not at pre-season intensity, but certainly with heavy weights, to increase their endurance capacity.

Training for speed

The final aspect of cardio-vascular conditioning is speed — working at maximum effort, for up to 30 seconds. Nobody can maintain their top speed for more than 30 seconds, so you train up to that 30 seconds. This aspect of conditioning is a combination of reaction of the neuro-muscular function and muscle and cardio-vascular efficiency. The better the foundation phase the greater the capacity the player has to maintain speed throughout the game.

The variations of speed running include shuttle runs, relays over 50 metres, 100 metre sprints, 50 metre sprints, wind sprints. Shuttle runs are ideal because they require a change of direction quickly. Recovery is usually double the working phase.

This phase of training (April-July) is very important in a game situation. The optimum distance to train is 50 metres as the player can hold maximum speed for that distance. One technique requires the players to sprint up to lines drawn on the ground, and then jog back. First you can work off the 22 metre line and the 50 metre line, then 75 and 100. The players sprint up and jog back, sprint up to the next line and jog back — the important thing is to use each jogging back as a rest period. In speed you work up to a maximum of 30 seconds, with a minute's recovery.

Pre-season weight training, especially with hill running and explosive strength training, definitely increases muscular efficiency. Most of us are lazy runners, and do only very quick steps, but you can increase speed by improving your technique. A player may be a lazy strider, and he has to learn to increase his knee lift in front and push out through the back. Reaction rate is innate, but it can be improved by specific training.

Furthermore there is a difference between small players and big players — the heavier person is not as agile. Bulk does limit explosive reactions. But by introducing hill sprints — step-ups — resistance training with weights, and so on,

these specifics can be developed. Youths who suddenly shoot up in height and lose their sense of control can help themselves by doing more skill work, but this is a natural phenomenon and there is no specific solution.

Specific conditioning also helps locks with their jumping. As a test they can stand against the goal post and put a finger mark within their reach, then jump up as high as they can and measure the distance. They should do special jumping, step-ups, hill running and so on, and watch the distance between the two finger marks increase. The point of this test is not to see who can jump the highest, but rather to give an indication of the player's explosive strength.

A speed training programme

Monday	Speed running
Tuesday	Team training plus anaerobic 6 x 200 metres and 4 x 400 metres
Wednesday	Speed running
Thursday	Team training plus aerobic 20-30 minutes easy
Friday	Speed running
Saturday	Team training or game
Sunday	Recovery aerobic run for 30 minutes

A misconception about conditioning for fitness during the season is that by just playing the game your fitness is maintained. It is natural that the skill levels will improve, the body also is more conditioned to the physical context. However, it is important to maintain regular cardio-vascular conditioning as outlined in the programme.

Suppleness conditioning

Suppleness is one aspect of conditioning that has been disregarded in the recent past; it was important in the 1950s, when the Swedish type of P.T. was popular, then it was ignored for a time.

Suppleness is the ability to take a joint through its full range of movement. The arm for instance, has a ball and socket joint, and it should be able to move in a full circular motion. The knee, a typical hinge joint, should be able to perform the full backward and forward movement of flexion and extension. We must consider the feet, the knees, the back, the hips, shoulders and elbows — all the vulnerable areas that feature in rugby injuries. In many cases the ability to take a joint through the full range of movement is lacking in our players and this affects the player's ability to reach maximum speed. To develop flexibility apply the overload principle by gradually and progressively forcing the muscles to stretch while moving a joint through a complete range of motion.

The knee would be one of the most underdeveloped areas. There are two muscle groups here that need to be developed: the quadriceps and the hamstring. Many hamstring injuries result from poor footwear or unfavourable ground conditions, or they just happen, but often the problem is that many players develop the quadriceps muscle (which is at the front) and underdevelop the back muscle. Naturally, suppleness is involved: players should be stretching the back muscles more, because these don't work as much as the front muscles do.

The shoulders are another vulnerable part. The players should be developing bulk to protect the joints, which are very susceptible to injury: bangs in tackling and so on. The deltoid, the biceps and triceps areas are the pulling and pushing muscles, and given the current maul situation these are the ones you need to develop.

To develop this suppleness, judo and jujitsu, falling practice and so on, are adequate, but gymnastics alone provide the most effective grounding for all major sports. Gymnastics develop balance and co-ordination as well as the tumbling and rolling movements used in rugby. Gymnastics also provide a particularly useful foundation for the younger player.

As you get older gymnastics enable you to maintain suppleness, although then the suppleness relies more on activity experience. If you've practised gymnastics in your younger days suppleness has probably become an established neuro-muscular pattern. The important point is to specifically develop the stretching aspect of conditioning.

I watch a lot of representative rugby and club rugby, and my impression is that many referees are not adequately conditioned. Usually they are approaching middle age, possibly vulnerable to coronary problems and therefore need to take more care. Obviously the same conditioning programme should apply. Older muscles are less resilient and they are more susceptible to injuries.

One cannot emphasise enough the importance of static stretching which is based on yoga. (See diagrams p 19.) This allows the muscle or group of muscles being stretched, to work separately and effectively. You probably remember when your teacher instructed you at physical education classes, 'Touch your toes, go on, get down there. Bounce, bounce, bounce.' But you were working both muscle groups at once — the antagonistic muscle groups as well — and you were not benefiting at all from it.

Developing skills

In pre-season and during the season the individual must practise his or her own particular skill, or skills, separately away from the team and then with the team; skills such as kicking, tackling, side-stepping, swerving, and so on. Backs practise their skills, and forwards theirs, and then practise together as a group. In a club the resources of the senior rugby players can be of great help to the junior players.

Skill involves efficient utilisation of many factors in varied combinations. Some of these factors are strength, power, endurance, co-ordination, timing, agility, flexibility and judgement.

Practising a skill effectively requires repetition for it to become ingrained. In team training, a second five-eighth may touch the ball only two or three times in 15 minutes, because by the time the players have travelled from one end of the field to the other in a ruck and scrum, he has touched the ball only that many times. When the opportunity occurs so rarely you cannot expect the skill to be acquired, much less perfected. Obviously, to develop the necessary skills, individual and group practice demands more intense activity and experience. It is better to have more balls and do a lot of work in smaller groups.

There should never be any difference between left limbs and right limbs, and if a player has limited skill in either the left or the right foot it is only through lack of practice. Repetition is the only solution. The skill then becomes ingrained and automatic. Repeating movements over and over again, aiming at perfecting a move, also raises the question of the player's self-motivation.

Coach Fred Allen (facing camera) gives a team talk during All Black Trials, December 1969.
Auckland Star

The coach's influence

Coaches have to 'read' each player, and this is where tests can help them. They can then encourage the players who need assistance. The players who are successful and are in the senior rugby team will be self-motivated already and only need to be guided in what to do and when to do it. Other players who are not as confident and skilled, perhaps need to work more conscientiously.

Posting graphs of performances on a notice board is effective and doesn't seem to have any negative effect on a player's performance — probably he will be even more aggressive in the approach to his work. The player thus has immediate feedback and can compete against his previous results as well as compete with other players. A coach can provide only outside motivation; the individual player must be his own most important motivator. Success is the best motivator and achieving a certain goal is motivation in itself.

Unfortunately a player tends to over-react if he sets his own goals, tends to look at the end result instead of the intermediate achievements. Therefore, a coach must be able to keep a player to realistic goals or challenges. Because individuals participating in an identical training programme improve at different rates, the coach must use any written programme as a guide only.

Coaches don't need to know everything about physical education, however: there is always someone to inform them. They don't need to be experts in their own right: they need to know only the basic principles. They should write down everything, keep a team diary and have as complete a record as possible for reference and improvement.

Careful conditioning will delay the onset of fatigue in a player and thereby enable him to maintain a high rate of performance over a longer period of time. This in turn enhances his enjoyment of the game and benefits play overall.

ales' most hallowed patch of turf, still affectionately known to most as Cardiff Arms but now more correctly called the National Stadium. As ardiff Arms it will forever hold a place in New Zealand's rugby heart.

ter Bush

Hugh Burry on

Strategy

- **The objective of planned movements is to create space for the attacker.**
- **The whole team should be aware of planned moves from set play.**
- **Surprise is the key.**
- **Moves must be carried out with speed, strength and subtlety so that space is created for the attacker.**
- **Transfers of the ball should be kept at a minimum to reduce the chances of handling errors.**
- **Keep it simple and do the simple things well.**

Modern rugby is a very sophisticated game. The wide use of cine and television photography has enabled coaches to analyse every facet of the game from their armchairs and to work out precisely why teams won and lost, why some moves succeeded and others failed. It is a far cry from English rugby of the mid-1960s, when in that country coaching was regarded as a way to get players to cheat more efficiently.

One day, I watched a top club win perfect possession from four successive line-outs and chain-pass the ball along their backline, no doubt hoping that one of our backs had either not been taught how to tackle, had disappeared into a hole in the ground, or had gone off the field to relieve himself. As none of these conditions occurred, the net result of this unenterprising play was that they were pushed gradually back to their 22 metre line where our troops finally won the ball and, from a smoothly executed set move, dropped a neat goal. After the game, I asked the opposing team what moves they practised. It turned out that they never trained together and they relied on the hope that one of their players would be too fast/clever/strong, for his marker.

Times have changed. The drawn match between the All Blacks and the Barbarians at the end of the 1974 short-tour was a complete contrast and, from a connoisseur's point of view, perhaps one of the greatest games of all time. On that occasion, Greek met Greek. Such was the quality of the play, that only an unstoppable surge or an outrageous fluke could produce a score. All Black, Andy Leslie's try was an example of the former. Three superb drives ended in a ruck a metre or two short of the goal line, and when the ball was smoothly delivered, Leslie, with excellent body position, was just able to find space to squeeze across the goal line.

Strategy is the overall word for the methods by which we hope to defeat the near-perfect defence. It has to do with the concept of space — how we create space or recognise existing space and how we hope to put our striker and the ball into that space. A criticism of New Zealand rugby might be that we have spent too much time thinking about what we were going to do, and too little time thinking about where the opponents were and what they were doing.

The basic tenet in planning a successful strategy must be that we asume the opponents to be competent defenders and that the exceptionally gifted player (such as the brilliant Welsh wing three-quarter and 1971 Lion, Gerald Davies or the powerful 1970s All Black three-quarter, Bryan Williams) is rare. We therefore aim to give our striker a metre's start or to confront one defender with two attackers. Of course, there is always the chance that the opposing team contains a player who has a defensive weakness which can be exploited, but this is basic knowledge and lies outside the scope of this chapter.

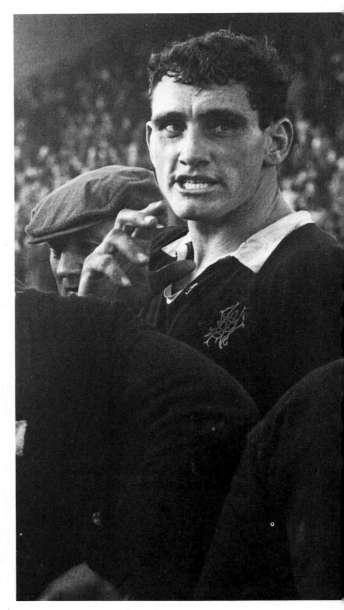

New Zealand prop Ken Gray sorts matters out at half-time.
Evening Post

A strong back-row forward and a consistent try scorer. Played for Christ's College (1st XV); Canterbury 1955, 56 (University) 1957-60, 62 (New Brighton) also NZ Universities 1956. Selected for NZ Trials 1957, 59. In 1960 represented NZ in South Africa. Coached Canterbury B 1963 and Guy's Hospital team (England) 1966-75; staff coach Rugby Football Union 1972, 73.

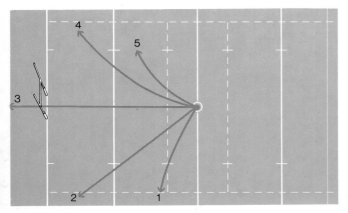

Some variations in the kick-off to start play from half-way

1. The kick high to the forwards:
   (a) for tapping back on the run; or
   (b) if an opponent catches the ball, your team-mates tackle the opponent and regain possession.
2. The deep kick behind the forwards if the defensive backs are out of position — bounced into touch.
3. The kick over the dead-ball line to take advantage of the wind and force the opposition to restart play at the 22 metre mark.
4. The kick for your wing, should his opposite be out of position — usually associated with a 'dummy' kick-off.
5. A variation of the 'silly' kick, again where the opposition wing or full-back is out of position.

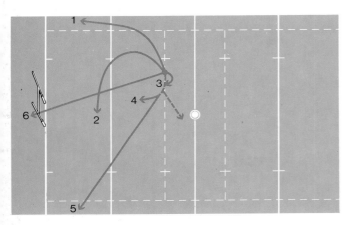

Some variations in the offensive penalty kick

1. The long touch-finder with a winger following up to force the opposition either to kick or to run the ball into touch.
2. The high up-and-under to put pressure on the opposition's backs under their goal posts.
3. The tap kick retrieved and run by backs or forwards.
4. The fast, short kick placed high — over the forwards as they are re-forming.
5. The long, bouncing corner-flag kick followed up by your winger on the run with his opposite out of position.
6. The standard kick at goal — place kick or drop kick.

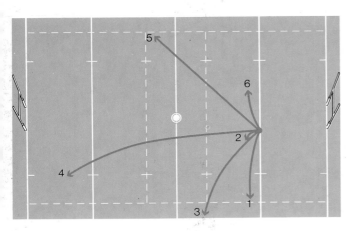

Some variations in the kick-off to start play from the 22 metre mark

1. The standard kick to the forwards — high, so that your forwards following up have the opportunity of getting under the ball and retrieving it.
2. The short, quick drop-kick, able to be retrieved by the kicker or a close team-mate.
3. The bounce-out touch-finder behind the opposition's forwards.
4. The long kick to a space behind a full-back who is in the back line out of position.
5. The kick behind the opposition's winger — for your winger to run up on and force mistakes in the opposition's defence.
6. The kick to the unmarked winger or centre — close.

33

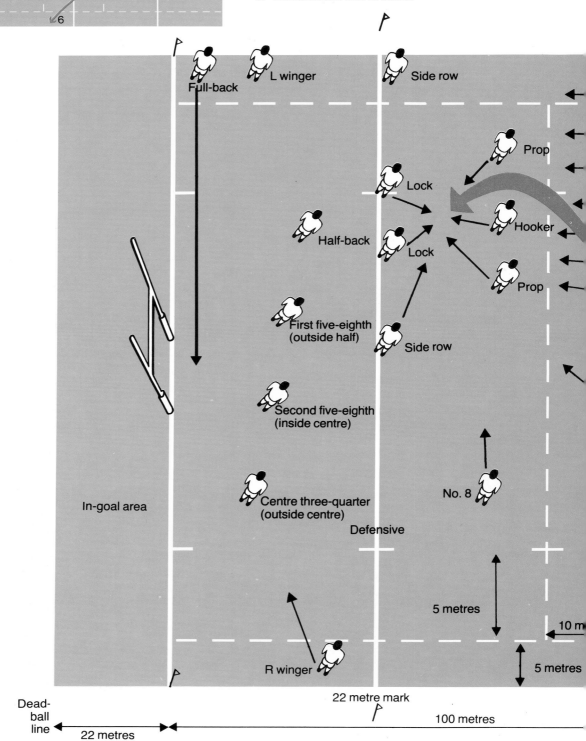

Some variations in the defensive penalty kick

1. The short tap kick, swung to the backs or forwards for the drive or for a kick at a more advantageous position.
2. The long low kick for your outside backs when their opposites are out of position.
3. The long bouncing kick to put pressure on a full-back already in the back line and out of position.
4. The high up-and-under to put the ball where your forwards can drive and commit the opposition.
5. The grubber kick to a fast team-mate running hard on to the ball, with the opposition still regrouping.
6. The standard kick to touch.

Full-back

L winger

Side row

Prop

Lock

Half-back

Lock

Hooker

First five-eighth
(outside half)

Prop

Side row

Second five-eighth
(inside centre)

No. 8

In-goal area

Centre three-quarter
(outside centre)

Defensive

5 metres

10 m

R winger

5 metres

Dead-
ball
line

22 metres

22 metre mark

100 metres

The field markings and measurements, and basic positions of the players at the kick-off at half-way

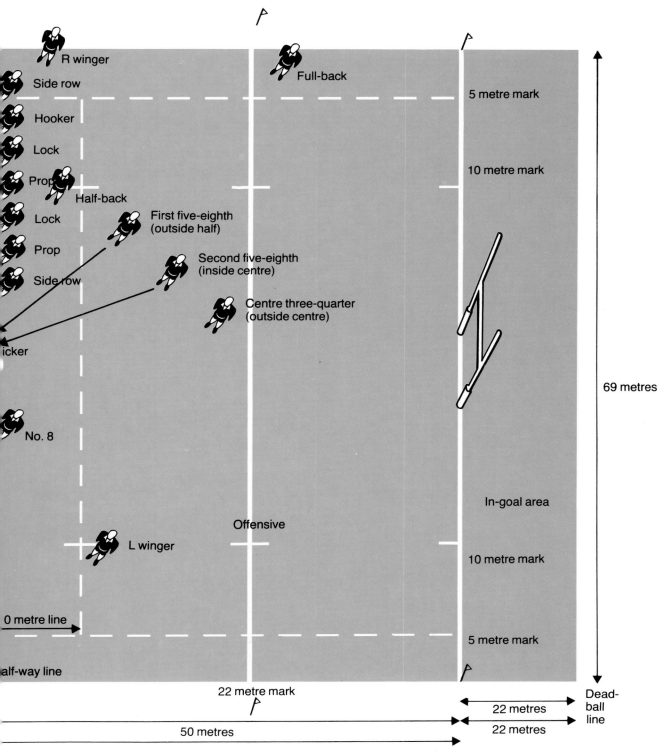

R winger
Side row
Hooker
Lock
Prop
Half-back
Lock
Prop
Side row
icker
No. 8
L winger

Full-back
5 metre mark
10 metre mark
First five-eighth (outside half)
Second five-eighth (inside centre)
Centre three-quarter (outside centre)

69 metres

In-goal area
Offensive
10 metre mark
5 metre mark

0 metre line
alf-way line

22 metre mark

50 metres

22 metres
22 metres

Dead-ball line

Basic positions for the kick-off at the 22 metre mark

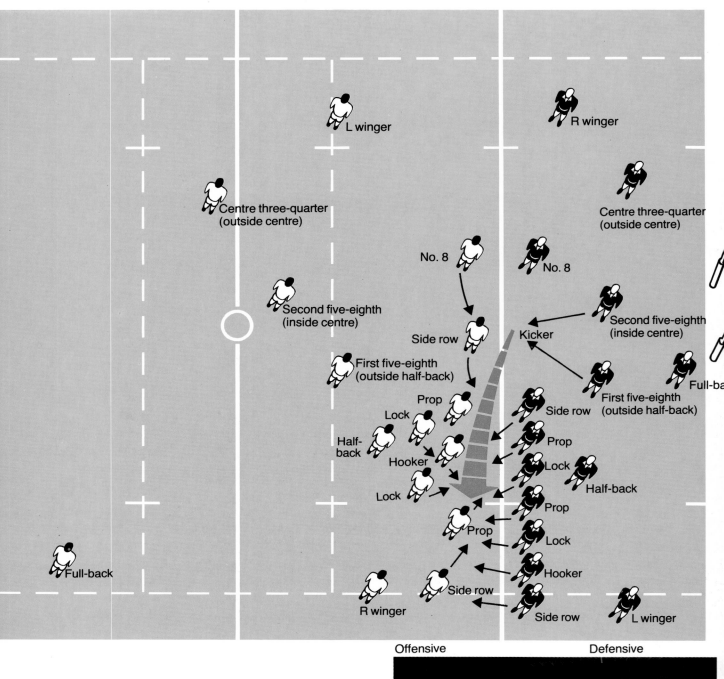

L winger

R winger

Centre three-quarter
(outside centre)

Centre three-quarter
(outside centre)

No. 8

No. 8

Second five-eighth
(inside centre)

Kicker

Second five-eighth
(inside centre)

Side row

First five-eighth
(outside half-back)

First five-eighth
(outside half-back)

Full-ba

Prop

Side row

Lock

Prop

Half-
back

Lock

Hooker

Half-back

Lock

Prop

Prop

Lock

Side row

Hooker

R winger

Side row

L winger

Side row

Offensive

Defensive

Wales, in a huddle, await the finish of the traditional All Black haka.
Peter Bush

Basic positions for a defensive penalty

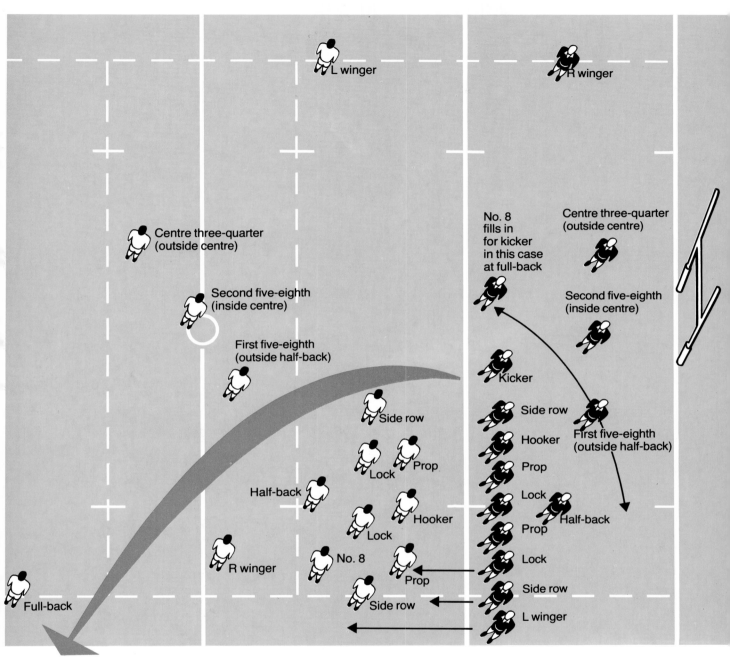

L winger

R winger

Centre three-quarter (outside centre)

No. 8 fills in for kicker in this case at full-back

Centre three-quarter (outside centre)

Second five-eighth (inside centre)

Second five-eighth (inside centre)

First five-eighth (outside half-back)

Kicker

Side row

Side row

Hooker

Lock

Prop

Prop

First five-eighth (outside half-back)

Half-back

Lock

Lock

Hooker

Prop

Half-back

Lock

R winger

No. 8

Side row

Prop

Side row

L winger

Full-back

Kick off! An International gets under way. Wales v All Blacks.
Peter Bush

Basic positions for an offensive penalty

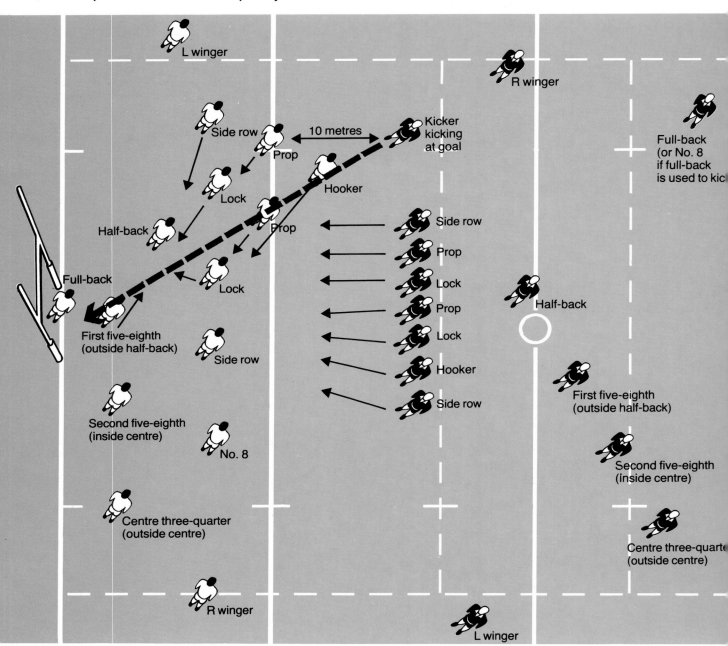

L winger

R winger

Side row

Prop

10 metres

Kicker kicking at goal

Lock

Hooker

Full-back (or No. 8 if full-back is used to kick)

Half-back

Prop

Side row

Full-back

Lock

Prop

Lock

Prop

Lock

First five-eighth (outside half-back)

Side row

Hooker

Half-back

Side row

Second five-eighth (inside centre)

No. 8

First five-eighth (outside half-back)

Centre three-quarter (outside centre)

Second five-eighth (inside centre)

Centre three-quarter (outside centre)

R winger

L winger

Athletic Park, Wellington. Though rugby is pre-eminently a game for the 'live' spectator, the wide use of cine-photography and videotape has 'enabled coaches to analyse every facet of the game from the depths of their armchairs and work out precisely why teams won and lost, why some moves succeeded and others failed . . .'

Peter Bush

Objectives of planned moves

There are various objectives of planned moves. They include:

- To score a try
- To kick a field goal
- To achieve a favourable position from which to launch further attack
- To unsettle the opposition
- To exhaust the opposition

Of these, the first two are the most important, they provide the greatest opportunities for skill and planning, and will be dealt with at length in this book.

The third is best exemplified by the peel around the back of a line-out which leads to a midfield ruck/maul and is followed by the strike by first five-eighth, wing and possibly full-back, back towards the sideline. This move was exploited beautifully by the All Blacks against England in 1967 for Earle Kirton to score. (A cautionary note: never attempt this against a poor team with a slow-moving pack. You find that your backs run straight into a bunch of stragglers jogging towards the already disintegrating ruck, who enthusiastically rubbish the ball carrier and gallop off with the ball before your forwards can pick themselves out of the ruck!)

A good example of unsettling tactics was the variation of line-out length, with long or short throws and quick throws before the line-out had even formed, which enabled the 1977 All Blacks to upset and eventually overcome the French pack that was dominating set play.

Welsh coach Carwyn James, one of the greatest thinkers on the game that we have known, may have lost admirers in 1972 by coaching the Llanelli forwards (who were to play against the All Blacks) to sometimes bring up only six players at a line-out when it was their own ball. When, after the line-out was formed, they moved in to be the regulation one metre apart, the All Blacks discovered that seven into six won't go: the man at the back was penalised for being off-side, with a kick at goal being the reward for what might be regarded as gamesmanship, rather than constructive rugby. Carwyn justified this tactic by pointing out that it was very unsettling for the New Zealand forwards. He was right!

Attempting to exhaust the opposition may be the best tactic when your light, mobile pack is confronted by a pack of no-neck monsters. The only chance then is to encourage them to run around the field chasing your backs, who are tearing round like demented blowflies. (On the other hand, if *you* have the dreadnought pack, keep the ball in hand and drive ruthlessly at your opponents, committing them to make tackle after tackle until physical exhaustion beats *them*.)

Why moves work

It was (probably) Charlie Saxton the renowned 1930s New Zealand half-back, Otago selector, and manager of 1967 N.Z. team in British Isles and France, who, in the 1940s, introduced and popularised the concept of the three Ps, possession, position and pace. These are still the vital ingredients of any attack. In thinking about moves, it is also necessary to remember the three Ss, space, surprise and strength.

The concept of space is very much a part of association-football thinking but tends to be neglected in rugby. Look at it this way — if it takes about a second for one player to pass the ball to another when both are running flatout, about 8 or 9 metres of space have been used up. On this basis, getting the ball from half-back to wing must use up at least 30 metres; and against an aggressive defence, you don't have 30 metres. Hence, the need to minimise the number of ball transfers you plan to make before breaching the defence.

The other aspect of space is the relationship of the number of defenders to the area of field to be defended. The density of defenders is obviously greater when play is taking place within the 22 metre line than when it is around half-way. There is, in the former case, only a small area for which each player is responsible, and being close together they can easily support one another if the need arises. On the other hand, because the distance to the goal line is short, there is a much greater chance of outflanking the cover defence. The object of a move is primarily to reduce the density of defenders so that you present an overlap or two-to-one situation, or leave your striker free with space to use to beat the last defender. A back should always beat a full-back caught in midfield, but should never succeed when he has only 5 metres along the sideline. A good example was when the very fast 1955 Wallaby wing, Garth Jones, was let loose in midfield at Athletic Park. As he approached All Black full-back Kevin Stuart (noted for very strong tackling), he feinted left but went right at such velocity that Kevin's dive left him a couple of metres short of Garth's flying heels.

A wonderful opportunity to use existing space occurs in counter-attack from an opponent's long kick along the touch line after a line-out. If the ball is still in play, the full-back has the chance to develop play across to the open spaces on the other side — provided that the other backs in his team have retired quickly with the kick. With both packs of forwards committed to the area along the touch line, there should be plenty of space for the skills of deceptive running — swerve, sidestep and change of pace — to be employed. The Lions of 1971 were masters of this art of counter-attack, and Gerald Davies' try in the second test at Lancaster Park, Christchurch, was a good example.

Surprise is, of course, an essential ingredient of a successful move; if the positioning or signals of the attacking players make it obvious what is planned, it is not too difficult for the defending players to regroup in anticipation of the danger. So here is the opportunity for the really crafty team to devise false signals or have players who will not actually participate in the move standing in strange positions looking fiendishly cunning.

A good example of surprise was seen in the movement that led to All Black back-row forward, Vic Yates' try against the French at Lancaster Park in 1961. Yates had detached from a scrum near the 22 metre line and about 15 metres from the left touchline in French territory and was standing behind the scrum towards the left side. When the All Blacks won the scrum, Neil Wolfe, the first five-eighth, sprinted around the blind side (left) and Des Connor, an outstanding post-war half-back, dummied a pass to him, but actually delivered a superb long backhand pass to his right, finding Yates who was then sprinting through the hole left by the French first five-eighth who had moved to the blind to cover Wolfe. As the French back row (equally fooled) had done likewise, Yates was able to gallop between the goal posts without a hand being laid on him. The abiding memory is of two irate Frenchmen standing waving and gesticulating at each other as they debated whose fault it was, before the ball was actually grounded for the try.

Strength can, of course, be completely unsubtle. The tactic of detaching a very large and burly No. 8 (such as the exceptional back-row and lock forward All Black, Brian Lochore) from a scrum and giving him the call to run straight at, through, or over the opposing first five-eighth is crude but effective; the comparatively puny target is sorely tempted to execute a defensive side-step. By and large, however, we are concerned more with strength in numbers, bringing up more players to the attack than the defence can cope with. The simplest example of this is the introduction of the full-back into an open- or blind-side attack.

Creating space

There are many ways in which space can be created, the simplest being overlap play. As previously mentioned, the introduction of the full-back is a simple and effective manoeuvre, the main problem being to persuade a full-back to hang back long enough to ensure that he receives the ball, sprinting to get into position and without having (by his movement and positioning) telegraphed his intentions to the opposition. Too little is made of the potential for an attack that is initiated by the full-back receiving the ball from a scrum in a defensive position inside the 22 metre line and bursting down the short side, accompanied by wing, half-back and back row. Surprise, again, is the important factor. An overlap can be created on the short side by the No. 8 picking up, taking out the blind-side flanker and giving to half-back, left-side flanker following around, or full-back to leave the opposing wing confronted by two attackers. Obviously this move goes best down the right side of the scrum, as the opposition half-back is on the left side after our put-in and can't get into the play.

Overlaps or clean midfield breaks can be achieved by the entry of the blind-side wing into the line. It is virtually impossible to engineer an overlap situation on the open side from a scrum, because of the shortage of space to pass the ball, but the appearance of the blind-side wing either inside or outside the first five-eighth can pose problems for the defence. Ross Smith, the Canterbury wing, exploited this move brilliantly in the 1950s, often side-stepping clean through the defence. Bryan Williams is perhaps the greatest exponent of the entry between the centres. All Black three-quarter Grant Batty's great try against the Barbarians in 1973 came as a result of this move.

Dummies

There is more to the dummy than the mere gesture of appearing to pass the ball, but retaining it instead — as is so brilliantly carried out by Hugo Porta, the world-celebrated Argentinian first five-eighth, who specialises in the dummy *kick*. Dummy runs and vocal dummies are also important deceptive ploys. Take, for instance, the commonly used long pass to cut out one of the midfield backs, which may break up a defensive pattern and create enough space for the full-back to enter the line successfully. This move is much more effective if the player who is to be missed out cuts inside as if to take a scissors pass. If he takes off early and ostentatiously, the defence — and particularly the cover defence — hesitates to ensure that he isn't the ball carrier. It makes good sense to carry out a real scissor movement as a prelude to the dummy. Nothing is lost, as the 'crash ball' run

An excellent example of a reverse dive pass. Dave Loveridge — All Blacks v France 1st Test Paris, 1981.
Peter Bush

by a big strong second five-eighth inside his first five-eighth is a favourite move to set up second-phase ball. This move, nevertheless, has been grossly overused at all levels of rugby during the past decade, consequently with a small chance of a clean breakthrough. The deception is increased if, at the moment of the dummy pass, he shouts 'Yes!', 'Now!' or 'Inside!' to ensure that the opposition players are distracted and look to see what he is up to — the vocal dummy. Vocal dummies *must* work, because there is a reflex (automatic) movement of head and eyes towards the source of a loud and unexpected noise. The same applies to players sprinting off down the short side when play is going to be made on the open side. There is no point in making a dummy run unless the opponents see you and have to detach a player to cover you. One further point about dummy runs: if there is a star player in the team, use that person as the dummy and give the ball to some anonymous but efficient character who isn't considered a great threat by the opposition. J. P. R. Williams would surely have served Wales even better as the dummy, instead of satisfying his masochistic urge to be knocked about by seizing the ball and charging heroically into the biggest, roughest forwards he could find.

Pivot play

A few years ago, France scored an extraordinary try against England. From set play, the ball was transferred swiftly along a line of backs who either accidentally or by design were virtually stationary. The ball then reached the full-back. He passed to his wing who was sprinting through on a clear overlap to score unopposed. The explanation for the exceptional success of this move was simple:

- The striker, when he received the ball, was moving straight up the field instead of across, giving the cover defence no chance.

- Because the players were not moving upfield using up the precious yardage, the defence could not reach them in time to prevent the final pass being made.

Space had been created. Clearly this style could not be successful as a routine, as the defence could jog across the field and pick off the striker as he received the ball; but as an occasional variation, it was successful. Jack Gleeson, All Black selector-manager-coach in 1970s, encouraged this principle in the style of first five-eighth play that was developed by the 1978 All Blacks.

The use of the No. 8 as a pivot from set scrums originated from the Bay of Plenty. The No. 8 detaches from the scrum and receives the ball standing still, facing the half-back and close to the off-side line. The second five-eighth makes a dummy run between the No. 8 and the scrum, but the ball is transferred to the first five-eighth who races across from a position behind the scrum and takes the ball from a very short pass and thus suddenly appears among the opposition backs whose timing has been unsettled by covering the dummy run. Usually a clean break results. One obvious variation is to set up the No. 8 and then pass the ball instead from half-back to the full-back coming fast on the blind side. The drawback to this move is that with the recent improvement in scrummaging techniques, it is now difficult to avoid being pushed off the ball with only a seven-man scrum.

One or even two pivots can be used in tap penalty moves with good results. Dummy runners work off both pivots on either side, and it is very difficult for the opposition to judge where the striker will appear and cover the vast number of possibilities that exist. The same principle might be applied to play from scrums using the No. 8 and one of the midfield backs as the pivots. The defence has to spread wide to cover all contingencies, and the element of surprise presents a very real possibility of projecting the striker through the first defensive line.

Decoys

In many of the moves that have been mentioned, the element of surprise can be increased by ostentatiously positioning decoys in suitable positions. Thus in planning a blind-side move within the opposition 22 metre line involving half-back (or No. 8), full-back and wing (as exploited with devastating effect by the Going brothers, three New Zealand players who developed some remarkable combinations), it is well worthwhile to place the first five-eighth in a position where he looks like a man about to drop a goal. With any luck, the opposition inside backs and back row will rush at the first five-eighth while the real move proceeds in an area unpopulated with defenders.

Committing the defence

Another way of clearing a space of defenders is by committing them to a tackle. The French do this beautifully by deliberately forming a maul at the tail of a line-out after a deep throw in. This immediately involves the opposition back row. When the ball is worked back from this maul, it may be taken away upfield by a large prop or lock who is confronted by only a relatively frail first five-eighth. Another simple example is when the No. 8 picks up from a scrum and takes out the opposition flanker as he transfers the ball to his half-back following him round the scrum. In each case, an area has been cleared of defenders to allow space for the striker to develop an attack.

Kicking for space

Lastly, the kicking attack has to be mentioned. The major objection to this form of attack is that hard-won possession is gratuitously given away and the ball now has to be won back. Against this is the indisputable fact that it is much easier to kick the ball up the field than it is to carry it. Furthermore, the threat of a kick into an area that is unoccupied by a defender may spread the defenders and leave a space in which a running and passing attack can be developed. Take the classic dilemma of the opposing left wing when you win good possession from your own put-in at a scrum on the right side of the field after a line-out. This player has to defend a corridor about 15 metres wide. If he stands on the off-side line, your scrum half comes round the scrum and kicks it behind him for your wing to chase. If he stands deeper to block this type of kick, the half-back gives a flat pass to his wing, who now has space to run in and must at the very least cross the gain line. The defending wing can't be in both places at once, there are no other defenders available to help out. Thus either way, you have developed the momentum of an attack. Gareth Edwards exploited this situation brilliantly during the 1974 Lions test series in South Africa.

In summary

The objective of planned moves is to produce the momentum of an attack across the gain line. These tactics must use strength of numbers or of physique, they must contain the vital ingredient of surprise, and they must produce space for the striker to exhibit qualities of speed, strength, subtlety or agility. It is not too much to expect that at each set play a planned move should be called and that the whole team should know what is on. Above all, keep in mind the fact that each transfer of ball from hand to hand involves the chance of error and therefore the fewer transfers the better. Keep it simple and do the simple things well.

Australian half-back Ken Catchpole has problems. While he tries to wrest the ball from All Black hooker Bruce McLeod, Kel Tremain (left) and a scowling Colin Meads move in.

Green and Hahn Photography

Jim Stewart on

Forward Play

- **The main purpose of forward play is to obtain good possession, though the modern rugby forward is interested in wider participation in the game.**

- **Successful efforts in serving line-outs, rucks and mauls require a total commitment to learning the skills. Good possession is the platform by which points are scored by the team.**

- **There is no alternative to constant drilling to achieve technical perfection in the battle for good forward possession.**

- **A fast, aggressive forward who is first to the breakdown to control the ball is an essential player in any team.**

- **Young players look forward to a total involvement in the game, and the wise coach will plan team strategy with this in mind.**

It is not unusual for a coach to proclaim to the forwards that their sole purpose in life is to win good ball possession for their backs. No one is going to minimise the importance of this, but it can get to the stage where such a philosophy of forward play is very stultifying for forwards, especially those who have imagination and inventiveness, and who justifiably want and can contribute creatively to a much wider role for the forwards. There are many forwards, of course, who are entirely fulfilled after 80 minutes of slogging from ruck to scrum to line-out, meeting their commitments there to the full, and contributing ungrudgingly to the overall performance of the team. They are the salt of the rugby earth. A prominent All Black forward once told me after his return from a tour of Wales that he firmly believed several Welsh forwards would like to dispense with the backs and get on with 80 minutes of good scrummaging and mauling. It sounded like an interesting game, but more appropriate for weightlifters than rugby players.

Which brings me to the point I really want to make. This is that if we become too preoccupied with ball winning capabilities, to the exclusion of mobility, development of ball-handling skills, linking of forwards into joint activities with backs — in fact, to the exclusion of what I would call 'total participation' — then we lose a lot from the game. You can be sure, also, that success rates will be lower.

Establishing priorities

I may be wrong, but I'm inclined to think that the tremendous success of British players' scrummaging and mauling techniques in the early 1970s, from which we all learned so much, has been partially responsible for what appears to be a loss of balance in British rugby in the late 1970s. Similarly, through our obsession (and success) with second-phase rugby in New Zealand during the 1960s, we

neglected our first-phase game, until we were handed out a lesson in scrummaging and mauling by the 1971 Lions.

Now, before my Southland, Otago and Canterbury colleagues think that I have gone soft on 'basics', I hasten to reassure them that I haven't. For there is no way that we can develop a team, at whatever grade it is playing in, without a full commitment by the coach and the players to basic ball-winning capabilities. The scrum, line-out, ruck and maul have to be regarded as basic rugby techniques, the individual skills of which have to be mastered, and in which a deep commitment by the whole group is developed and nourished.

I suppose the most common axiom in rugby is that 'you've got to win up front first'. But it all depends what is meant by 'winning up front'. We have all seen games lost by teams winning 70 per cent of the ball.

In my time coaching Canterbury we did this more than once: the Lions game in 1971 was one, the Ranfurly Shield game with Marlborough in 1973 was another — two rather traumatic experiences. But the fact remains that a team starts from well behind if it is not getting 50 per cent of the good possession. I would lay down some specific objectives which, if they are met, greatly increase the probability of developing a really good balanced rugby team, which all the players will enjoy being in.

Firstly, maybe most importantly, when it is your put-in at scrum you must be able to lay up good ball. It sounds simple, and hardly worth saying, but it really is crucial. Put another way: it hardly interests me at all whether hooker A takes two tight-heads to hooker B's one. What really interests me is how much pressure scrum-half A was under to clear the ball from his put-in, compared to scrum-half B. So much of the game is, or should be, directed to forcing attacking scrums, with your loose-head, and so much is lost to the composure of the whole team when this advantage cannot be exploited. Correspondingly, the ability to convert the opposition's loose-head to 'bad ball' yields an immense technical and psychological advantage.

New Zealand v Australia, Second Test, Sydney 1962. An almost balletic clash of forwards with Waka Nathan (white head stripe) conducting. The Australian forward R. Hemming is endeavouring to salvage the ball while being grappled by Colin Meads. His team mate R. Thornett (foreground) has just been toppled by I. N. MacEwan.
Sydney Morning Herald

Played club rugby for Canterbury University, Lincoln College and Massey University. Represented Canterbury 1950-56 as a front-row prop and occasional hooker. During this period also represented NZ Universities and toured with this team in Australia. Coached Canterbury University team 1956-59 when it won the Canterbury competition each year. Selected and coached Canterbury provincial team 1967-73 during which time it captured the Ranfurly Shield twice. Currently co-coach of the Lincoln College senior team.

All Blacks v Lions, Third Test, Dunedin, 1977. All Black prop Bill Bush (on knee) has successfully kept up the forward momentum of this driving play by giving the ball on to wing Brian Ford.

Scott A. G. M. Crawford

43

West Wales and New Zealand packs fighting for possession, All Blacks v West Wales 1978. An outstanding example of good support play with Gary Seear scoring for New Zealand.
Peter Bush

Mastering the skills

A high level of confidence and competence can be achieved only by mastering the skills of scrummaging, body positions, feet positions, gripping procedures, and timing, all through hard repetitive training. There is no easy way to achieving high levels of performance in scrumming. It requires total commitment to hours of practice.

Secondly, it has to be understood by coaches and teams just how much influence line-outs have on the course of a game. There has been some despair about our line-out game in New Zealand since the major changes in the rules, particularly that related to spacing. I find many coaches more frustrated by inability to develop sound line-out play than by any other facet of their coaching. Again it is only by a full commitment to repetitive drills, including positioning, timing, support play, ball maintenance and distribution, that progress will be made. But the important point is that it can be made, despite the difficulty of overcoming the impediments that current line-out laws place in the way of effective line-out work. If musicians were involved in coaching rugby, which regrettably is not very common, I'm sure they would talk about orchestrating the line-out. Because that's what it is all about — getting everyone, winger, jumper, support players, to know their parts perfectly, and then ensuring that it is all put together harmoniously by constant practice and attention to detail. Carrying the analogy a little further, the scrum-half should be seen as the conductor — calling the tune and demanding the attention of every player.

The third objective is to win the battle for second-phase possession. It has to be clearly understood that the strike force has to be at the scene first. No amount of skill and commitment at the ruck, or maul, will compensate for being beaten to the break-downs by the opposition, or even by one member of the opposition if their support play is good. This is why the fast, pressurising, ball-hungry, open-side flanker (or line-out No. 8), with ball-handling skills, is so dominant in modern rugby. No team can afford to be without such a player. Nor should sight ever be lost of the role of backs at the break-down — if they are the nearest to it, it's their job to go in after the ball, and get it.

Beyond this I have only one other point to make about the ruck and the maul. This is that the principle enunciated above, concerning scrummaging, still applies, namely that good possession for you or bad possession for the opposition will result from forward momentum imparted by low body positioning and driving. It is surprising how many of a team's inadequacies elsewhere can be compensated for by total commitment of eight forwards to hitting the break-downs hard and low, and keeping on hitting.

Developing the skills

Returning to my first point, there can be no philosophy of forward play that does not place first emphasis on ball-winning capabilities. But beyond that there is a whole array of individual and group skills which should be consciously developed if the full potential of a team is to be realised. It is important to the future attraction of the game to young players, and to spectators, that these skills be developed strongly. They include co-ordinated passing and driving, linkage moves with backs from set play and counter-attacks, continuity development at break-downs and from mauls. We lose a great deal from the game if we do not place the appropriate emphasis on these exciting aspects of the forward game.

J. J. Stewart on

The Scrum

- **A strong scrum is vital today and is achieved by constant practice and understanding of the correct techniques.**

- **Head up, back straight, legs bent and pushing off the balls of the feet — this is the best body position.**

- **Grips must be strong and maintained throughout the scrum. A static foot position is best.**

- **For a team, the ideal scrum is to win the ball with as little movement as possible.**

- **After-match analysis of scrummaging is helpful and should lead to more effective scrummaging as the season progresses.**

In modern rugby the scrum has become of vital importance — more important than it has ever been before. From a device to restart the game, it has evolved into a unique structure whose dynamics and discipline directly affect other areas of play. If your scrummaging is sound, your performance in rucks and mauls should also be sound. Conversely, the team that is unable to produce a good scrum is at a major disadvantage in any game.

To perform well in this situation of intense physical confrontation requires more than a few hours' practice. The days when hooker and half-back could stay on after an evening's practice to practise their 'combination' are long vanished. Good match scrummaging can be achieved only after many hours of meaningful practice throughout the season. It is the result of the players assiduously practising their individual body position skills and scrummaging techniques and applying them to a unit — a platform to obtain a usable ball — upon which a successful team pattern can be structured.

The secret of good scrummaging is for every player to understand what is required and what the whole scrum is about. Some details are often given great emphasis but are not really that important — for instance, whether (or not) locks have one foot well forward, and which foot. The main thing is that their feet be reasonably close together, with the weight on the ball of the foot, ready for the forward drive.

Training with a scrum machine

There has been considerable debate about scrum machines. Very popular a few years ago, they are now considered by many to be inferior to training with a live scrum. The problem, however, is to get a live scrum to push against, one that will be available frequently and for the length of time that allows for the necessary work. For the majority of teams, at any level, such an opposition is only rarely available, so that leaves us with the scrum machine. It does not need to be too sophisticated. As long as it is reasonably substantial to push against, and isn't uncomfortable for the front row, it is satisfactory.

The scrum machine is fine for ensuring correct body positions and for organising and practising the concerted push. It is no use for practising the hooking action — in a live scrum the hooker usually can see what is happening, but against a scrum machine in trying to see he is likely to hurt his neck. So during training with a scrum machine, never put the ball in.

John West sorts out problems. France v All Blacks. All Blacks left to right: Murray Mexted, Mark Shaw, John Spiers and Andy Dalton.
Peter Bush

Played for Massey University 1941, 43, 44; Auckland Teachers' College 1946, 47, and New Plymouth HSOB 1948. Represented Manawatu 1944. Coached New Plymouth Boys' High School lower grade 1948-49, 1st XV 1950-64. Selector-coach for Taranaki, 1963-69, and Wanganui, 1970, 71. Selector for the North Island 1972-77, 81, and for NZ 1973-77; NZ coach 1973-76. Co-manager of the 1955 NZ Colts in Australia and Sri Lanka. Assistant manager of All Blacks touring Australia and Fiji 1974; Ireland, Wales and England 1974; and South Africa 1976.

Body position

Body position is all-important in scrummaging, and the first principle of correct body position is that the spine must be straight. This is achieved by lifting the head, which will keep the neck straight, and tilting the pelvis backwards, which locks the spine. This is easier to do if the knees are slightly bent.

Players should practise assuming this position away from the scrum. Try it first with the body tipped about 45 degrees forwards on the hips. Try walking around in this position. The result is a rather unlovely, duck-like waddle, but the spine is locked and the back is straight. Then it is a matter of

holding this position, as the trunk is bent fully over to the scrum position. The feet should not be wide apart, the secret is in the position of the knees; and if players find their back curving as they go over, a little more bend in the knees will solve the problem.

At all times in the scrum, as mentioned earlier, the feet should be reasonably close together, with the weight on the ball of the foot rather than on the heels. The feet can move forwards or backwards, away from each other, but never outwards. If the stance is too splay-footed it shifts the centre of gravity of the player, and any consequent foot movement will upset the balance of the whole scrum. It only takes one player with incorrect body position in a scrum to produce a weak scrum.

Pushing positions in scrum, ruck and maul

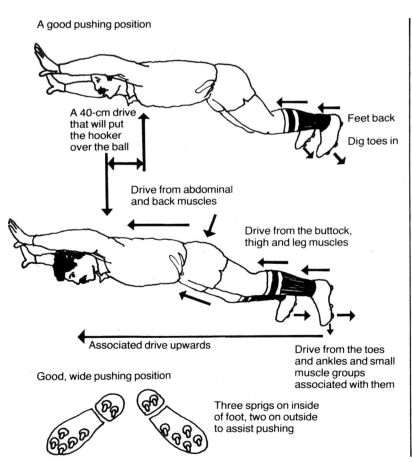

A good pushing position

A 40-cm drive that will put the hooker over the ball

Feet back

Dig toes in

Drive from abdominal and back muscles

Drive from the buttock, thigh and leg muscles

Associated drive upwards

Good, wide pushing position

Drive from the toes and ankles and small muscle groups associated with them

Three sprigs on inside of foot, two on outside to assist pushing

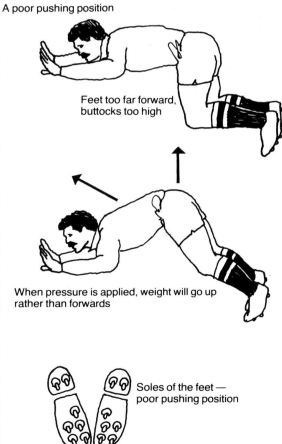

A poor pushing position

Feet too far forward, buttocks too high

When pressure is applied, weight will go up rather than forwards

Soles of the feet — poor pushing position

Binding the scrum

The front row is the platform for the entire scrum. Assuming that each has good body position, their main requirement is to be tightly bound together, both through the shoulders and through the hips. They are responsible for their own binding through the shoulders; the flankers are responsible for binding them through the hips. If the front row is 'spread' by their opponents, the resulting scrum is a disaster.

Binding through the shoulders is best done by each player taking a high grip on the team-mate's jersey. (An arm around the waist will not do it.) The jersey grip needs to be up by the chest, and sufficiently across the jersey so that no slipping is possible. The loose head, for instance, should with the right hand reach around the hooker and grab a handful of the latter's jersey on the left side. This is a long way for the loose head to stretch, but the hooker can help by turning slightly to the right, as the scrum is forming, to allow the grip to be taken.

The loose-head is on the difficult side — it is the hardest side on which to maintain the desired body position and avoid being split away from the hooker. The tight-head is not in the same danger of being split — in fact, the tight-head is usually trying to split the opponents.

Just before the scrum goes over, the loose-head prop should have the right shoulder tucked in behind the hooker. As the front row goes over and the opposing tight-head finds his position, the shoulders will come square on.

The middle row must bind together as the scrum is setting. Locks must bind on to each other very tightly, again using the jersey to do so. All members of the middle row should be in their positions behind the front row, before the front row goes over. Flankers must not wait until the locks are in, before binding on to the scrum. Their job is to bind the front row through the hips. Consequently, as the front row players join their opponents in the pushing position, they must feel the flankers' pressure at once, binding them together through the hip line. This requires a sharp initial butting pressure, which must be maintained.

As the scrum is setting, the locks should put their out-side hand through the prop's legs and grab a handful of jersey, just above the waist line. As the front row goes over, they should reach higher and change their grip for one higher on the chest. A grip in the open front collar is a good one, but some players may not be able to reach that far.

The best position for the back row is between the locks, binding them tightly and pushing each lock forwards as hard as possible. The No. 8 should always adopt this position on the tight-head, unless, of course, a tactical plan demands that he remain off the scrum entirely when opponents are putting in the ball.

There are advantages in packing the No. 8 between the left flanker and lock, if the ball is being hooked very quickly and is getting out of control in that difficult area behind the scrum. But it must be recognised that pushing power is being lost if this is done.

A firm foot position is vital for all players in the scrum. Therefore the less foot movement (and foot replacement) there is the better. For this reason, the scrum should form as near the mark as possible, so that there is a minimum of foot movement between the scrum forming and the final scrum.

The body position and binding of forwards in the scrum

The application of weight from the scrum, focused on the inside shoulders of the two front row supports

The Scrum — how the locks bind in on the front row

The crutch method of attachment

The Scrum — grips by the loose-head and tight-head flankers and the No. 8

The loose-head flanker   The tight-head flanker

The standard method of attachment

The No. 8

The Scrum — a side view of the drive

Drive line is low, hard, up and under the opposition as legs straighten

All Blacks using scrum machine. Up front, from left, Bill Bush, Tane Norton, Kerry Tanner.
Evening Post

Setting the scrum

Since the laws demand that the ball be put in as soon as the front row is ready, the other five team-mates should get into position as quickly as possible. Strictly speaking, the front row is not permitted to wait for them.

Common faults in scrum setting are:

- Loose binding through the shoulders by the front row
- The middle row not going down together, with consequent loose binding of the front row's hip line by the flankers
- Poor body position — bowed backs, splayed feet
- Loose gripping throughout, too loose scrum

The front row should 'ripple' in. The first player to make contact is the tight-head, followed by the hooker, and then the loose-head.

Pressure from the middle row and back row should be on at once. A sustained push is required — and this can be exhausting work.

With every player in position, their backs set, feet in position, weight on the ball of the foot, and pushing, the half should be signalled that the scrum is ready. The hooker can do this with a hand sign, or perhaps the tight-head lock, who should have the best 'feel' of the state of readiness of the scrum.

There must be some communication to the whole scrum that this point has been reached; and when it has, full and sustained pressure should be exerted and the ball put in.

Very little foot movement should be made and, if it is necessary, it should be in very small steps (ideally, only centimetres) straight up the field. The final push comes, from digging the sprigs in, transferring the weight from the ball of the foot to the toes, and straightening the knees. This total push must be sustained until the ball is out of the scrum, and everyone must contribute. It is most undesirable if this push disintegrates into a 'jerk'; then the scrum will start to go backwards against a good opposition scrum, with dire consequences for your half-back.

The main objective should be to hold the line, not to go forwards. If the opposition can be pushed back, it is a bonus; but it won't happen very often with well-matched teams. The ideal is to set a scrum that wins the ball without moving in any direction at all. This is the perfect platform for the half and the half's backline to launch an attack.

Analysing the faults

Common faults with scrum dynamics are:

- Scrum not ready when the ball goes in
- Scrum moving about — poor foot position, front row split by opponents
- Jerking, rather than long sustained pushing
- Scrum going backwards once the ball is hooked — push unsustained, relaxing grips

After each match, there should be an analysis of the scrummaging and an honest airing of any weaknesses displayed. This way the team should increase the effectiveness of its scrummaging as the season progresses. In such an atmosphere — if scrum improvement is one of the team objectives — a prop, for example, should have no hesitation in telling his flanker that he is pushing him too late or insufficiently, or is not sustaining his push.

Scrum patterns will keep on changing as the game (in all its facets) continues to evolve. But there is no part of the game that so uniquely belongs to rugby. It may be hard work, but it is honest and rewarding — and fun too, when you perfect it as a unified team skill.

Young players scrummaging. Good scrummaging can only be achieved after many hours of meaningful practice throughout the season. The team that cannot produce a good scrum is at a major disadvantage in any game.
Christchurch Press

Stamina, strength, speed, suppleness and skill. The five S's needing cultivation to be able to play good rugby especially at international level. All Blacks v Springboks. All Blacks: flanker, Ian Kirkpatrick, front row, Bill Bush, hooker, Tane Norton.
Peter Bush

John Graham on

Attack & Defence from Scrum

- **All scrums can be 'attacking', irrespective of their position in the field. If the eight forwards move quickly into position, go down with control with the aim of making a forward movement then that scrum will be an 'attacking scrum'.**

- **In attack the No. 8 and the open-side flanker follow the ball, the blind-side flanker moving behind the scrum in support of the play and the remaining five team-mates going straight to the play.**

- **In defence the flanker ensures that the half-back passes, the open-side flanker and No. 8 are moving to the play and the blind-side flanker is moving back in defence.**

- **Depending on the player's running and handling skills, a No. 8 may be used as a dummy half or dummy first five-eighth. The scrum must be moving forwards if the No. 8's decision is to pick up the ball.**

The scrum as a basis for attack

The scrum has changed considerably in the past five or six years and as a result has become a more important aspect of the game. Now it can be a means of destroying an opposing team — in the past it was more a means of restarting the game.

Most coaches who want to run a successful team must have a good scrummaging eight. If their team can't scrum well in every scrum, whether it's a defensive scrum or an attacking scrum, they will have trouble in that game, and I imagine that one of the key aspects of coaching is to create a situation whereby the team can attack backwards and forwards from scrums. So, you need to think of all eight forwards and their function as a scrummaging unit before you can consider specifically the function of the loose forward, for example.

I believe you can attack from a scrum anywhere. In other words, you can attack from a scrum on your goal line if the other team is putting in the ball, simply by pushing them backwards; that might be considered a defensive scrum — it's defensive in terms of its position on the field. All scrums, I believe — your ball or their ball — must be seen as attacking scrums. What you do when you've won the ball (or lost it) is a different matter, but if the scrum goes down it must be seen by your team as an attacking scrum.

Forming the scrum

Ten years ago the method of form-up was not particularly important. Now it's critical. The speed with which you form up, the method in which the grips are taken, the way the front row forms, and the positioning of the hooker towards the loose-head, on your ball, and the tight-head positioning on to the hooker on your ball — all these things are extremely important, and as a coach I would place great emphasis on how we form our scrum. We go from there to where the hands grip, which hand or arm goes round the body — how it grips, where it grips and the tightness of the grip are extremely significant. The distance of the scrum from the point of contact with the opponents is also important. There's no point in positioning your eight bodies in the right place and the grips tight, and then moving the whole eight a long way forward to meet the opposition. The scrum has to be in the exact position, with the front row bending to hit the opponents with the minimum of movement of legs, arms and trunk. These are some of the factors that any coach needs to emphasise before going into particular aspects of necks and feet and inside feet up and outside feet up, and so on, which are all part of detailed coaching of the scrum. Form-up, grips and proximity to the opposition are, therefore, in my mind, the three primary aspects of forming the scrum.

Protecting the scrum-half

To start with, we want the ball won while moving forwards. Our scrum-half can't function properly otherwise, so our aim must be not to go backwards. If you hold your ground, you are doing reasonably well. If you go forwards, you are doing even better. That's the first requirement for protecting any scrum-half.

Channelling the ball is the next important factor. Where does the half-back pick up the ball? Because the rules are absurd in not prohibiting the defensive half-back from following the ball through a scrum, channelling becomes an important part of the game; and this means having the skill to push the ball to the No. 8's feet who can then push it away from the offensive half-back. I suppose the loose-head flanker can push a little wider thus causing the scrum-half to go around him — all these are simple methods of protecting the scrum-half. The two best methods are, firstly, going forwards as you win the ball, for that forces the defensive half-back to move backwards (and then you can release it while they're on the backward movement); and secondly, channelling the ball away from the defensive half-back's movement around the scrum. I would add a further point: the half-back does not want to receive the ball from a screwed scrum, so the scrum must stay straight to ensure controlled ball to the half-back.

A dive pass by Marcel Pugeot. France v Marlborough, 1968.
Peter Bush

Considered an astute, fast-moving loose forward and a determined, authoritative captain. Played for Auckland 1956, 57 (University) and Canterbury 1958-65 (Christchurch HSOB); also for the South Island 1958, 61-65; played in the NZ Trials 1958, 60-63, 65; for NZ Universities 1957; New Zealand XV 1958. Represented NZ 1958 against Australia, 1960 toured South Africa, as captain in several matches. In the 1961-64 seasons he played in all internationals and succeeded Wilson Whineray as captain after the 1963-64 British tour.

The position of the No. 8

I am generally opposed to taking the No. 8 out of the ideal pushing position with his head between the two locks. Between the loose-head lock and the loose-head flanker, the No. 8 is not an effective pushing machine and is certainly not as effective in maintaining a tight grip on the locks' bottoms to keep them in the right place. But occasionally, if the hooker is very quick, or if a player of the calibre of the 1970s All Black Sid Going was the defensive half-back (he was very good at getting around on to your own half-back), or if your scrum is right on top, you might have to put the No. 8 into that area to control the hook.

Wheeling the scrum

I'm conservative in this, and I think you need a well-formed scrum to start talking about wheeling the scrum. When we win the ball, I believe we want to win it going forwards, and going straight forwards; and the less wheeling motion the better, unless it's a planned move from the scrum.

There is definitely a place for wheeling the scrum: you can wheel the scrum on their put-in. If you do this, it effectively stops their forward movement, and most well-coached scrums now attempt to wheel the opposition scrum on their put-in. It also throws your half-back around on to your opposing half-back, and your flanker as well. Wheeling the

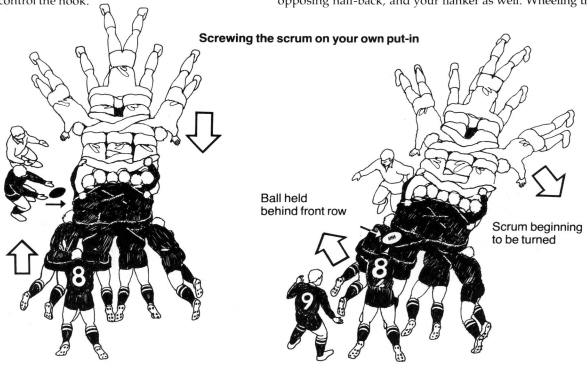

Screwing the scrum on your own put-in

Ball held
behind front row

Scrum beginning
to be turned

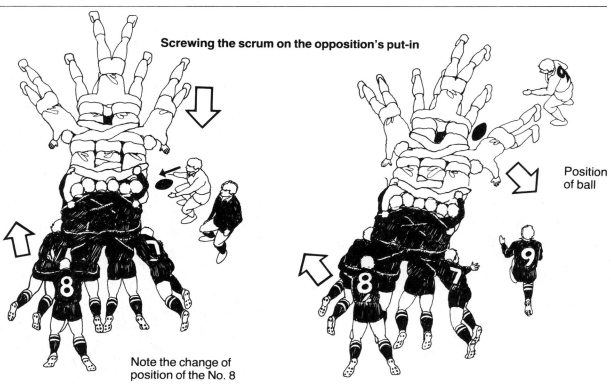

Screwing the scrum on the opposition's put-in

Position
of ball

Note the change of
position of the No. 8

scrum can also be an attacking move, especially close to the opposition line when it pushes the opposing half-back and flanker away from the ball. All Black Gary Seear scored against Ireland in 1979 from a quarter wheel and a No. 8 pickup. Alex Wyllie, an impressive New Zealand loose forward, used this very effectively, as does Canterbury Province still.

The front row, side row and back row break off with the ball at toe

New Zealand v Australia. The Australians move up in defence from a scrum as Mark Donaldson passes to All Black backs.
Peter Bush

Wallaby No. 8 Greg Cornelson breaks from the back of a scrum. Behind him is John Hipwell.
Col Whelan

On winning the ball

Let's assume first of all that we're using our backs from the scrum. And that the half-back is passing the ball out to the first five-eighth, I believe there must be a set break formation for our loose forwards in support of our back attack. The open-side flanker and No. 8 will go straight to play, to follow the ball. The No. 8 will be automatically slightly behind the ball because of his positioning in the scrum. The flanker will be slightly in front of him initially. He goes straight across the field towards the ball carrier. The No. 8 moves directly to play — that is, he follows the ball. Any cover defence that's required from loose forwards comes from the blind-side flanker, who moves around the rear of the scrum and then provides greater depth in defence if the ball is dropped. Certainly it enables this player to support the attacking play if we have an attack that goes up to or across the advantage line.

Corner flagging by forwards

I've always been opposed to any form of corner flagging. Certainly under the present rules it is not necessary. The backs should stand deeper at all times, and this makes it easier for backs to cover. A loose forward was corner flagged in the old days because of the close line-up of backs, and therefore if a break was made, it was a clean break right through; and you would find the covering forward picked up the opposition back at the extreme lateral extension of the play. Under the present rules we need no corner flagger from forwards — we want the forwards going straight to play.

When the ball is lost

When we lose the ball from a scrum, the first job of the flankers is to make sure the half-back doesn't run. Some coaches do allow the half-back on one side of the scrum to take the place of the flanker, and thus release the flanker to

Attack and defence from scrum — the normal defensive screen when the ball has been won and is being fed (note the positions of the open-side and blind-side flankers and the No. 8

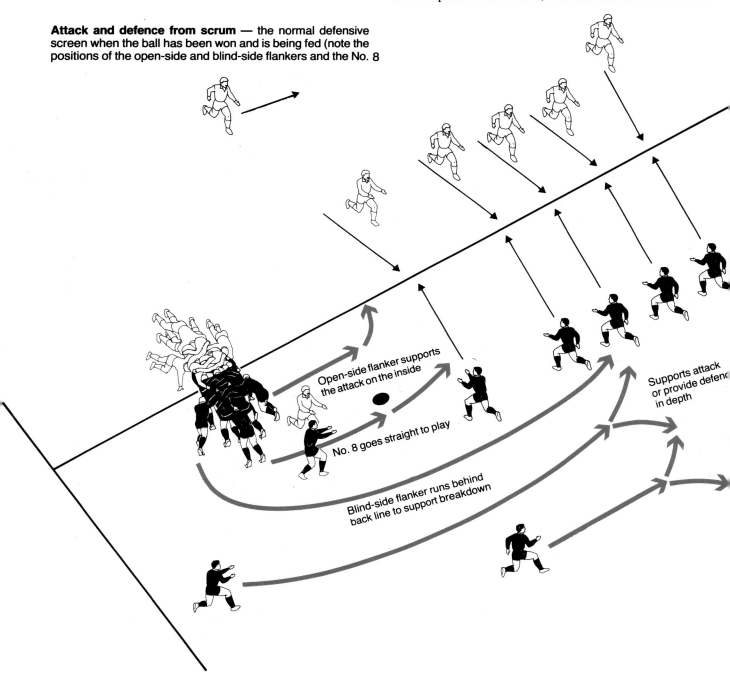

Open-side flanker supports the attack on the inside

No. 8 goes straight to play

Blind-side flanker runs behind back line to support breakdown

Supports attack or provide defence in depth

go straight to play. I've never believed in this. I think it is the job of the flankers to make sure the half-back passes the ball, or is not running with the ball. It's also the flankers' responsibility to make sure that if there are any ploys around the scrum by the opposing No. 8, or by loose forward in conjunction with the half-back, they are stopped before they reach the advantage line. For that reason I think it is simpler and clearer for defensive loose forwards not to move into the open field until the ball is away from the scrum.

To go back to the No. 8. We've lost the scrum ball and the ball is now passed. The first objective has been achieved, the flankers have forced the ball to be passed to the first five-eighth or to a back. At that point, if the play has gone open side, the open-side flanker moves straight to play, the No. 8 moves straight to play and the blind-side flanker again provides cover defence. If a loose forward is running deep — and he would do so only if the ball has got out to the outside backs — then it is the blind-side flanker's job to provide the cover, not the No. 8's. I believe there are two

offensive-defensive forwards from a scrum on a lost ball, open-side flanker and No. 8. The defensive player who gives you depth is your blind-side flanker.

Communicating verbally

It is essential that the players — the loose forwards, in particular — know in which direction the play is going to go. Every time the ball is put into a scrum by a half-back, a clear sign is needed to indicate the direction of the ball.

Our key man in the scrum when the ball is being put in by the opposition is our tight-head flanker, because he sees the half-back — he's right beside him — and he calls the play for the rest of the scrum. He watches the opposing half-back's hands, and when the hands move our tight-head flanker calls 'weight' when the ball is about to come in. Also he should listen very carefully for the opposition's signals, so that if their signals are 'left' or 'right', 'one' or 'two', 'rock' or 'lamb' (which simply mean 'right' and 'left') the tight-head

Attack and defence from scrum — the normal defensive when the opponents have won the ball and are sending it out along their back line

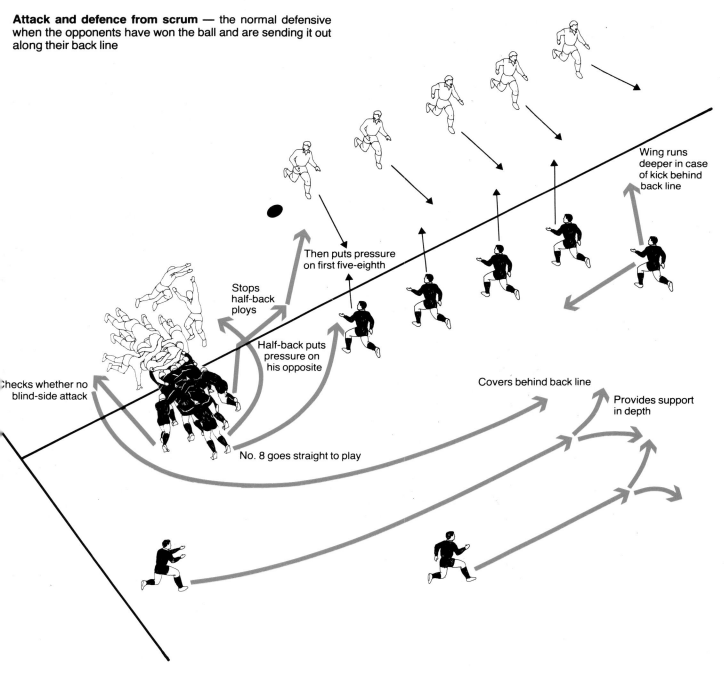

Wing runs deeper in case of kick behind back line

Then puts pressure on first five-eighth

Stops half-back ploys

Half-back puts pressure on his opposite

Checks whether no blind-side attack

Covers behind back line

Provides support in depth

No. 8 goes straight to play

flanker translates for the rest of the 'dummies'. 'Concrete-mixers' like front-row forwards must have that translated for them. So if I'm tight-head flanker and Sid Going comes up and says 'lamb', I say 'right' — which means I've got to think more than a little bit. It's a small but very important thing; and good teams, well-coached sides, will do that very well. Unfortunately the majority of sides don't do it well at all. They simply don't find out the direction of play. Too many loose forwards, for example, stand up at scrum time and look around to see if they can find out what's going to happen — and that's disastrous for your own scrum, because unless the whole eight go down together the scrum will not function at all. You can't be deciphering the signals of the opposition by standing up while the rest of your other five are in contact with the opposition. Of course, when we put the ball in, the half-back *must* indicate the direction of play from the scrum.

When the ball goes to the blind side

On the subject of attacking and defensive positions of loose forwards on the blind side: Obviously the half-back's most effective supporting forward initially must be the No. 8, because as soon as the half-back moves right or left the No. 8 is immediately on-side. The blind-side flanker is still ahead of play, until play reaches him, so your most effective supporting forward on attack on the blind side must be your No. 8 — therefore he becomes a very critical player. Gary Seear, for example, in the second Test against Australia in 1978, did this very well.

A competent open-side flanker also, when the play is on the blind side, can become the next most effective supporting player. He knows it's going blind, he has a good ear, and he knows we're running away from him and he can leave the scrum quickly to support a blind-side move.

With the knowledge that the ball is coming back into play,

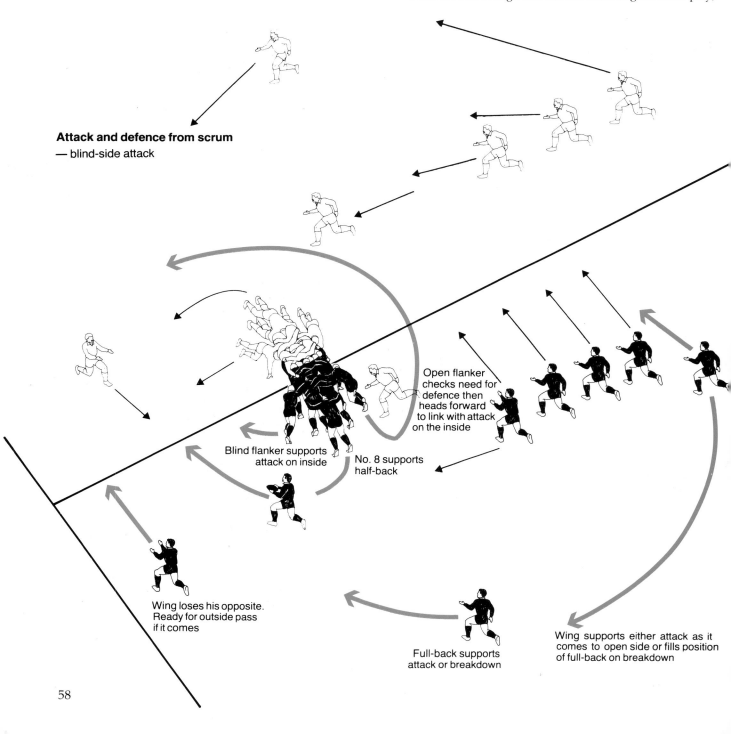

Attack and defence from scrum
— blind-side attack

Open flanker checks need for defence then heads forward to link with attack on the inside

Blind flanker supports attack on inside

No. 8 supports half-back

Wing loses his opposite. Ready for outside pass if it comes

Full-back supports attack or breakdown

Wing supports either attack as it comes to open side or fills position of full-back on breakdown when you're running a blind-side move, the rest of the forwards run straight to play, straight towards the touch line (and not worrying about a centre kick).

One of the backs would be responsible if the ball reached the winger and he centre-kicked. I wouldn't ask any loose forward, or any other forward, to try to anticipate a centre kick from the blind side. Or for that matter, from the open side.

However, the games of Ron Jarden and Bill Clarke can be classified as a particular case. If you look carefully, their centre kicks always occurred when the ball had gone right across the flank. In other words, the ball had gone open side, and the centre kick came from open-side play rather than from blind-side play. I think it would be wrong to ask loose forwards, when a blind-side attack is being mounted, to look for centre kicks. Nine times out of ten they would be running in the centre field and the ball wouldn't be there, so your best attacking forwards would be running away from the ball

Lions v All Blacks, Wellington 1977. The Lions are developing a strong back attack from a scrum.
Peter Bush

Attack and defence from scrum — defence against a blind-side attack

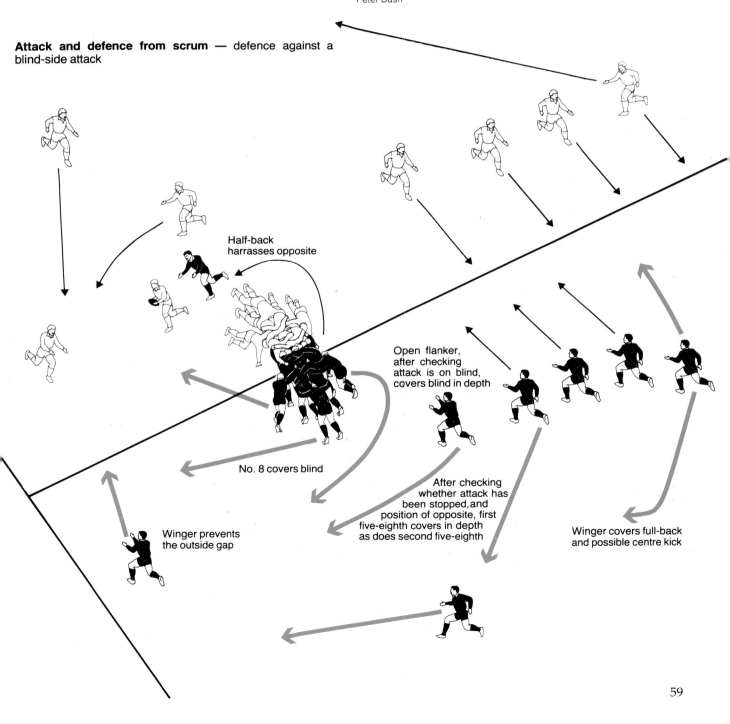

Half-back harrasses opposite

Open flanker, after checking attack is on blind, covers blind in depth

No. 8 covers blind

After checking whether attack has been stopped, and position of opposite, first five-eighth covers in depth as does second five-eighth

Winger prevents the outside gap

Winger covers full-back and possible centre kick

instead of to it. Rugby is a game of percentages, and the centre kick percentage is very low.

What would be our defence against the opposition running on the blind side? Starting from scratch there is a wide blind on defence — a very dangerous position for any scrum to be in — I'd naturally want our scrum to go forward. The first defensive strategy is to scrum well and give the opposition bad ball.

This means that everybody pushes, including our hooker. After we've pushed them back, or made it difficult for them to win the ball, the first forward to leave the scrum when there is a wide blind side must be the No. 8. Many coaches teach that when there is a wide blind, the No. 8 moves earlier than usual. When a ball is lost, the No. 8 stands up and looks to see that play is going to the blind side. In fact some coaches, myself included, have coached the No. 8 to automatically move blind side first when there is a wide

blind. This means that the most effective defensive forward is on the blind side early. And all good teams are going to use the blind, from scrums, when there is a blind. It's logical, when you have a wide blind side, to run your backs that way. You can take it as a set rule that the No. 8 gets off and moves blind. He is your best offensive-defensive forward on a wide blind when you've lost the ball. The other two flankers, also, have a set job: no one moves around the scrum. The half-back doesn't run blind — if he does run, he's chopped. He can't be allowed to set up a move like the Canterbury/Alex Wyllie move with any loose forward around him on the blind side. If he does, it is the blind-side flanker's job to nail *one* man — if he puts one out of play, he's fulfilled his role. His main task is to allow no one on his side to cross the advantage line. The open-side flanker covers around the back of the scrum on to the blind side and provides your third loose forward as in-depth cover.

Attack and defence from scrum — defence against centre field attack

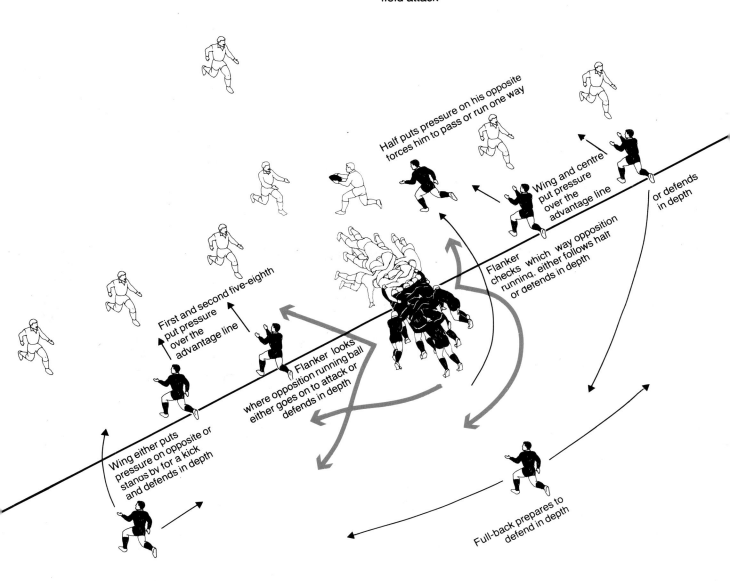

Half puts pressure on his opposite forces him to pass or run one way

Wing and centre put pressure over the advantage line

or defends in depth

Flanker checks which way opposition running, either follows half or defends in depth

First and second five-eighth put pressure over the advantage line

Flanker looks where opposition running ball either goes on to attack or defends in depth

Wing either puts pressure on opposite or stands by for a kick and defends in depth

Full-back prepares to defend in depth

Defence from the scrum against a kick

To defend against good kicking from the scrum is much more difficult to legislate for. For instance, the grubber kick is something that some backs use very well. I would use my No. 8 in this situation. If we've lost the ball and there's a player who chips a lot (1978-79 All Black Eddie Dunn is a good kicker, open and blind), I believe it's the No. 8 who has to deal with such a defensive situation. The No. 8 has the time and is deeper at the base of the scrum anyway when the ball is lost, to move out into the field more quickly. The No. 8 then becomes the key defensive loose forward if you're against any back who is kicking. That is for 'the box', the small chip, or the grubber. The longer kicks are the problem of the backs rather than the loose forwards.

The dummy half-back

On the question of a dummy half-back, I suppose the commonest strategy is the use of the No. 8 breaking off to create an extra man as half-back, or driving forward (as did Alex Wyllie) to create secondary phase by letting in the loose forwards. Mounting these attacks depends on having a stable scrum. The No. 8 can't detach himself to pick up the ball (if he's the first man to pick it up, and generally he will be) unless the scrum is stable and moving forwards. He can't do it moving backwards. If the scrum is going backwards, and that move is called, the No. 8 must pick it up and take his chances, there is no point in passing.

Let's assume first of all that the No. 8 is going to pick up the ball and pass it to the half-back. The only thing required then is a stable, forward-moving scrum. The No. 8 pushes first, and when the ball has come back to him he takes out one

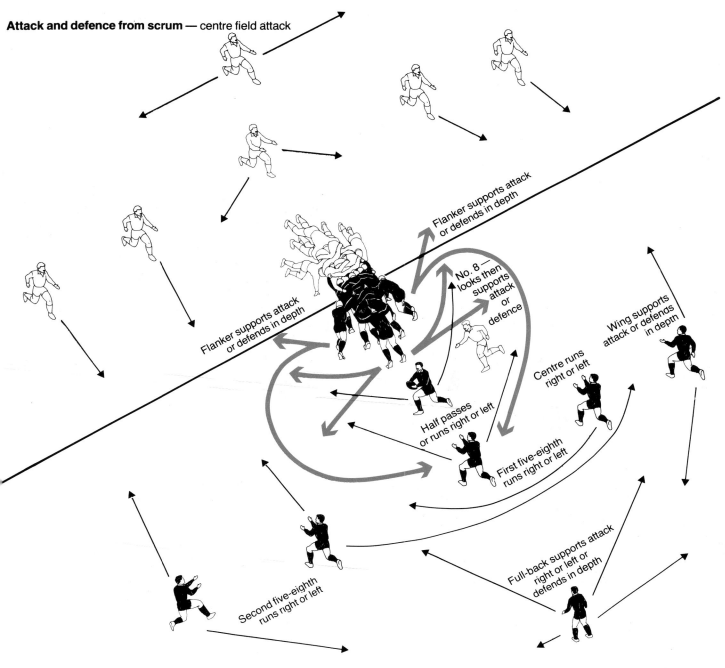

Attack and defence from scrum — centre field attack

Flanker supports attack or defends in depth

Flanker supports attack or defends in depth

No. 8 — looks then supports attack or defence

Wing supports attack or defends in depth

Half passes or runs right or left

Centre runs right or left

First five-eighth runs right or left

Second five-eighth runs right or left

Full-back supports attack right or left or defends in depth

opposition player and passes to the half-back. Whichever way the play goes, the open-side flanker or the blind-side flanker becomes the immediate supporting loose forward, and the other loose forward comes around the back of the scrum to support that move. If it's the No. 8 who is to receive the ball from the half-back, that's a more difficult exercise and one that I don't think should be used as much as the traditional one where he takes the ball himself. One reason against it is that he can't push as well. The No. 8 has to move out to play dummy, or to play first five-eighth (which is in fact what he is doing); he is off the scrum too soon; and you lose the effectiveness of a very strong No. 8, such as 1970s All Black Laurie Knight or Gary Seear — you want them in there scrummaging. If you intend to use the No. 8 as a battering ram at first five-eighth, you must assume you will lose scrummaging power.

I'd stress that point again if you were considering using the No. 8 as a dummy half. The No. 8 can push, pick up the ball and pass. Or he can push, pick up the ball and run. Those tasks are easier to perform than asking him to be the first five-eighth with the half-back passing to him. Brian Lochore continually used this method, but it was possible in Brian's day because there wasn't so much emphasis on scrummaging. Scrummaging as we know it today has developed only in the past seven or eight years — you must all be in and push.

Defence against the Wyllie-type move

Correctly executed, the Canterbury/Alex Wyllie move is almost infallible — though it hasn't been as effective in recent years as it once was. I think Canterbury overuse it and therefore are predictable in certain areas of the field. In defence you would certainly coach your loose forwards to combat it; you'd tell both your flankers that a 'Wyllie' could run either side. Wyllie's great value, before we devised ways of stopping him was that he could run either way, that he stood square behind the scrum and therefore had both options open to him. Both flankers would have to be on the alert to tackle a 'Wyllie' as soon as he moves; the interceptor, has to be the flanker, no one else is capable.

Whichever way he runs, the flanker becomes the critical defensive forward initially, with quick and very immediate support from the No. 8. It must be a holding tackle for the ball near the line. If you can hold him and the ball, you've performed well. Hold him with the ball and push him back, then you've performed exceptionally.

If you're a good attacker, you take a flanker out of play by forcing him to tackle, and then spin and put the ball on to your own flanker who's coming up in support — aiming at creating a gap between your opponents' half-back and first five. The great value of that move is that you create at least a strong, attacking maul and you haven't lost the ball.

Attempted push-over in a scrum

How do you defend yourself against a push-over try? There is only one way of stopping it, and that is to go to ground. It's illegal, but you must do it. If your opponents force you backwards, and you're on the move, you must go to ground; and the only people to do that are the front row.

If you've got the ball in your scrum and your opponents are pushing you backwards, you need to clear the ball quickly. You must coach your side — particularly if you know your side is not competent enough to hold a strong scrummaging side — that the ball has to be put in as soon as you make contact with the opponents. Put in the ball and let it travel straight through your scrum. Don't fumble around with the ball in your scrums. Don't give the opposition a chance to become settled. It's the speed of your form-up, and the accuracy and quickness with which you can attack the opposition and move the ball in and out, that's the most

effective way of opposing a very competent scrum. Certainly it isn't the three-man scrum, that's a waste of time, and an admission of failure and incompetence.

In terms of morale for a side, if you can win a push-over try it's one of the finest achievements — because really you've eliminated another forward pack. The best person to do it? I think either the loose-head flanker, because the ball should be somewhere in front of his eyes, or the No. 8, or the half-back who is probably the most effective because he can see it, and he's not pushing. Once you go for a push-over the whole eight need to push very hard and thus the half-back becomes the player best able to score. All Black Mark Donaldson scored magnificently against the 1978 Wallabies.

The loose forwards' role

For a start, I'd oppose any specialisation in the loose forward positions — for example, blind-side/open-side flankers. I believe it is far more important to talk about loose-head and tight-head flankers — that is where the specialisation is necessary. The loose-head flanker pushes differently from the tight-head flanker, he sees more of the ball on his side's put-in and much less of it on the opposition sides' put-in. He needs to concentrate on watching the ball go through the opposition's scrum, as it's difficult for him to see it. A very technical point this. Also the loose-head flanker will find that the opposition half-back runs his side most often — it's the natural side for the opposition half-back to run. I could say a lot more about this sort of specialisation and I believe that New Zealand coaches ignore it almost completely. I would specialise in my flankers therefore — their jobs are quite different — and obviously the No. 8 is a totally specialised position in the scrum and *must* be seen as such.

I feel that the importance of ball-handling skills in the loose forwards is increasing. This is partly because of an increase in the importance of the maul, but it is also because new rules have created a situation where there is more flow and the forwards get into the backline more often, which means that loose forwards have the chance to run on to the ball carried by backs more often than when I was a player. The kick into touch rule has also helped. (I always pushed with my outside foot back, but I think you are a better pushing unit if both your feet are back.)

Loose forwards *cannot* function unless the tight forwards are functioning properly. There is no way that the flankers can leave the scrum if they are going backwards. If you are struggling all the time to hold the opposition in set play, particularly in long, hard scrummaging, you certainly won't be an effective loose forward. There is a maximum time for you to push in the scrums. You just can't continue pushing and pushing. I can't give you specific rules, but the loose forwards must be sensitive to this aspect — they must learn when to stop pushing in the scrums and concentrate on defending and attacking. I believe a flanker or half-back can call this. The Lions on a recent tour of New Zealand had loose forwards who spent too much of their time pushing and therefore weren't as effective in supporting back movements or in helping in defence, because they spent too much time on the scrum. You must make flankers aware of this, you must coach until it's understood by the players.

What would I expect of a loose forward? He must be able to tackle; he must be able to grovel for the ball; he must have sure hands, the intelligence to assess play; and he must be conscious of the importance of appropriate, low body position. He must be assertive and fearless. He must be able to function within the loose forward trio and within the team's pattern.

Australia v New Zealand 1972. Sid Going keeps a careful eye on the Australian half-back.
National Publicity Studios, Wellington

And what qualities would I look for in choosing a loose forward group? It is very important to choose three complementary players. In other words, you wouldn't choose three Gary Seears, just as you wouldn't choose three Leicester Rutledges. You want a dynamic aggressive loose forward who is quick and sharp and accurate, who moves around the field, will grovel on the ground and can range freely off the set plays. Examples would be All Blacks Graham Mourie, Graham Williams, Dick Conway, John Graham and Bill Clarke.

You want a competent No. 8 who can play at No. 7 in the line-out, who is strong and scrums hard, who can make the moves around the scrum we've been talking about, but who won't be as wide-ranging as your first. New Zealand examples would be Gary Seear, Laurie Knight, Brian Lochore and Peter Johnson.

You want also a player in between — a tight/loose forward (if you like) who has speed, strength, can play at six in the line-out, a rare individual indeed. Examples would be 1960-70s All Blacks Barry Ashworth, Ian Kirkpatrick, Waka Nathan and Kel Tremain. All must be capable of intelligent analysis, as they have to follow set patterns, perfectly. All must be able to *tackle*

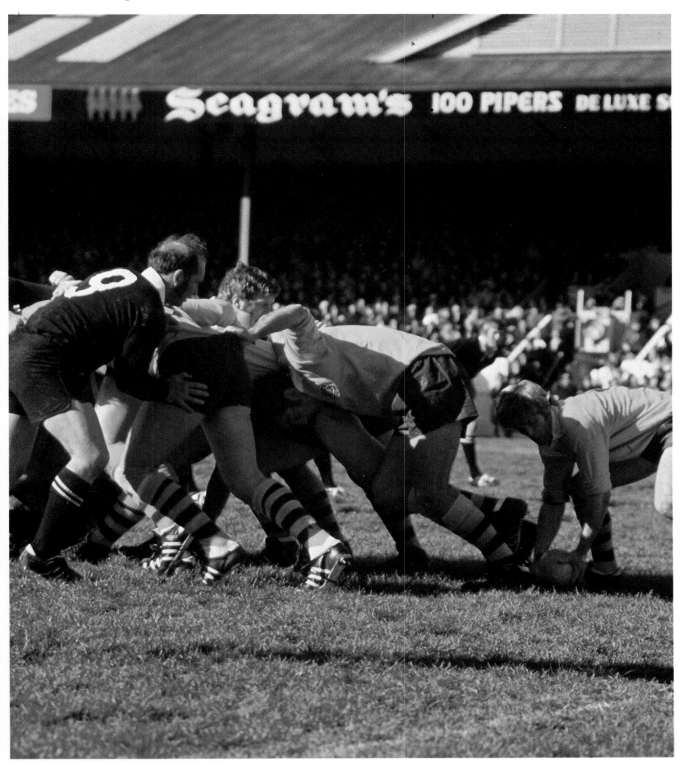

Tane Norton on

Hookers

- **To be a successful hooker, good scrummaging is required from the remaining seven forwards.**
- **The attributes of a good hooker are: quick reflexes, agility, reasonable strength, extreme competitiveness, ability to remain cool and ability to co-ordinate and motivate team-mates in the scrum.**
- **The method of binding should be well understood, and particularly the requirement of the loose- and tight-heads in assisting the hooker to find and maintain his best position for hooking.**
- **The communication between half-back and hooker is crucial. The half-back must be aware when the hooker wants the ball in.**

I think the most important aspect of good, strong scrummaging is pride. The success of the scrum depends on a team effort, rather than the particular skill of the hooker, and the hooker is only as good as his other seven forwards. I'd like to stress this point.

The attributes of a good hooker

I don't think height, for example, matters too much; it is really the physical attributes — co-ordination, agility — of the hooker that are more important. There have been short hookers, for instance Denis Young, the indestructible 1950s and 60s All Black; and fellow New Zealander Frank Colhurst, a much taller man, but both were outstanding hookers.

There are certain special skills or aptitudes a hooker needs. Firstly, quick reflexes, agility with the lower part of the body, and a certain degree of physical strength.

As for mental attitude or temperament, I think the hooker must be competitive and, of course, have pride in hooking skill. He must also have the type of personality that allows him to develop team effort, particularly with his props. He must be able to withstand psychological pressure and not be put off because of the geographical position of the scrum. He

The All Black scrum — the basis for successful hooking. Front row All Blacks: Gary Knight, Andy Dalton, John Ashworth, with moustache.
Peter Bush

A consistently first-rate hooker and all-round forward. Played for Mid-Canterbury 1961 (Methven) and Canterbury 1969-77 (Linwood); also for the South Island 1971-75; NZ Trials 1970-72, 74-77; NZ Maoris 1969-75, 77. Represented NZ 1971-77 — a sequence of 27 consecutive internationals. In 1977 he captained the All Blacks in their win against the Lions. Also captained NZ Maoris team on Pacific tour, against the All Blacks 1973, Fiji 1974, Tonga 1975, and against the 1977 Lions.

must be ice-cool on attack and on defence. He must also — and this is most important — be a motivator of the scrum. It is the hooker who motivates the front row and motivates the pushing middle row. In short, he has to be a leader.

His first priority must be to win his own ball. The top hookers are at the top not because of the tight-heads they win but because they have always retained their own ball.

Tight-heads in the scrum

Early in my career I was the type of hooker who went for tight-heads all the time, working on the premise that the more I did so the greater were the chances of success. As you reach the levels of the top club sides, the provincial sides and the international sides, you come up against skilful packs and hookers, and it is very difficult to get tight-heads against them. Sometimes you might decide before scrum entry to go for a tight-head, but when the scrum goes down it is impossible because of your position to strike for the tight-head. If you have indicated to the scrum that you will try for a tight-head and it becomes impossible, you need a code call to alert them to the fact that you are not trying and you can then revert to your eight-man push.

I believe that the top hookers today are very selective, maybe striking three or four times during a game. You have the advantage of surprise and you can select your position for its attacking potential.

On other occasions, you can concentrate on an eight-man push, thereby destroying the quality possession of the attacking of the opposition side on its loose-head. Bad possession for the opposition may be of greater advantage to you than the ball itself. You may not win the ball but you can make it quite unpleasant and uncomfortable for the opposition hooker and front row.

Binding on the front row

I am a strong believer in the hooker's binding over the shoulders of both props. Personally I do not alter that position at all, not even for tight-heads, although I know that some hookers bind under. I am against this because of the risk of injury. Once committed the hooker who binds under is trapped and I believe that this technique should be banned. I am also aware that some hookers bind with one arm over and one arm under; for instance, going for a tight-head the hooker will bind with his left arm over and his right arm under, allowing him to get closer to the opening of the channel with his right leg. I did not have to use that technique as I was supple enough and agile enough to get across in the normal way.

I know that many locks now prefer to bind between the legs, coming up with the hand grip on the chest, taking a mid-stomach position initially and then getting a second grip well up on the chest. That technique is said to help the locks get under the buttocks of the props. I see a danger in that technique in that it may encourage the lock to pull the chest and body of the prop downwards, thus affecting the vision of the hooker and creating pressure on the hooker's body and therefore limiting leg movement.

Another technique is for the lock to bind on the inside leg of the prop, coming up through the crotch and across on to

The Scrum — grips by the hooker

Under the shoulder

the hip, binding with the hand near the waistband of the trousers. That technique avoids the pulling-down danger, but again the locks would have to ensure that they did not slip down on to the hamstring muscle and the knee joint of the prop, again causing a loss of stability and forcing the front row down and in turn affecting the hooker.

I personally encourage locks to bind with the old-fashioned outside grip, particularly on the loose-head side. It seems to be a matter of preference and comfort and confidence. The test is whether there is an effective shove or push and a stable platform. If that is achieved it probably matters little which technique is used. However, I must stress that binding must be tight.

The hooker must first bind tightly with the loose-head prop. I like the loose-head prop to step behind me and come up under my left arm. The tight-head prop then joins to form the complete front row, also binding tightly under the hooker's right shoulder. It is important on the loose-head side for the loose-head prop to pull the hooker over and around to face the channel and mouth of the scrum, and it is probably preferable to have the right hand of the loose-head prop up about the chest or rib cage of the hooker to encourage and assist the hooker to drop and turn his right shoulder. I must emphasise that it is important for the loose-head prop to pull the hooker towards, and not away from, the mouth of the scrum. Some props make the mistake of pulling the right side of the hooker back and away from the scrum, making the hooker's right shoulder position impossible and of course taking his feet further away from the ball. Conversely when the hooker is going for the tight-head strike the loose-head prop should try and turn him the opposite way: that is, towards the tight-head side by pulling back and around, or by pushing the hooker towards the tight-head prop and thus the mouth of the scrum on that side.

The tight-head and loose-head props must bind firmly in such a way that the scrum will never split.

The method of entry into the scrum

Scrum entry is most important, and it is then that you build up a good rapport with your props and the rest of your scrum. On your loose-head the front row must come down together with the tight-head prop leading in slightly. The key point on the loose-head is the position of the right shoulder. It is crucial that the hooker turns his right shoulder and lowers it and gets beneath the opponent. This takes him closer to the mouth of the scrum and also allows him to swing with his right foot to strike the ball. If I had a bad shoulder position, I would take the scrum right back and break it up and start again. I believe that my biggest weapon and advantage in hooking was my ability to use my shoulders. I must stress again that shoulder position and dropping of the right shoulder is critical.

On the tight-head my body position was quite different. I tried to get under the opposition hooker and lift him, putting him into an uncomfortable or awkward position. I would ask my loose-head prop, my loose-head flanker and my loose-head lock to push me across to the right-hand side and again it was the use of my shoulder and the upper part of my body that was all-important.

In my opinion, at the top provincial level and the international level it is the hooker's strength in the shoulders and agility in the hips that are important. In short, the ability to arrange a good body position rather than have speed of foot is critical. In some international matches I have felt extreme pressure from the opposing front row of the scrum and it was a struggle even to be able to move the foot. It is in these situations that you rely utterly on your own props and scrum.

It is very important to ascertain the scrum mark and for the hooker to form up in relation to that mark. I prefer the hooker

The Scrum — where the players position their feet

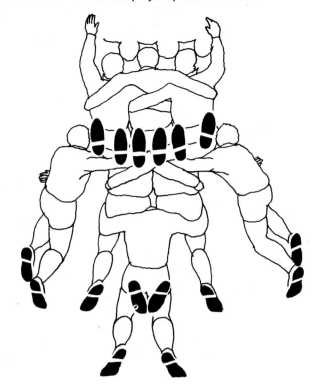

Position of feet for
the eight-man shove

to be the key man, because after all he is the one who has to hook the ball. When the scrum goes down it should come on to the mark with a short step. This will ensure a balanced scrum and will have the players in a proper pushing position.

I like to have my prop with his right foot well across and forward before entry. As he comes forward with the front row, he moves his outside foot perhaps slightly forward of his right foot.

The loose-head prop's function on the loose-head side

The key function of the loose-head prop on your put-in is to keep a clear channel and to provide good visibility for the hooker to see the ball. Accordingly, the loose-head prop should lead with his left hand and come up and under the arm of the tight-head prop, and he should endeavour to get his arm as high up and as far round the back of the opposing prop as possible. This means he can keep his back in a straight position, and he allows no area of the arm to be available to be pulled down or levered down by the opposing prop. I should mention that it is just not body or arm position that matters. On the 1970 tour of the United Kingdom one of my loose-head props, Graham Whiting, had long hair that hung straight down, and when he propped on the loose-head side those five or six centimetres of extra hair made it impossible for me to see the ball. He obliged by getting a hair cut.

Lions v New Zealand, Third Test, 1971. Tane Norton moves quickly to support Sid Going.
Peter Bush

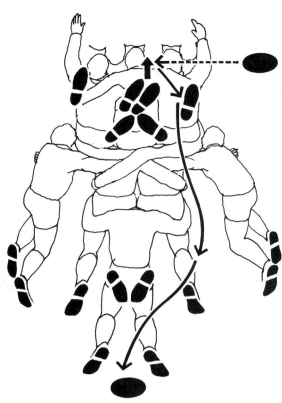

Position of feet for
tight-head strike

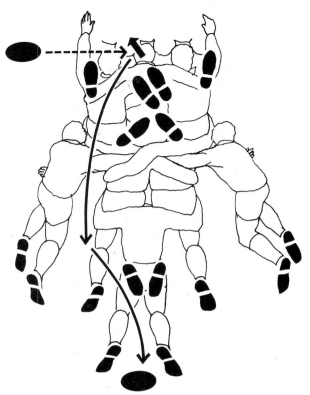

Position of feet and channel
for loose-head strike

The tight-head prop's function on the tight-head side

On the tight-head side the tight-head prop's role is quite different. I want the tight-head to make his opposite's task as difficult as possible and his opposite prop's position as uncomfortable and awkward as possible. Accordingly, I would be asking my tight-head prop to apply maximum pressure in an effort to split his opposition prop and hooker. The loose-head prop, flanker and lock can all contribute to this pressure across the scrum. I must emphasise one point. The loose-head prop never even lifts his front foot to hook the ball. He does not bring his foot around to trap the ball. Once the ball leaves the half-back's hands the responsibility is for the hooker to hook it. The loose-head prop concentrates on stability and maintaining his correct body position. If the ball is heading out the wrong channel or the mouth of the scrum, then the problem is with the half-back or hooker, not with the prop. I want the loose-head prop with his feet well spread, but his inside or right foot must not get in the way of the ball.

Communications between hooker and half-back

The combination with the half-back is critical. It makes or breaks the hooker, in the same way as a line-out thrower makes or breaks the jumper. I was extremely fortunate at provincial level to have a great combination with Lyn Davis, the Canterbury half-back. I informed my half-back that I had a particular foot position in the scrum when I was ready to hook. The half-back would wait until he saw my feet in this particular position before putting the ball in. On some occasions I used a call signal for timing on the put-in, but usually I relied on the half-back's hand position on the ball as he put it in. The advantage of the hand signal on the ball was that the call could distract or mislead the opposition hooker, making him strike early or late. I know that some players use hand signals. I rarely used such signals, but if I did it was only to indicate that I was ready for the put-in and I then relied on a second signal or call for the actual put-in. I would prefer to have the half-back concentrating on my feet position so he knows that I am ready and comfortable — and if he is looking for a hand signal he is taking his eyes away from the hooker's feet.

I used to practise a lot on my own by using the end of a bed to prop or lean against and striking with my foot at a mark on the floor; I would sometimes do the same drill on a post, door-frame or goal post. I liked to get together with my half-back during a training session and often practise with him while I leant against the goal post. I paid particular attention to this early in the season or when I was hooking with a new half-back.

I should stress at this point that the hooker should never doubt his half-back. If you start losing confidence in your half-back, things will only get worse. Also if you mess up a strike and lose the ball, never blame the half-back but tell him that it is your fault and not to worry. If you grizzle at him he will lose his confidence and he will get worse. Complain about anything else, but don't complain about your half-back. Try to sort it out in a quiet and constructive way.

The Scrum — hooking from the tight-head (the forwards illustrated in standing positions)

The Scrum — hooking from the loose-head (the forwards illustrated in standing positions)

Relationship with the props

The relationship of the hooker with the props is similar to that of hooker and half-back. You have to have confidence in each other. I've often made the point that my Linwood club props could have made good provincial props — such was my confidence in them. Again, I've often remarked that the Canterbury provincial props would make good props at international level, and this was often proved. What I'm saying is that the hookers and front row props become oiled to one another. As I said earlier, it's pride that is all important. And the hooker has an important role in developing this pride and the sense of loyalty. He is the monitor and he is the motivator.

All Blacks v Scotland, Eden Park 1981. NZ front row: Gary Knight, Andy Dalton, Rod Ketels.
Peter Bush

R.A. White on

Locks

- **Locks need to be strong and tall, with jumping ability, a hard determined mental attitude and ability to hold a scrum firm.**
- **Binding scrum locks must maintain a straight back, head up, with flexed legs to develop a powerful forward thrust.**
- **Because of their height, locks are the line-out jumpers generally; therefore proficient ball skills are required, and practice at increasing their ability to leap is essential.**
- **Consistent practice with the line-out thrower will develop confidence, understanding and greater success in two-handed takes.**
- **Locks, because of their size and strength, play a large part in rucks, mauls and drives down field. Speed of movement can be developed with practice.**
- **Locks must have a continual appreciation of the opposition's options of attack and defence: when leaving a ruck, scrum, maul or line-out, vision is not always perfect, and as each second lost is 8-10 metres from the ball, the locks must combine anticipation with their assessment of the opposition's options.**

Locks are the powerhouses of the scrum — big, hard, strong, mobile and intelligent. Strength is more important than size, but at top level — for example, at provincial and international levels — you also need line-out height. Height does not always mean jumping ability, and coaches should bear this in mind when making their selections.

The importance of strength must be emphasised, and my preference in a senior team would be a stronger man of 190 cm (6 ft 3 in) rather than a weaker man of 200 cm. Nowadays, at the top international level a lock of 190 cm (6 ft 3 in) is on the small side, and we are usually looking at men 195 cm (6 ft 5 in) to 200 cm (6 ft 7 in). A player of the height and calibre of the outstanding 1970s All Black lock and line-out exponent, Andy Haden, (at 6ft 6½ in, reputedly the tallest New Zealand representative), is an excellent choice in the line-out, although his contemporary Frank Oliver has been particularly useful in All Black sides in a totally different role: as a consistently determined player in the ruck, low-driving and hard.

Returning to the role of a lock, let us not forget that rugby is an 80 minute game and scrums, line-outs and mauls are only a percentage of that time. All players have their own special skills and locks are no exception. Winning means total use of all natural abilities, not just position skills.

The lock in the scrum

The key role of the locks is to provide the power and strength in the scrum. The locks, above all others, provide the drive. Their other vital task and in fact their first priority, is to bind the scrum together. This is the task from which they derive their name — locking the scrum.

The locks, the No. 4 and No. 5 middle row players are right in the centre of the scrum. We sometimes talk about the front five which is made up of the front row and the two locks. We all know how important the front five are to the scrum; and the locks are the core of the five. Scrum strength and stability start with the binding of the locks. It must be firm and tight.

The locks bind around each other with vicelike grips, pulling the upper part of their bodies together and forcing their inside legs and hips together. If the No. 8 can get his head in comfortably at the start of the scrum, then the locks are bound too loosely. If the locks are correctly bound, the No. 8 must force his head in between their thighs. Once the jaws of the vice open up and the No. 8 positions himself, the vice locks again.

As the locks apply the weight to the front-row props, there is sometimes a tendency to push the body of the prop out of line and to the outside, and it is here that the flankers play their part by keeping tightly bound to the lock and applying the pressure forward and inwards on the prop. The flankers must bind on to the body of the locks on their side of the scrum and they must be firmly bound as a middle row of four. They are poised as the pushing rams or pistons in the scrum. The props in the front row form the pillars on which the weight and drive is applied. But it is the locks who provide the greatest weight and drive.

Locks must have the right mental attitude and approach, particularly to the scrum. They are not the glory men. Much of their work goes unseen. They must appreciate their pushing and scrummaging role and take pride in that role. They must be dedicated to their task — keen to get to the scrum formation, determined to apply all their strength, and patient in keeping the drive on even after the ball has been won and is being cleared behind them. For them it is just not a question of winning the ball, but of maintaining the pressure to improve the quality of the possession.

For me, strength is the priority and a hard determined mental attitude secondary. I would want strong, hard locks who will give their guts for the team.

Where lock strength is needed

Let us analyse where locks need their strength. Firstly, we frequently overlook the need to have strong fingers, hands and wrists. The hand grip of a lock is important, in the scrum particularly but also for binding in the ruck and binding and wrenching in the maul.

Locks also need strong arms to bind to each other and to keep the scrum well knit and tight. They should have broad shoulders, and shoulder and upper body strength generally.

They need to engage with the front row with their heads in a slightly extended position — chin up off the chest, eyes

An outstanding lock-forward who commanded much admiration. Played for Fielding Agricultural College 1st XV 1941, 42; Poverty Bay 1949-57 (Gisborne HSOB); also for North Island 1949-56; NZ Trials 1950, 53, 56; New Zealand XV 1949, 52, 54, 55; Rest of NZ 1956; Poverty Bay-East Coast 1949, 55; Poverty Bay-East Coast-Bay of Plenty 1950. Represented NZ 1949-56: 1949 against Australia, as Poverty Bay's first All Black; 1950 against the Lions; 1951 against Australia; 1952 against the Wallabies; 1953-54 as a tourist of Britain and France; 1955 against the Wallabies and 1956 against the Springboks. Served as president of Gisborne HSOB club.

looking up and not to the ground. It is important to maintain this position so that the head doesn't drop down, causing a nosedive effect with consequent loss of power and stability. In short, the locks need neck strength to maintain their head position, which is vital for maintaining their overall body position and the stability and structure of the scrum. Yet coaches often consider that neck strengthening exercises are important only for the front-row forwards.

It is frequently said that locks must be strong in the back. That is certainly true, for they must be able to maintain a good straight back to obtain maximum pushing power.

Locks must also have strong leg power and thrust. They must have the ability to flex and bend their legs and then to snap them into a strong pushing action. Again, they must have the ability to straighten their legs to a locked position, keeping their legs and the scrum locked against the pushing power of the opposition scrum. The term 'locking the scrum' is sometimes used in this sense.

Locks must have a sense of balance and the ability to transfer weight from foot to foot with a minimum of movement. I believe that this is a neglected art and one that should receive more attention, both for scrum situations and for the ruck and maul. Experts can tell us more about the mechanics of leg power and ankle power and mobility, and we should become informed on these matters. But in practical terms, I would emphasise the need for locks to move their feet or to adjust their feet by short, quick

Lions v All Blacks, Third Test, 1977. English lock W. Beaumont goes high to make an attempted one-handed deflection to his half-back D. B. Williams (far left). While the two-handed take is a safer procedure, the one-handed tap allows the player to get very high in the air to meet the ball. For example, a lock 195 cm (6ft 5in) tall with his arm stretched vertically upwards has his fingertips approximately 245 cm (8ft) above the ground. If he makes a vertical jump of 60 cm (2ft) then his hand can deflect the ball at a height of more than 3 metres (10ft) above the ground.
Scott A. G. M. Crawford

71

movements to maintain a good balanced pushing position without affecting the overall stability of the scrum.

I prefer to have locks using the balls of their feet for ground contact, with feet slightly splayed, thus utilising full ankle power and maintaining maximum contact and grip with the ground. In my opinion, it also adds to stability.

We can improve our overall strength and endurance by the appropriate training programmes. Today it is not enough to rely on natural ability. We can do finger-flicking exercises, press-ups on hands and fingers, and wrist strengthening exercises. Numerous exercises developed by rowers can be successfully adapted for rugby players to develop such strength. Most coaches also accept the value of weight training; but do get professional advice on this, and remember that weight training programmes for rugby players should be designed to develop power and speed, not body bulk.

The locks' grip

I cannot overemphasise the importance of the grip. Firstly, the grip of the locks on each other: the actual position of the hand will depend on the bulk of the partner and the length of arm of the lock. Get a comfortable position which is effective in keeping both locks bound together at all times. (I like to think of the middle row as being the knuckles on a closed fist. As you look across the top of your hand, the knuckles cannot be separated and yet they are the centrepiece between fingers and the palm of the hand.)

The grip position of the locks on the props is a matter of debate. Today most locks bind with the outside arm through the prop's legs. But many players were brought up on the method of binding with the outside arm around the prop and not between his legs. Some top hookers and front-row forwards still maintain that there are advantages in this method — All Black hooker, Tane Norton, for one, recommends the method particularly for his own loose-head. The method does help to keep the body of the props in line — 'spine in line'. It is important, however, that the outer arm is up high enough to allow the flanker to bind under the buttock of his prop. If the arm forces down, it can make life difficult for your own flanker.

The Scrum — grips by the locks

To ensure a tight grip,
the locks' legs are initially crossed,
then uncrossed just before going down

With the underarm and between the legs method, there is some encouragement to get well down and beneath the fleshy buttock of the prop. Some locks take an initial grip on the lower part of the front of the jersey of the prop and then take a second grip going higher up on to the chest. An advantage is that it encourages the locks to maintain tight formation with their front row. If this method is used, I recommend the higher position on to the chest of the prop. A second advantage is that it allows a clear pushing position for the flankers on their prop.

There is one danger, and that is that the lock pulls the prop down, thus lowering the height of the scrum's front row and causing loss of stability.

Some coaches are now suggesting a third grip, with the arm coming up between the legs and across the groin on the inside leg, with the hand grip on the waistband of the prop's trousers near his inside hip. This is said to help props keep straight on; and it would avoid the pulling down danger of the chest grip.

However, this can lead to another possible danger, and that is the lock's shoulder position. Sometimes, the lock's shoulder slips down the back of the prop's leg on to the lower part of the hamstring and then on to the back of the knee joint, causing total destruction of the prop's stability and pushing power.

Some of our older props used to lift up on the heels and then sit down on to the shoulders of the locks, making sure that the shoving shoulders are in the correct position. Too often, the shoulders get too high up on the fleshy part of the buttock and slip further up when the pressure is applied. The shoulder must be below the buttock. With the head tilted slightly up and the neck slightly extended, the lock will achieve the correct position when weight is applied.

Footwork in the scrum

The ideal position of the feet is a matter of debate. As a matter of preference I like to get the inside leg forward when the two locks combine. As the scrum enters and joins with the opposition front row, the outside foot comes forward. I believe that maximum power and better balance is attained if the feet are more or less even immediately before the main application of weight.

In the modern scrum it is important to keep the feet well back, with the legs cocked or flexed ready for the explosive thrust forward.

If the position of the feet has to be changed this should be done with very short steps. This is particularly so if the scrum is being forced back. However, if locks feel the scrum is being forced back, they should endeavour to lock their legs by straightening them and if possible maintaining a stationary foot position.

As the scrum moves it is crucial that the grip and binding of the locks are maintained, eyes up and head up with the neck kept in the slightly extended position, and the back straight. I must mention again the importance of balance and the need for locks to think about balance during every scrum. The locks must be thinking about their feet position, and they must be flexible enough and strong enough to make adjustments when necessary. If they don't make these adjustments, they will either be misapplying their weight or be outmanoeuvred.

The locks' other requirements

The modern game is all about support and the locks have an important role in this respect. The loose forward trio, by position and physical attribute, should be arriving in a support position ahead of the locks — particularly from set scrums and line-outs. Often the locks will form the hard driving and binding force of the ruck and maul. They need the skills of binding and driving. Locks should leave the training field with the words 'bend', 'bind' and 'drive' ringing in their ears.

In the mauling game, the locks need the ability to turn an opponent with possession around, to make the ball available for his own team or to rip the ball away from the opponent ball-carrier. Arm and hand strength are again important.

As a firm believer in the ruck and maul that drives forward, I look to my locks and tight five to develop that drive and momentum.

Locks sometimes have problems other than just their opponents — in this case the sun. Brian Lochore and Colin Meads shade their eyes.
Evening Post

Line-out skills

In the line-out locks usually find themselves in a jumping role. But they also have a support role: binding or wedging on to the jumper.

When there is an apparent loss of ability for the good two-handed take, locks may find themselves picking up a 'bobbled' or 'tap' ball in a position two back from the nominated jumper. In this role they need efficient eye and body co-ordination, alertness and quick reflexes.

Locks should always be seeking advice on how they can jump higher. They need to think about their particular jumping style and develop techniques to increase their jumping ability. Get on to the toes and balls of the feet rather than stand with flat feet. The thrust from toes and ankles should be co-ordinated with straightening of flexed knees; power will be lost if knees are flexed too much or if they are kept too straight. Develop an explosive jump and use drive with the arms. Spring comes from reflex action, calf muscle strength and quadriceps strength. Use drills to develop them.

I think too many locks stand out too far from the line-out and then jump in on an exaggerated angle. [I wonder how they ever get near the ball.] Stand ahead of your marker and as a rule endeavour to jump forward of him.

Two points are worth mentioning. Firstly, effective jumping depends on accurate throwing in and fine co-ordination and communication between thrower and jumper. Spend more time practising with your thrower. Secondly, pay more attention to different types of throw-ins. Japanese teams could teach New Zealand players a thing or two about this.

Finally, one point about general body position. The locks, in the modern game, more than ever need to have the ability to run with a firm forward body lean and the ability to use a shoulder on contact with the opposition, making the ball available for team-mates or for the ruck or maul platform. This includes the ability to carry the ball in both hands and to keep it secure and protected on contact. The locks will always be the men in the powerhouse, but more than ever they have their responsibilities in general play also.

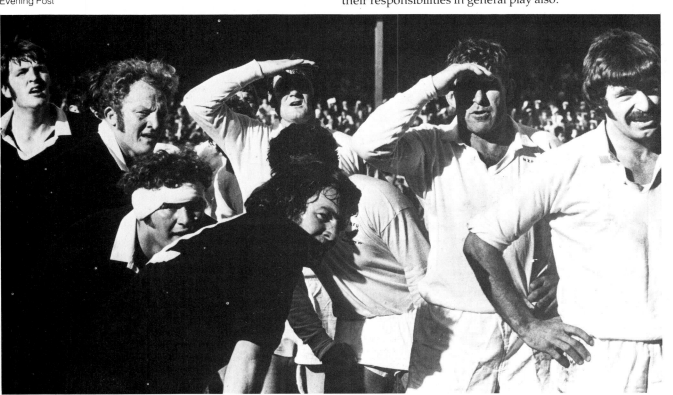

Waka Nathan on

Loose Forwards

- **In the scrum loose forwards should bind firmly, push hard, and assist in controlling the hooked ball from the scrum.**
- **From the line-out the physique of the loose forward decides if the player is a ball winner, a defensive or attacking forward or used in a protecting role.**
- **The three loose forwards form an attacking and defensive pattern from set plays and each should be familiar with the others' duties, specialisation between blind- and open-side flanker should be avoided.**
- **Speed to the breakdown is vital and the ball should be kept moving forward, avoiding any development of the maul situation.**
- **The attributes of the loose forwards are: ball handling skills, speed and aggressiveness in the tackle and the ability to give and take a pass.**

Loose forwards in the scrum

First of all, the front five are very important. When the front five are doing their job they make it so much easier for the loose forwards and enable the 'loosies' to do their job well. How do they fit in at scrum time? Well, it means that everyone has to push, and that includes the No. 8 and the 'loosies', especially at ball put-in time. When the half-back puts the ball in, they must all contribute to that initial push.

Some flankers pack with their hands on the ground to get balance and position at an angle, and manipulate themselves around; then they can push straight down the line of the scrum. (Some years ago, flankers used to put their seats out and try to push in towards the centre.) But comfort is one of the most important things, because if you're comfortable in rucks or scrums you're going to perform well. Much is up to the flankers themselves. If they feel balanced with a hand on the ground, then that's all right, so long as it fits in with what the rest of the pack is doing. I believe that on the open side the flanker should have a hand on the ground for balance; and on the blind side, perhaps up a bit — with the person gripping the other guy. The open-side flanker should have the inside foot up, and the blind-side flanker the outside foot up. As to the job of the flankers in channelling the ball when it has actually been hooked ...Take the eight-man shove, for instance, when you want to hold the ball in the middle row. Invariably it bounces round a bit, and the loose forwards do have a role in keeping the ball in the channel; and, of course, we do lead the wheel, the No. 8 and the blind-side flanker do control the ball.

After the scrum

I think that the whole game of rugby is a patterned one. Especially with loose forwards. If I can tackle a second five-eighth from the side of the scrum, it's because I've practised it enough to be able to do it in my sleep. Once the scrum is over, the three loose men do have different functions. What is important is that the loose forward trio perfect their pattern together.

For instance, the blind-side loose forward generally has the job of seeing that the opposing half-back doesn't run. He must see that the opposing first five-eighth doesn't run — and there invariably he has to tackle. He's got to decide whether to do these things, whether it is better to go around the front of a scrum or around the back of his scrum. It's a personal preference.

There are times when we see the No. 8 run very deep, particularly on defence — corner flagging — and I think this is probably the best approach. Anticipation has a lot to do with it. Some players have it and some don't. The deep No. 8 is probably the safest bet, because he's going to get to the

All Blacks v Lions, 1966. Waka Nathan evades Jim Telfer.

Evening Post

74

A powerful side-row forward and dynamic runner with the ball. Played for Auckland East Roller Mills team and Otahuhu College 1st XV 1956, 57; for Auckland 1959-63, 65-67; also the North Island 1960, 61, 63, 65-67; in the NZ Trials 1961-63, 65-67; New Zealand XV 1960, 66; Rest of NZ 1960; NZ Maoris 1959-61, 65, 66. Represented NZ in the 1962-64 All Black tour of Australia (1962), England (1963), Ireland and Wales (1963-64), Lions (1966), Britain (1967). In his 14 internationals he never played in a losing side. NZ Maori selector 1971-77.

breakdown, he's going to make a tackle and he's got it all covered. So if there is a breakdown, he's going to run into it — whereas if he runs flat and there is a breakdown, he's got to run all the way back and he's actually right out of play. If he's deep and keeps inside of the ball, he is on the spot.

On specialisation of the flankers

There has been much discussion about using specialist open- and blind-side flankers, but I'm not one for specialist loose positions. I think the flankers have to be flexible. They have to do so many things. To concentrate on one specialist position, such as open-side or blind-side, could unbalance the scrum.

I think left and right are more important than concentrating on open- and blind-side play. Perfecting your scrummaging on the left and the right will be more important to the pack as a whole. What you need to do is develop the flexibility to be able to move into the inside backs on the open side, and then, the next time you are blind-side flanker, be able to cover the action on the blind side as well.

But it's a matter of preference . . . Some flankers probably like playing on the open side, and whether such a player would cover the open side of the field all the time will depend upon the team patterns — if it fits, then so be it.

Creating moves from a scrummage

To what extent and with whom do flankers combine to create moves from a scrummage? In most cases, the half-back running on the blind side or on the open side. Then, of course, there is the first five-eighth combination with the loose forwards. But I think mostly it's done between the loose forwards themselves. If they can get the ball and drive, say, ten metres, your pack is all there coming into the play and you can really set off your back movement.

So even if the half-back involves your first five-eighth, you've got the bulk of your backs in position and you are moving forwards, so your chances of a worthwhile attacking position are good.

You can also use both sides of the field. That is, with the half-back running open and bringing the ball back to the loose forward, or even the No. 8 coming off the back and creating a situation where he can move to either side of the field.

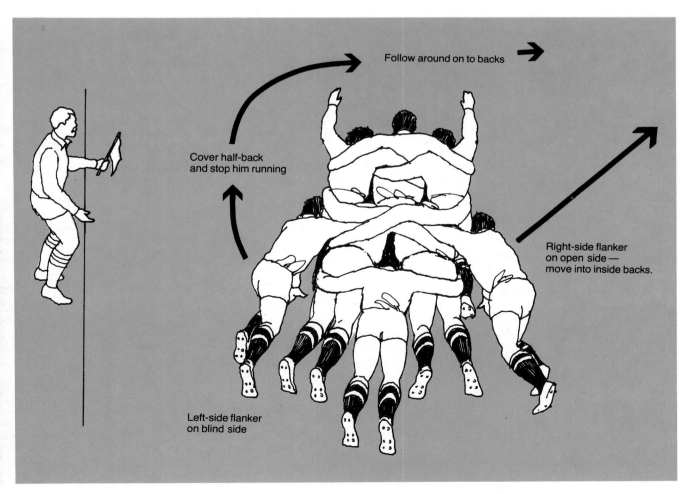

Follow around on to backs

Cover half-back and stop him running

Right-side flanker on open side — move into inside backs.

Left-side flanker on blind side

It seems important that the half-back gets down the field far enough so that the loose forwards can get up a bit of steam and run into the play.

From a line-out

In line-outs I used to play in the No. 8 position initially, though as I got slower I moved into No. 6. As I wasn't a very strong jumper, I played only No. 7 in the line-out for my club. For New Zealand I played at No. 6 and more often at No. 8 position.

My main duties at No. 8 from the line-out position on defence were, firstly, to crowd the inside backs and make them crab across the field, and invariably to tackle the inside backs. In the attacking position from the line-out — in the back movements — to be first to the ball, whether the ball was in hand or on the ground. The main thing I considered was that if we did win the ball and if it did go out to our backs, I would join the backs in the passing movement and, if they were tackled, I was there to set it up or carry it up and keep it going.

When I was on the back of the line-out to put the pressure on the inside backs, I had to ensure that I wasn't cut out of the play. You have to be a bit of a gambler there. Firstly, you must always keep inside the man — once you go outside, you'll really be cut to ribbons. So I made sure I was always inside the man and if I felt that he was going to have a try, I'd make certain of him. I knew that I'd have to put myself out of the game if I missed him in a tackle. Quite a few times I did — but there again, quite a few times I didn't. I think that's the main thing: the No. 8 in the line-out has to make the inside backs do something. Either they kick the ball out, or hold their pass, or they're tackled — he must do that job — either make them do something hurriedly or force them to lose possession.

A couple of times I deliberately went outside the ball carrier. I remember one occasion when Kel Tremain, John Graham and I were the 'loosies'. The idea was to go outside the man and push him back in. Tremain bagged him and Graham did the rest — we had him fooled. But the basic job is to force the opposing backs out and create errors.

With all loose forward play the three must work together. In the position of No. 6 you must first of all upset the opposition half-back and move across after he has got rid of the ball. If the No. 6 upsets the half-back, this makes it easier for those in No. 7 and No. 8 positions in the line-out; and if things have gone well, the ball shouldn't have gone beyond second five-eighth without us. The other important thing is to help the jumper at No. 5 and ensure that if he got the ball it remained our ball.

With the recent changes in the laws to open the line-out and set the players apart, it has certainly made it easier for forwards to get through to the half-back — no doubt about that. Once the ball leaves the middle of the line, it's really anyone's ball.

Incidentally if 'tapping' the ball is considered, if you haven't got good line-out jumpers it's frankly better for the opposition to get the ball, with your players in No. 6, 7 and 8 positions working to put pressure on your opponents.

I think that if a loose forward can jump and run — if the player is lucky enough to have both those skills — it is most important to have him at No. 7 position in the line-out.

The player in the No. 7 position in line-out is one of the ball-getters, on attack especially. So this player has to be the tallest of the three — at senior levels at least 190 cm (6ft 3in). And he has to be able to run, pass and tackle. Ian Kirkpatrick, for example, although he has played in No. 6 and No. 8 positions is, in my mind, the ideal No. 7 because he could do all three things. So the No. 7 invariably is a ball-getter and also has to do what the others do in set play: notably cover, run with the ball, and tackle.

With the No. 8 position in the line-out, I don't think height is as important. The most important attribute about him is ability to anticipate — a lot of speed, strength and anticipation.

In a line-out the loose forwards are usually placed in positions No. 6, 7 and 8. The front of the line-out becomes the blind side during a maul developed from that line-out. To cover the blind side of that particular maul you might consider bringing the other loose forward to bolster the blind-side wing. Perhaps as the maul develops, one drops off to create a two-wing position initially, before the drive. It could be quite a useful thing too, really, because if there is a breakdown there, a forward who is prepared to go forward and drive will be on the spot.

The maul

With the new tackle ball rule you no longer have to play the ball with the foot before picking it up from the tackle and maul.

I think that the maul tends to frustrate the player (the spectator, on the other hand, sees it as a skill). Quite honestly, I don't think it helps the game. Rugby has all sorts of players — short, skinny, big — and maul play seems to need only the big and strong.

My main objective at a breakdown was to keep the ball moving forwards, and once it was stopped to get it back as quickly as possible. That was the only way — once the ball was stopped it went back. Now once a maul is stopped so many times, it is just a mess.

All Blacks v Ireland, 1976. Ian Kirkpatrick takes the high road.
Evening Post

Piet Greling, Springbok loose forward, in full flight.
Peter Bush

The loose forwards' positional play

At kick-offs players such as the superb All Black line-out performers, Peter Whiting and Andy Haden, who are not really very fast, invariably beat the loose forwards to the ball. Where the loose forwards should be at the kick-off really depends upon the pattern. In some teams the loose forwards are up there amongst the first; in others the taller and stronger second row forwards tap the ball down to the faster loose forwards on the drive. In this case, they've got more opportunities than you to get the ball because they're much taller.

Colin Meads, the legendary All Black lock and loose forward, didn't chase the ball from the line-out but his brother Stan used to. Haden and Whiting were masters at this.

With centre kicking and its influence on the positional play of the flanker . . . Well, you can often guess that there is something in the mind of a player who is about to centre kick — just the way he is running, perhaps. Most forwards anticipate and, if there's any chance of a cross kick, say 'I'll be there.'

When it comes to a ruck the open-side flanker and the No. 8 are usually first to the breakdown. The No. 8, who is normally first to the ball, makes sure that the ball is on our side by driving over it. If he can pick it up and hand it on, fine; but if he can't, he's got to be the first there and over. Invariably the open-side flanker should be second there. The loose forwards have got to work this out — the ideal

combination of the pack with the man who covers. The combination is very important, especially for this sort of thing. In the normal ruck, it is often the hooker or the lock as the last out of the scrum who end up on the flank.

Bob Graham, Lew Fell and I had rather a good combination. One of the things we did was talk prior to the game — in the dressing room — about one another's role. On the field of play invariably we never spoke. I'd say to myself that I've got to be there with Lew, or I've got to be there with Bob. I always hoped they'd say the same thing, that they had to be there with me. At training twice a week we would work together to develop this until it became automatic. Now and again, if somebody wasn't on the spot supporting you, you'd scream out 'Where in the hell were you?' This friendly rivalry makes you work harder.

The attributes of the flanker

Ball handling skills come first. The loose forwards have to be able to handle the ball well; they must be able to take and give a pass. Secondly, speed — especially over the first 10 or 15 metres. So often one of them has to be first to the ball: to kill it or get it away, or carry it on. Those two attributes are musts in today's rugby. Thirdly they must be able to tackle hard and low.

Dragging the first five-eighth into a tackle

Half-back

First five-eighth

Side row runs deliberately wide and suggests to the five-eighth that a gain exists inside

Nathan

Tremain

Graham

But waiting for him are two deadly tacklers and he is cut off from support

All Black Bryan Williams eludes a tackle and Stu Wilson awaits the pass. All Blacks v Wallabies.
Peter Bush

Wilson Whineray on

The Front Row

- **The props must be big and strong enough to withstand pressures from behind and from the opposition; to be able to maintain a stable platform to ensure the hooker can be successful on his loose-head.**

- **All feet back on the opposition put-in ensures an eight - man push to put pressure on the opposition scrum.**

- **Props should move quickly to rucks and mauls where their strength and skill may be used to gain possession.**

- **A tall prop may assist in jumping for the ball in a line-out but usually supports the line-out jumper and is in the position to collect deflected throw-ins from touch.**

- **Props should push straight, maintaining a steady front row to assist the hooker. Twisting and buckling in an attempt to unsettle the opposition are negative qualities and are not part of the game.**

Responsibilities in the scrum

The basic responsibility of a hooker is to win his own ball in the scrum. It doesn't matter very much if he gets tight-heads or not. What does matter is that he is not beaten for his own ball, because if he loses it other unpleasant things happen — his backs are in trouble, if they're too deep. He must win his own ball, but he can't do it on his own — it would be silly to expect him to. I believe that the basic responsibility of the front row in scrums is to provide a ramp for the hooker to operate off, which means they must endeavour to play their part in keeping the scrum stable, not moving around — because it's terribly hard for a hooker to keep shuffling his feet all the time, and the ball may come in when he's on the wrong foot. The priorities are to keep the scrum stable; transfer the weight of the scrum and help it move forward, at the appropriate time; and to give the hooker a good look at the ball.

On your own put-in, the loose-head prop's responsibility really is to make sure the hooker has a clear view of the ball. He should try, if anything, to come up a shade with the left shoulder so that the hooker can see the ball clearly. Also he must make sure he gets his feet out of the way — I don't believe he should help the hooker to strike the ball (he shouldn't need to) but he should make sure the channel is opened up so the ball will come through into the second row of the scrum. The tight-head should be lower, and I think almost becomes a third lock — he's really in a pushing role.

There's probably a difference in the physical type required for the position of loose-head prop and that of tight-head prop. Each position 'feels' different, and most props prefer one side of the scrum to the other. I played all the time at loose-head and preferred it. More players seem to prefer tight-head — it's a more even push on the shoulders — but I used to feel constrained, maybe because I didn't play there very often. All things being equal I would put the bigger prop at tight-head, because the scrum is unbalanced slightly because of the loose-head situation. If you can put your bigger, stronger player into the tight-head position I think it's wise. That's why generally we've seen fellows like Ken Gray, the indomitable 1960s All Black front-row forward who was 4 centimetres taller than I was and 10 kilograms heavier, and the invaluable 1950s All Black tight prop Kevin Skinner, again a taller prop, play in this position — while the thicker-set, squarer sort of player tends to do a little better on the loose-head.

I always felt that the tight-head was more physically demanding in some ways — that it was a very crushing position. The loose-head was more technically demanding. You really have to know what you are doing in the loose-head position, otherwise you may be 'popped out'. You have one shoulder in open space, which makes things awkward if a fellow is trying to bear down on you. You must get your feet out of the way in the scrum, and you can become twisted more because the weight is coming on you unevenly.

I've been 'scrummed down' on occasions in the loose-head position. Let's face it, if you have equal physical strength in a tight-head and loose-head, generally speaking the tight-head will win because he's got two shoulders to lever on, whereas the loose-head has one shoulder flapping around in space. Generally, bearing-down by the opposition is designed — when the half-back is putting the ball in — to force the loose-head down so that his hooker can't see the ball. As I said earlier, it is important to keep up enough so as to let your hooker see, and if the opposition can force the loose-head's head down, the hooker is striking blind. So the loose-head strike, which you have a 95-5 probability of winning, becomes 50-50 on a blind strike. And it does lead to troubles. It is largely illegal now, but it still seems to happen — and because of the possibility of a scrum injury, I would stop it quickly. It's quite illegal and quite wrong.

On the question of technique, if you are under pressure in the front row and the scrum as a whole, you should not have your scrum down too long. Form up quickly, go in firmly, put the ball in quickly, then you're away. The longer you are down there the more the effect of the heavier scrum will press on you and exhaust you as the game proceeds.

The real problem is to explain how a scrum 'feels right'. It is 'right' if you are sitting well on your lock, and he's in the right spot — there is a right spot, you can feel bone, hard solid bone — and you mustn't lose your lock, the prop mustn't lose his lock, and the lock mustn't lose his prop, they must become as one. Again, I found that I didn't require side thrust from my side row to hold me in. I'd rather have weight from a straight push. I could stay in if I had weight, and once the weight started to slip you'd fall apart as you went back. I would always ask (Kel Tremain was my side much of the time) that he came almost parallel to his lock.

The pressure and concentration shows on both front rows. NZ Maoris v South Africa, 1981.

Peter Bush

Acclaimed by fellow players, commentators and spectators as a conscientious rugby footballer, a skilful ball handler and an inspirational and dedicated captain. Generally he played as a front-row forward. Played for Auckland Grammar School 1st XV 1950, 51; senior club rugby for Wakaia, Southland 1952; Wairarapa 1953 (Martinborough); Mid-Canterbury 1954 (Rakaia); Manawatu 1955 (University); Canterbury 1956, 57 (Lincoln College); Waikato 1958 (City); Auckland 1959-63, 65, 66 (Grammar); also South Island 1957; North Island 1958, 59, 61-63, 65; NZ Trials 1957-63, 65; NZ Under-23 1958 (as captain); NZ Colts 1955; NZ Universities 1956, 57. Represented NZ 1957-65. During his All Black career he captained the team in 68 of his 77 appearances; first appointed as captain at the age of 23 in 1958 against the Wallabies. In his 30 Test matches as captain of the NZ team he sustained only five losses. Coached Auckland Grammar Club 1970-73 and Onslow in Wellington 1974. Named New Zealand Sportsman of the Year 1965. Honoured with the OBE in 1961.

I think if you're the loose-head prop it's important to have the right hip fairly hard on your hooker when the scrum goes down, with your right foot almost in behind your hooker's feet and your left foot near it, almost parallel but slightly advanced. As the weight came in, I always used to prefer to drive forward with my left foot, leaving a gap for the ball to come through. The inside foot doesn't move; and if it doesn't move, then you're leaving a good, solid block for your lock to keep on it, so he is really digging into your right-hand buttock. The movement forwards in the scrum really comes from the drive, or step forward, of the outside foot. It allows a drive of almost 30 centimetres — more than enough, unless the scrum is to be 'driven' or screwed . . . but this is different technique.

The tight-head, on your own put-in, would take probably a lock's position with legs flexed; and it would be a drive straight from the knees. (The loose-head can just straighten his knees too, but if he does, he has a foot in the way of the ball, so he has to drive forward to get that foot out of the way.)

If the ball goes right through the scrum, as happens occasionally, the tight-head has to be alert enough to get a foot to it. This doesn't happen very often, and if the ball does go right through it's a put-in again, so you've lost nothing. Frankly, if someone in the scrum brings up a foot to stop the ball going through, he can't push and therefore there is some loss of weight in the scrum.

Perfecting the timing of push and effort in the front row is all part of scrummaging technique. Because the front row is only one part of the scrum, the timing is usually based on a call from the half-back, or the prop, or occasionally from the side row. The ideal is that the weight of the push is applied at the time that the ball comes in, and not too much too soon, or you'll end up with a crooked put-in. I've found scrummaging not too hard to coach, because it's a technical thing and you can explain with diagrams, etc. You must work on your technique with constant practice. The scrum is a repetitive situation against a fixed position, and tremendous advances have been made throughout the world in understanding the techniques, because people have put their brains to work, and practised it.

Sometimes on the opposition's put-in, of course, you use an eight-man shove when you are trying to embarrass the opposition. Then everyone in your scrum would have their feet back — the loose-head and the hooker too. There is no attempt made to hook the ball, as your purpose is different — you are going to push, you're not interested in hooking. Every one in your scrum is pushing. You know they're interested in hooking, as it's their put-in, so their hooker will have his feet up and their front row will probably be giving less than a total push. They'll be expecting the ball, so their loose forwards will be starting to think of other things — where they go when they win the ball — then, if you get a good sharp quick shove on them, your eight is opposing to their six, so you have a good chance of moving them backwards.

The front row in rucks and mauls

The speed with which you are able to break from the scrum and move to a break can be the notable aspect of play. I believe that a loose-head prop (the tight-head is usually last out of a scrum, as he's totally boxed in) has the opportunity, if he is that way inclined, to get into broken play quite quickly. He won't be as quick as the loose forwards, but he should be there soon after. By dropping your right shoulder and just running off you can slip quite quickly from the scrum. Once the ball is gone, there is no point in staying around. Front rows in broken play are a bit like cruisers — the loose forward 'destroyers' are quicker and arrive at the breakdowns first. The front row players add more strength to thicken up the defence, or to run on to a pass, but to

generally support and exploit opportunities created by the loose forwards. The fellows that really do the damage are the big men of the middle row. If you can get men of 105 to 108 kilograms (16½-17 st) running hard, it takes two men to tackle them, and that's punishing. If I could somehow help bridge the gap between the quick fellows and the slower but stronger ones, I felt that was a valuable role. Often a prop can apply more strength to a broken situation — enough, anyway, to support it a little longer — till the big fellows arrive.

So I would be the person to support the man at the break. That was always part of my job. A prop is seldom first to a break-down — someone else had to do that. But they must try to arrive quickly. It's a state of mind — whether you want to or not. Some props couldn't do it if they wanted to, because they aren't physically equipped that way. Others have all the physical attributes, but haven't quite learnt that they can do it if they really set their minds to it.

In many situations on the field one advantage the front row forwards have over the fast players and the big players is in the rucks and mauls. Because they don't involve an all-out push, someone of about 183 centimetres (6 ft) in a senior match would be about the right size in rucks and mauls. The taller players have trouble — they're line-out people, really — the quicker men are often lighter. Rucks and mauls require arms and chest strengths, wrenching, pushing, moving around, and often 89 to 95 kilograms (14-15 st) is the right weight. In this area of rugby we can do a lot the others can't do. Mauling, pushing, heaving is a large part of our game. The Rumanians had a very good reputation for this. The French, too, the type of player like Domenech — they're very difficult to deal with.

With forward play, you have to create a ramp for your backs to work off. To do that, you've got to get as much ball as you can, retain it as long as you can, and try to go forward all the time, in every situation. A forward must say to himself, 'No matter how tired I am, I must keep going forwards, I'm going to knock this ruck forwards. I'm going to push this scrum forwards. I'm going to hold the line of the line-out', or whatever. If you are moving forwards — as any back will tell you — interesting things happen; they can start moving forwards before the ball comes. (Conversely if you are going back, they've got to shuffle back to stay on-side. They are in a bad position to defend.) If you are moving forwards, the loose forwards are starting to free up and get ready to move. If you ever see loose forwards playing well, you can know that the tight forwards have done a damn good job — they've given them a platform to run them off, given them a bit more freedom, and then they'll start making

Getting ready to go down — the All Black front row gets organised. Left to right, Gary Knight, Andy Dalton, Bill Bush.
Christchurch Press

the breakdowns first and putting pressure on their opponents. This should win them the ball from the breakdowns, and with the backs running into the ball the whole performance of the team will come alive.

Skills in the line-out

Let's take these two players and put them into the line-out. These skills that they have in the ruck and maul and in the scrum, how do they relate to the line-out?

Frequently your biggest prop might be able to do a useful job at the short end of the line-out, in No. 2 position. I think it's helpful if you *can* have one of your props as a supplementary line-out forward. The best teams I played in had at least three and probably four good line-out forwards, one of whom would be a prop, with a couple of locks and a big loose forward. The shorter prop frequently is a supporter to the main line-out jumpers, by trying to keep them from being molested — knocked off the line. He also supports the ball if it goes loose. If the ball is held and the ruck forms, then he is a worker and a strong man. He should be in his element once the maul or ruck forms.

Sometimes, of course, the ball is deflected to the half-back. In fact, I don't believe in line-out forwards trying to tap the ball back directly to the half-back. I think they should tap down to one of the props, who holds it, sets up the maul and then delivers it to the half-back.

Skills in the scrum

A hooker knows what's expected of him. To help with the ball, props must do what they can to keep the scrum moving forward and get their feet out of the way of the hooked ball. As I said earlier, buckling and bowing in the front row should be eliminated from the game by law. It has no purpose, it has no part in the scrum and is dangerous. Props must keep a straight back and bind tightly with their hooker.

Wheeling the scrum is not easy; that's the first point I'd make. We worked hard on the wheel on our British tour. It is a hard point to coach, and you need a competent pack to do it properly. Often a wheel takes place because the scrum happens to wheel on its own, and someone says, 'Right, we'll take the ball away!' But to consistently wheel a scrum in a controlled fashion, say three out of five, is hard to do. You need to hook, hold, drive, wheel. That's the sequence. You have to drive straight before you wheel (most scrums will hook it and then try to wheel). But you have to hook, hold and trap the ball — at the left lock, drive, and then wheel. Funnily enough the loose-head prop — and you always have to wheel to the left, of course, because of the overlap in the front row — you would think the thing for the left prop to do is to turn in, with his bottom going out to the left, but in fact you find it generally works easier if he drops his right shoulder at the last minute and breaks out from the scrum in the direction of the wheel. Under those circumstances, the ball would be behind the loose-head prop's feet, it would be with the lock so he would have to angle out and then take no further part in the play as it went past. It's a sort of squeezing-out effect, it seems to pull the lock round with it, don't ask me why — a physicist might be able to sort it out.

When the ball is out of the scrum you move to the breakdown as quickly as you can. Anticipate where the breakdown is going to be. You don't back up anyone. Run straight to where the ball is, or where you think it will be by the time you arrive. I don't believe in forwards backing up backs when the backs are running with the ball. Generally speaking, backs back up backs. I would run to the spot where I thought the next breakdown would occur. If there was the possibility of a centre kick from a player out on the sideline, it's frequently the job of front row forwards to dwell in midfield in anticipation. It's a matter of judgement as you look at play developing.

Wallaby half-back John Hipwell awaits the pass from a well-controlled maul. Wallabies v All Blacks.
Peter Bush

Preparing for play

Players should develop their physical strength, in their joints and in the big, bulky pushing muscles. People should not confuse strength with weight. I believe there is a right weight for every player, and to carry more weight than is 'right' is not sensible. You slow down a racehorse by putting weight on its back; and whether you are putting lead in your saddle-bags or fat around your midriff, it has the same effect. I knew, in the later stages of my career — when my body was stable — that I could stand on the scales and know how well I would play. When I was lighter I played a better game than when I was heavier — by a long way. Players who carry weight and bulk above what is 'right' for them would do a wise thing if they took it off. They'd play better, hit harder and feel stronger, if they trimmed down to their own best playing weight. There's an old Maori saying: 'It's not the size of the dog in the fight, it is the size of the fight in the dog.' And this is true.

If you are agile, if you run quickly and move quickly, you think quickly and react quickly. The whole system seems to speed up. But if you develop a plod syndrome, if it's a physical plod, then you'll plod mentally and in your reactions and you'll fumble passes and be generally clumsy in everything you do.

For the front row preparing to play as a group, both the scrum machine and scrummage against an opposition pack have value. The main value of the scrum machine is for heavy repetitive scrummaging, under somewhat artificial conditions. You have a big load on you — and on some of the modern machines you can measure how you are doing, you can set the height, and as the season progresses you know how much lower you are getting, how much the weight is coming on, how quick it's coming on, whether it's even — because of the gauges on each side. So scrum machines have great value in improving your techniques. The *real* world of scrummaging is against another pack, which is moving and

not stable. I think you should have a blend of the two if possible.

The only thing I've found in practice, no matter whether you practise for the All Blacks or for a senior club side, is to try to be sensible in a live scrum practice. Everyone wants to talk at once and generally fool about. You often end up with the backs in there, and they wouldn't know what it was about (nor should they — it's none of their business). In practice it's difficult to maintain a serious attitude. The coach needs to be firm and start speaking sharply: 'For goodness sake, we're going to be here doing nothing for the next half-hour if we're not careful. Now everyone just shut up for a while.' I think live practice is good, but it must be disciplined.

The ideal front row

Of the characters I've played with and played against, among New Zealand players I think Ken Gray and Kevin Skinner were magnificent front row forwards; and Ian Clarke was a very good loose-head prop — not that he wasn't a very good tight-head, but he was really the build of a loose-head. Of the overseas props, the one who gave me the most difficult time personally was Piet du Toit, the Springbok tight-head. He was the only one that I ever really found a problem. In saying that, I must say that my philosophy in scrummaging was to push straight, keep my back straight, and I wasn't interested in buckling and bowing, twisting or whatever, because if I started that it would upset my hooker, upset our scrum, and upset out loose-head hook that we wanted to win.

We've been blessed with some expert hookers in New Zealand. As purist hookers go, the outstanding one in my time was Denis Young — the finest hooker I every played with or against. The other two great hookers I played with were Ron Hemi and Bruce McLeod, both of whom were grand forwards in addition to their world-class hooking ability.

Ian Clarke — 'a very good loose-head prop' — is here seen tackling New South Wales full-back Terry Curley in 1957.
Dominion

All Blacks v Cambridge, 1963. New Zealand is making a strong attack on the short side — Ralph Caulton passes the ball to Wilson Whineray.
Sports & General Press Agency

All Black Gary Seear out-jumps Willie Duggan of Ireland and taps back from a line-out. All Blacks v Ireland.
Peter Bush

Colin Meads on

Lineout Possession

- **The line-out is the cause of many frustrations, and changes may have to be made to remove them.**
- **Great skill and constant practice are necessary for a good throw-in. The thrower must become expert at all types of throwing.**
- **Line-out positions should be flexible and all players should be fully aware of what they are required to do. Signals must be clear and understood by all players.**
- **Deflections from the line-out to the half-back must be controlled. Forwards not involved in the deflections must watch and control the bobbled ball.**
- **Possession by the opposition must be disputed.**

One team has forced a stoppage of play by propelling the ball (whether in possession or not) across the touch line. For the sake of discussion and consideration we call the team using stoppage the *offending* team and the opposition the *non-offending* team. As the majority of play stoppages are restarted by a line-out, it is not surprising that the majority of player and referee frustrations arise here.

The normal positioning of the pack in the modern line-out. If the winger is used to throw in the ball, the hooker would return to the front of the line-out.

Quite correctly, any possible advantage at line-out is allowed to the non-offending team. Whether the advantage is sufficient can be argued at length without a great deal of satisfaction under the present rules. Perhaps the International Rugby Football Board, which must be fully aware of the frustrations (for instance, two-men test-match line-outs, match-winning penalties, and so on), will rule further to ensure a very definite repossession advantage to the non-offending side. It may well be that a compulsory four-man line-out , or only a non-offending three or four man single-file line-out with the offending team 10 metres back, could be introduced to ensure the repossession. These are perhaps unorthodox ideas, but there is little doubt that all concerned with the game realise that moves are necessary to negate the frustrations which continue to beset line-out play.

Arguments that above-average-height players and that certain line-out skills should be retained are valid. Then again, the big players are very much required in all phases of play, especially in the 'scrum machine' and drives and mauls, and should not be lost to the game. The new non-direct penalty will assist the game substantially at line-out, but there remain areas of concern for player, coach and referee.

Hooker	1 Front row	4 Lock Jumper	3 Front row Supporting player	5 Lock Jumper	7 Side row Supporting player	8 No. 8 Jumper	6 Side row

Highly regarded throughout the rugby world, Colin Meads has become a legend, commanding admiration as a consistently powerful and resolute player. Generally a lock or loose forward, has played for Te Kuiti High School 1st XV 1950; King Country Juniors 1953; NZ Colts 1955; King Country 1955-72 (Waitete); also North Island 1956-59, 62, 63, 65-69; NZ Trials 1956-61, 63, 65-71; New Zealand XV 1958, 68; NZ Under-23 1958; Wanganui-King Country 1956, 65, 66, 71; King Country-Counties 1959. Began his All Black career in 1957 on a tour to Australia and represented NZ until 1971, his final season when he captained the All Blacks against the Lions. His total of 361 first-class matches is a NZ record. Awarded OBE.

A fine two-handed take by Andy Haden against the New York All Stars, Dowling Stadium 1972.
Christchurch Press

Winger

2

Hooker

1

Front row Supporting player

4

Lock Jumper

3

Front row Supporting player

5

Lock Jumper

7

Side row Supporting player

8

No. 8 Jumper

6

Side row

The throw

The large players in particular, will suggest that when the ball is returned from touch it will be won if the throw is correct. Should they miss, there is no thought that the opponent has more ability but rather the *thrower* is incompetent and must either practise with greater zeal or be replaced.

It is true that considerable skill is required. Once the signal is given the players have a right to expect the ball to be thrown exactly. To ensure this, the coach must encourage the thrower(s) to practise the skill with intense determination at team training and , more importantly, in his *personal skill training time;* if the player doesn't own a ball, the coach must acquire one for this purpose. There is no doubt, however, that the percentage of perfect throws will be below 100 per cent, and the pack must be coached to improve accordingly.

The signal

Communication, of tremendous importance throughout the game, is vital in the line-out. It doesn't matter who gives the signal, as long as your pack has the opposition guessing. Variations on the obvious are often rewarding.

The positions

Not too regimented, but following the coach's choice. A coach may try many combinations in the search for perfection. Players have preferences, and two-or three-men combinations are very effective and should be used when it's your own throw-in. Regardless of line-out length each player in it has an exacting task and must combine perfectly with his immediates. When it's the opposition's throw-in your forward leader should decide which variation of line-out positions should be used.

Throwing the ball in to the line-out — the overarm throw

Throwing the ball in to the line-out — the spiral throw

**The technique
of line-out jumping**

Side on

Front on

Hand up high to prevent interference. Hip presented to your opposite. Knees bent to create upward thrust. Fingers already outstretched.

Jump in and towards the ball, leading with the inside arm. In contrast, tapping the ball should be done with the outside arm — if contact is made with the opposition jumper, it will be made with the hip rather than with the shoulder.

Ball brought straight down, with elbows outstretched. Ball kept at maximum distance from the opposition.

When landed, the jumper should make the body as stable as possible, with legs apart and elbows outstretched, and ball held in a manner to make it as difficult as possible for the opposition to interfere with the ball.

Half-back positional play from line-outs. By standing inside the player catching the ball, the half-back can receive a pass and, sighting the team-mate he will pass to, passes the ball on in one action.

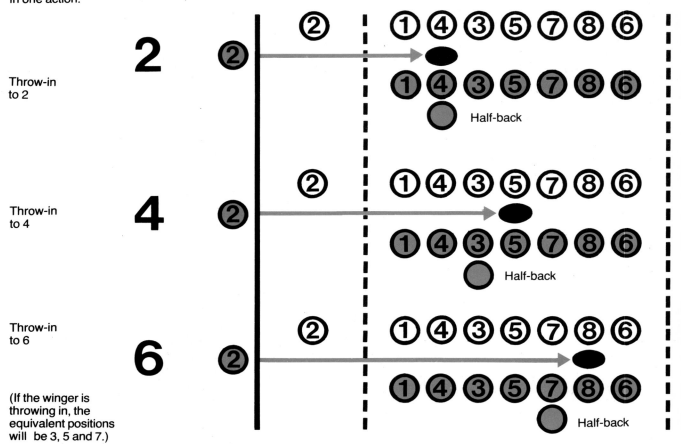

2

Throw-in to 2

4

Throw-in to 4

Throw-in to 6

6

(If the winger is throwing in, the equivalent positions will be 3, 5 and 7.)

By standing inside the player catching the ball, the half-back can receive a pass and, sighting the team-mate he will pass to, passes the ball on in one action.

The win

The ball-winning ability of the pack depends on the combination of all players in the unit and the preparation they devote to specialising. The 'jumpers' are able to practise in their own time. The coach should encourage the players to develop their abilities of the jump, noting each person's preference for types of jump, left- or right-hand deflections etc. The coach must enthuse about individual skills, and ideas for improving specialist positional play. Many of the winning techniques will be developed from the players.

Although very rare, the practice of two-handed taking should still be encouraged — it makes the big player get off the ground. Two-handers are appropriate for No. 2 and No. 6 positions. Probably the balls will be won mostly from much-practised, very slight deflections to another member of the line: 3 to 5, 5 to 7, 2 to 5, (and reverse) — there are many variations. There is surprise value in the No. 8 throw with drive and also to the front. Many of these exciting possibilities may fail in the game, but players will see their value if they are executed to perfection and they will continue to be enthusiastic to master them at practice sessions.

If you are a line-out jumper, keep your eyes on the ball.
Peter Bush

The line-out — the short throw to 2

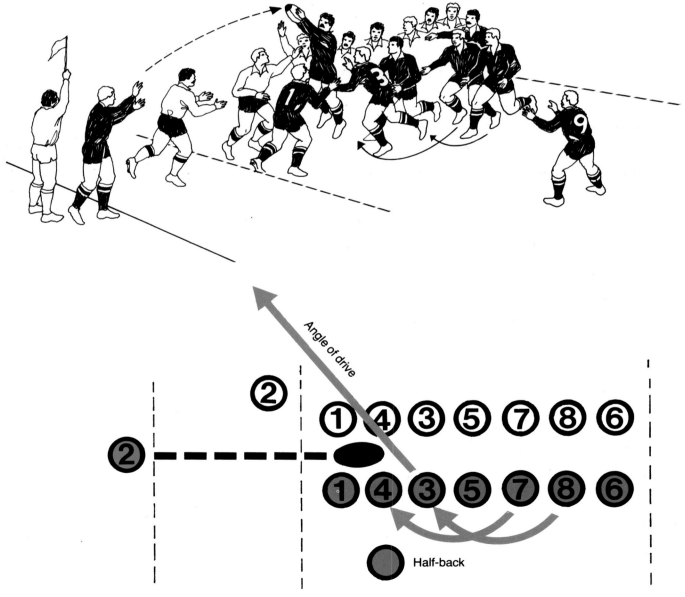

All Japan v New Zealand Universities. Japan demonstrates an excellent example of guided line-out possession.
Peter Bush

The line-out — driving at 6

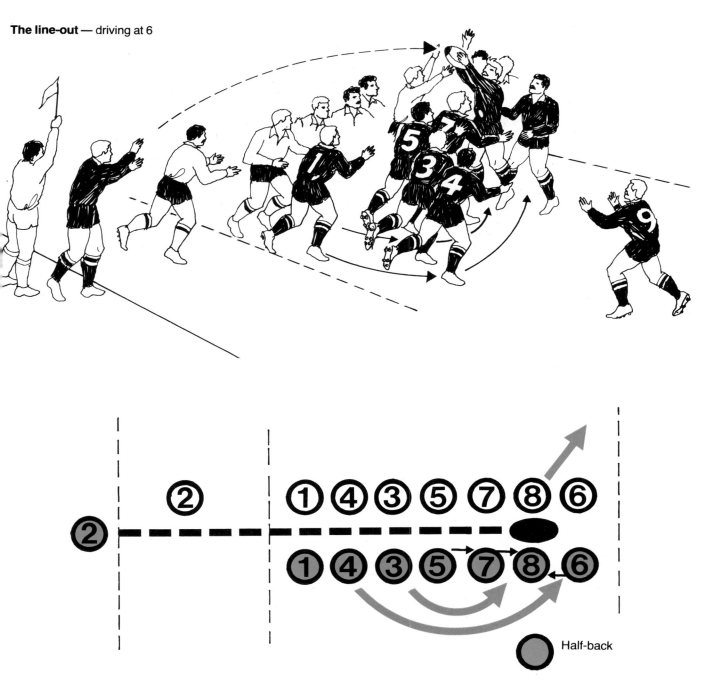

Half-back

The feed

Direct Attacking deflections direct to the half-back are of great value, but they require perfection and there is no room for 'slaps'. Direct feed must be immediate and the line must be held.

Moving The majority of wins that develop from deflection require the line to be moved ahead, committing opposition 'loosies', and fed at the half-back's request. Moving from the line of touch means, of course, that the opposition backs advance; and here the timing of an attack must be at the discretion of your half-back and first five-eighth. The effect varies.

Maul Probably a continuation of the 'moving feed', this has greater potential for a final peeling drive, punching at the opposition's five-eighths or to the short-side. Communication with your team-mates is essential, as the ball should be completely screened from the opposition. The maul requires full participation from the eight. It is rather exciting, with a great number of rewarding attacking possibilities and becomes a valuable second-phase attack where the opposition can be manoeuvred out.

The dispute

Very rarely will you be able to gain possession of the ball against the throw (when it's the opposition's throw-in), though this depends on the abilities of the opposition. They should not be allowed to get possession without a good 'fight'. It is helpful if your hooker is able to calculate the opposition's signals. Many tactics (mostly legal) employed to make line-out ball difficult for the opposition can finally result in valuable bonus wins. Should the 'little big men' be able to infiltrate to deny the opposition possession of the ball, your pack should endeavour to move the line-out, as the resulting scrum loose-head is a bonus.

The referee

Many referees agree that the line-out is most difficult to adjudicate . Perhaps the referee should not overcome this problem by answering with a scrummage for slight 'calculated miscalculated' throw-ins or small breaches of the many other line-out laws, but rather adapt the policy:

If won without *obvious* breach, *believe.*

If won against the throw, *be suspicious.*

If confident in ruling every line-out to the book, *be a liar.*

If guessing, *be a spectator.*

All Blacks v South Africa. Contesting line-out possession.
Peter Bush

Brian Lochore on
Attack & Defence from Line-out

- **The winger, front row forward or loose forward may throw the ball in, but whoever it is should be the best. Line-out calls should be clear.**

- **The extra player should be brought in from line-out play, either the full-back or blind-side winger, (the blind-side winger outside the second five-eighth).**

- **A quick drive at the end of the line-out, either by a peel-away or a drive at No. 7, can create an attacking platform to bring the backs into play.**

- **The ball may be kicked, allowing the blind-side winger to chase through on attack.**

- **In defence each back covers the opposition counterpart; and for the extra player each man moves in one, allowing the winger to be covered by the full-back.**

One of the most important people in any line-out is the thrower-in of the ball. The throw should be to the best line-out jumper in your team, and to a position required by the line-out jumper. I don't think many throwers practise enough. It doesn't matter in my opinion who throws the ball in (winger or hooker), so long as it is the person who can do it best. From a coach's point of view it is much easier to have a forward do it, as at practice sessions you can work with the forwards on their own, practising line-outs, while the backs are doing something else. I believe you can use a loose forward to throw the ball in if your hooker is not good enough, as the front of the line-out is a good place for a fast loose forward to operate from. So be flexible, but make sure you have someone very good throwing in.

Every team should have line-out calls or codes, so that all forwards and inside backs know where the ball is going.

Attack from line-outs

Attacking from line-outs is most important, for it is the only time that the opposition's backs have to be ten metres behind the advantage line.

The outside backs should generally be the key players in any attacking moves from a line-out, for the first five-eighth especially will generally be confronted by the opposition's No. 8. I would use the full-back as extra man fairly often. Also, I don't think the blind-side winger is used enough from line-outs, and when this player does come in it is too close in; I prefer to see him coming at least outside the second five-eighth, if possible outside the centre (for example, during the move involving All Black Tony Steele against the Barbarians in 1967, leading to Ian MacRae's try.) On gaining the ball from the opposition's throw in, the half-back or first five-eighth kicks the ball into the 'box' for the blind-side winger to chase. Other methods could be centre doubling outside winger; full-back coming outside winger.

Driving around the end of the line-out from a 'tap down' ('Willie away') is a good attacking move. The No. 7 or, if you have a tall No. 8, should be used. If you have no tall players at the tail of the line-out you could throw the ball right over the back so that your tail-end line-out player can move back to catch it. As a variation of this move (after using it a couple of times), have a drive straight on No. 7 who has caught the ball and brought it down.

The front of the line-out is also a good place to attack from. Use a short throw to No. 2 and the drive on No. 2 by the other forwards. Also try a quick throw to No. 2 and then a 'tap' back to the thrower.

Any moves from line-outs by the backs should generally be done by outside backs, and there are also many variations that can be worked out for the forwards. The key to the success of these moves is an accurate throw to your line-out jumper.

New Zealand gains possession from the line-out, and the Gazelles look to their defence. Pretoria, 1970. All Blacks from left: Brian Lochore, Tom Lister, Neil Thimbleby, Colin Meads, Alister Hopkinson. No. 9 Sid Going.

Greatly admired and respected as a totally committed and physically inexhaustible player, and as a dedicated and dignified leader. A back-row and lock forward, he played for Wairarapa College 1st XV 1956; Wairarapa 1959-71 (Masterton) as captain 1961-71, and Wairarapa-Bush 1971 (Masterton); also North Island 1964-69; NZ Trials 1961, 63, 65-70; Wairarapa-Bush 1959, 65, 66. His All Black career began with his selection for the 1963-64 British tour and continued until 1971. He was appointed All Black captain against the 1966 Lions, against Australia 1967, on the 1967 British tour, 1968 against the French tourists, 1969 against Wales and 1970 against South Africa. Captained NZ teams in 18 internationals. Coach of the Masterton club 1966, 67, 75-78; club president 1977, 78; successful Wairarapa-Bush coach 1980-81, taking the team from 2nd Div to 1st Div status. Honorary member of the Barbarians (UK). Awarded the OBE.

The line-out — the 'Willie-away'

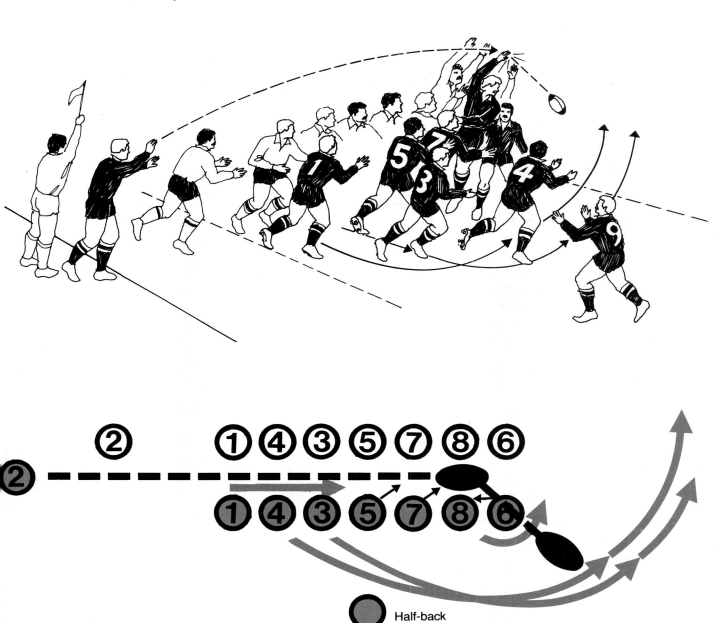

Half-back

One variation of the short line-out — a two-man line-out (as was the situation before Mexted's try against Scotland). Here the two-man line-out is stretched out, the ball is lobbed into a gap, and the No. 8 catches the ball in that gap and drives through. The half-back position is taken by a side-row forward, who will be committed to the drive if it is tapped to him.

The long throw-in

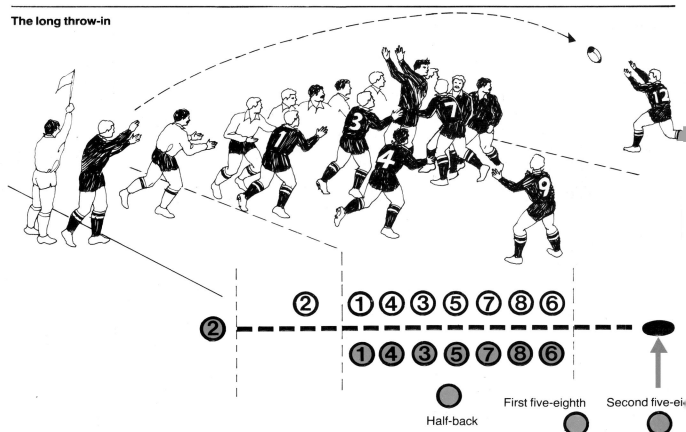

Half-back

First five-eighth

Second five-ei[...]

From the line-out — set-up for the feed

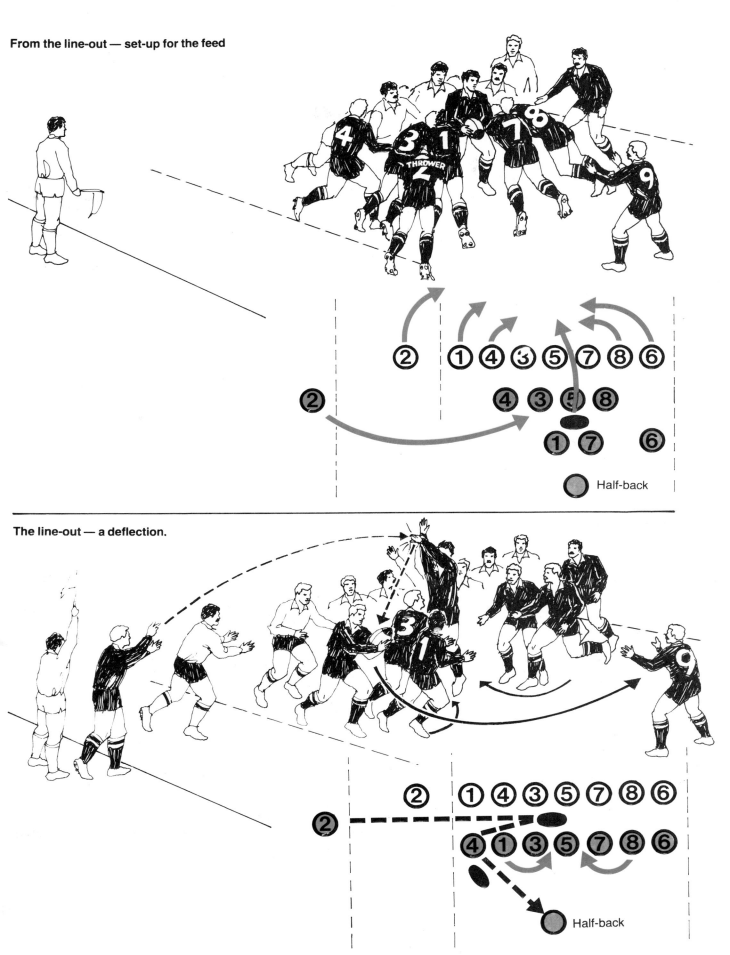

Half-back

The line-out — a deflection.

Half-back

One variation of the quick throw-in — in this case, player 13 has picked the ball up from in-touch and, before the opposition has arrived, has thrown the ball in to a team-mate.

Opposition has not yet arrived.

Defence from line-outs

In defence from line-outs everybody should know where they are going and whom they should be marking.

The front of the line-out is covered by the thrower-in of the ball, who should try to catch the opposing half-back to make sure he can't break down your blind side. The No. 8 should try to catch and disrupt any opposition backline movement towards their first five-eighth, by keeping on the inside and forcing him out. Those forwards not involved in jumping for the ball should try to get through the line-out to put pressure on the opposition's half-back.

All backs should come up to mark each of their opponents, each keeping slightly on the inside of them. If they bring an extra man into the back line, each player in your line-out moves in one, so that the overlap is on the outside and the opposition's extra man is covered by your full-back (your blind-side winger covering their full-back). The half-back does the job a No. 8 would do from a scrum — that is, covering behind the backs.

The best defence is attack: do your utmost to outjump the opposition on their throw-in and also try to work out their line-out code

Australians, from left: Hipwell, Pearse, Fay, Cornelson.
All Blacks, from left: Gary Seear and Andy Dalton.

Line-out defensive pattern

One variation of the short line-out

Half-back

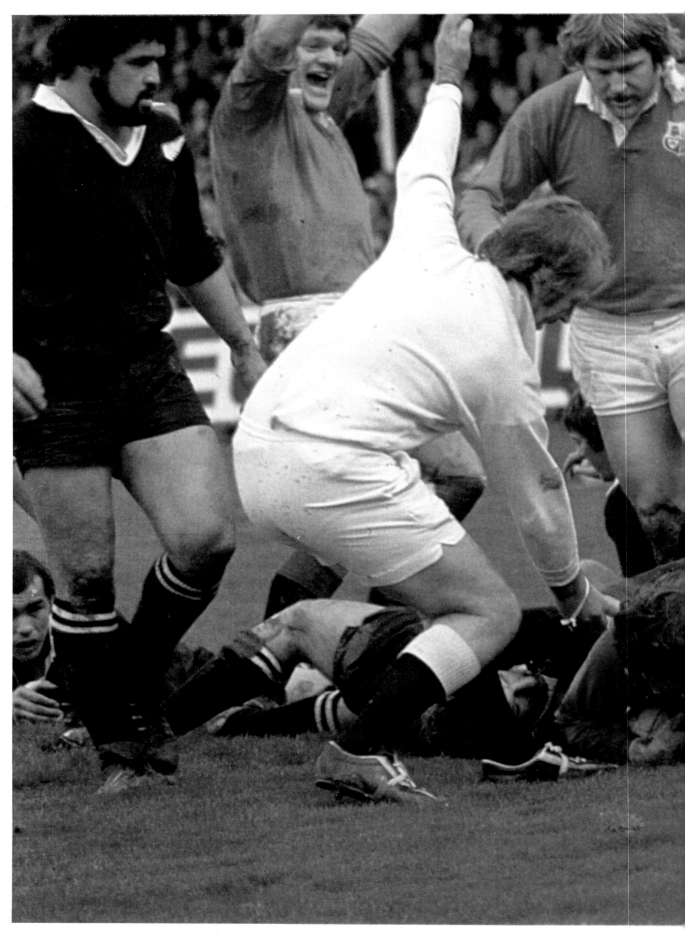

Willie Duggan, playing for the Lions, scores in the tackle from Bryan Williams. All Blacks Bill Bush and Doug Bruce look on in dismay.
Bush

Ivan Vodanovich on

The Ruck

- A ruck is formed when players from each team make scrum formation over the ball in an attempt to gain possession by foot.

- On physical contact with the opposition, the stronger scrum formation drives over the ball on the ground until it is behind their feet.

- Being first to the ball in the greatest numbers, getting quick possession while the opposition is off balance and out of position, this is the best ruck.

- The forwards don't need to take their set scrum positions. First to reach the ball form the front row.

- Body should be low, with strong grips; with all forwards watching the ball and applying weight in the best position to clear the ball.

The ruck and the maul are the key platforms for launching an attack from secondary-phase play. Today's rucking technique, developed from that used by Vic Cavanagh for Otago in the 1940s, has long been a strong aspect of the New Zealander's rugby style, whereas mauling as a science in this country stems from the innovations of the 1971 Lions team and the 1974 Rumanian team. There is still considerable confusion about their definition and application, and the best thing is to refer to the current International Ruby Football Board Laws of the game for a clear exposition.

Although a maul may become a ruck, and a ruck a maul (depending upon what happens to the ball), in the strict sense the players in a ruck concern themselves with gaining possession of the ball on the ground, usually by foot, and players in a maul with the gaining of possession of the ball off the ground, and by hand.

Forming the ruck

Rucking, carried out positively by a forward pack that knows what it's about, can lead to some of the most exciting set-pieces in the game. Movements from this important attacking platform not only make for good rugby but can also produce valuable points.

The first essential is for the pack to get to the loose ball, tackled player, or whatever has precipitated the ruck, as rapidly as possible. Players naturally find this easier if they are going forwards to the ball, and consequently the rucks most likely to produce advantages are those occurring behind their opponents' advantage line. But players should also be ready to go backwards to the ruck situation, and should practise for this eventuality. Flankers should be fit, fast and ball hungry.

The ideal ruck must be based on the 3-4-1 scrum formation — three players in the front row, four in the middle row. A solid platform must be created by the first people to the breakdown. There is an obvious correlation between good rucking and good scrumming, and all of the forwards in the pack must be able to operate effectively in any one of the scrum positions when the ruck forms. It's unimportant which one of them arrives first at the breakdown point: whoever it is must become the basis of the three-man front row, with the others making up the composite unit as they arrive on the scene. (Formation of this type can be essential to winning the ruck.)

The essence of good rucking is the players' body position. This should be low, with the back horizontal and the feet in a pushing stance, not too wide apart, with weight on the toes. Though arriving players should join the ruck with speed and vigour, they should not in their enthusiasm bind too high up on their team-mates and start pushing on a point above the hip rather than below it.

The initial stages of a ruck.
Evening Post

A leading figure in New Zealand rugby coaching and administration. Usually played as a front-row forward for: King Country 1949 (Taumaranui); Wellington 1949-60 (Marist OB); Wellington rugby rep 1952-60 playing 127 games; Wellington Colts 1950; North Island 1955, 57, 59, 60; NZ Trials 1956-60; New Zealand XV 1955 — his All Black debut; Rest of NZ 1954. Coached Marist club 1961-64. Member Executive Marist OB. Member Wellington RU for five years. North Island selector 1966; NZ selector 1967-74. Coach North Island team 1967-69 and All Blacks 1969-73. Member NZRFU executive committee since 1969. Chairman Maori Rugby Advisory Board since 1973. Assistant-manager/coach of 1970 All Blacks in South Africa. Manager NZ Sevens Team to Scotland 1975. Manager NZ Maori Team that toured Australia Tonga, Western Samoa and Fiji 1979. Member NZ executive to International Rugby Board 1979. Coached in Canada, USA, Rumania, South Africa, Tonga, Western Samoa, Fiji, Australia and Japan.

Setting up a ruck from your possession

When a player from your team falls on the ball, he must, under Law 19, either immediately play the ball, or move away from the ball. You, following up, have the option of picking up the ball or driving over the top of the ball to create a ruck. Probably this will also mean stepping over your team-mate to ensure he is in your side of the ruck.

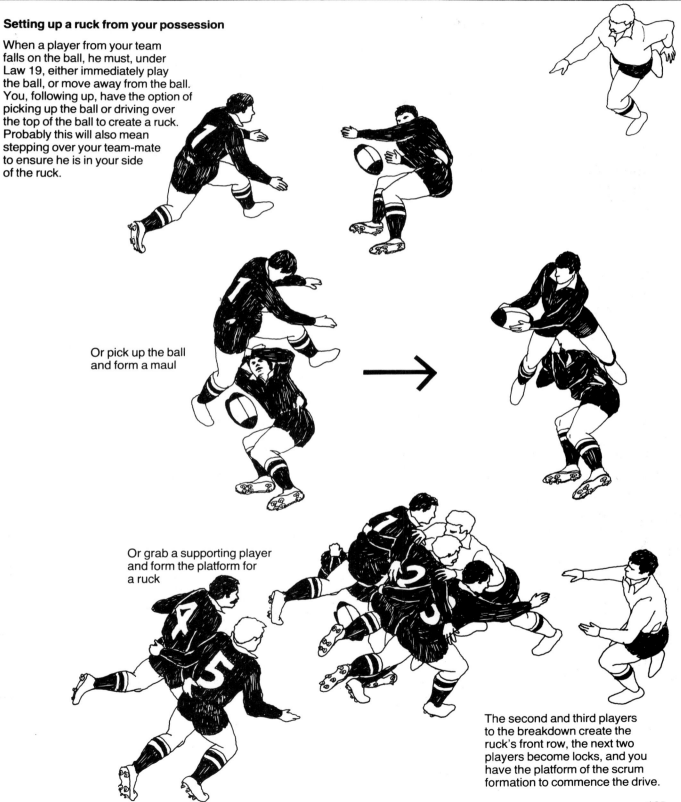

Or pick up the ball and form a maul

Or grab a supporting player and form the platform for a ruck

The second and third players to the breakdown create the ruck's front row, the next two players become locks, and you have the platform of the scrum formation to commence the drive.

Setting up a ruck from your opponent's possession

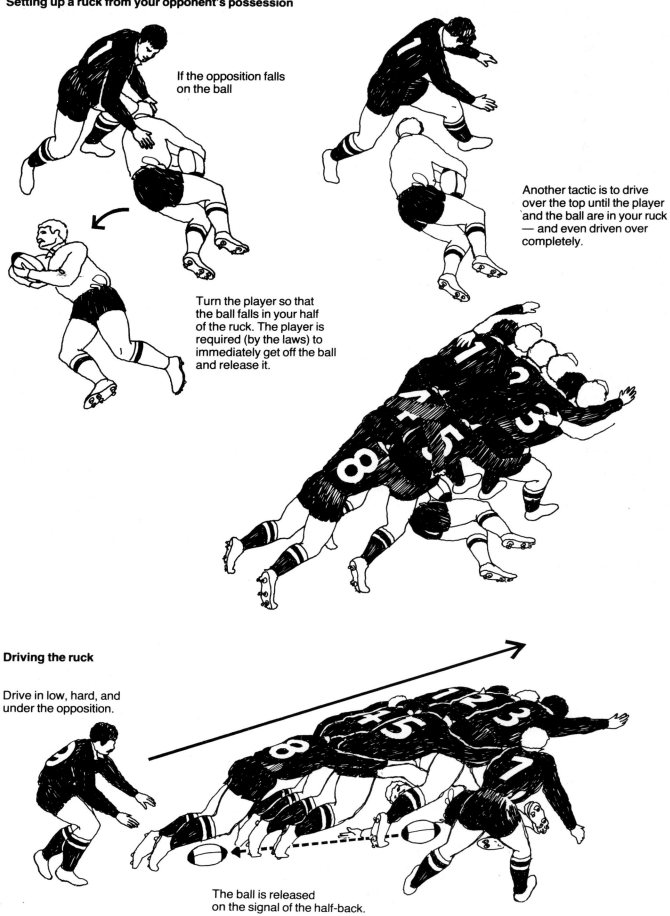

If the opposition falls on the ball

Turn the player so that the ball falls in your half of the ruck. The player is required (by the laws) to immediately get off the ball and release it.

Another tactic is to drive over the top until the player and the ball are in your ruck — and even driven over completely.

Driving the ruck

Drive in low, hard, and under the opposition.

The ball is released on the signal of the half-back.

The essential points

- Get there first.
  Keep on your feet and keep your feet close together.

- Bind in a 3-4-1 formation, getting your shoulders below the hips of your fellow forwards.

- Get a good grip — reach out to bind on as you line up to the ruck. A good arm(s) grip is essential. Hit the ruck already bound, if possible with your shoulders rather than your heads.

- Back-pedal the opposition. The idea is to *push*, not to spread the legs and anchor the ruck. Rucks are won by pushing and driving over the ball and not by heeling.

- Look for the ball and continue to do so until the ruck is over. Hook or hold it on command from your scrum-half, until the ruck is good and tight.

If the position is correct, the ruck can drive forward towards the opponent's goal line, can contain all the opposition forwards and control the ball. At the start of the ruck, the ball should be covered as soon as possible. Any player who can arrive at the breakdown and secure possession of the ball, maintaining it at the pick-up point, has made a major contribution to winning the ruck. If forward movement is maintained, even if your side does not win the ball, it gets the ensuing scrum put-in.

As mentioned earlier, every forward in the pack should be drilled so that each person can act confidently in any of the scrum positions when a ruck forms — so that the No. 8, say, can act as hooker, or the prop go down as lock. It is fatal for a loose forward who is in an ideal position to become a front row man in a ruck to be expected to hang back because some other forward had been nominated for that role in a set scrum. This used to happen too often in New Zealand. Many will recall how the Lions in 1971 won the third test at Athletic Park, Wellington, by a morale-boosting try after they had pushed back an unready All Black pack slow to the ruck.

On the other hand, speed and decisiveness in getting to the ruck should not degenerate from what should be a controlled set-piece into an indecent melee. Each arriving forward should assess the situation and place himself into the appropriate vacant position and stay on his feet and drive.

Players who clamber on top of their team-mates in the mistaken notion they are doing something constructive only ensure the collapse of a ruck and the loss of a chance to control the ball.

Common faults in rucking

- Too slow to the ruck. Reasons: Lack of fitness; faulty anticipation.

- Body position too high. Reasons: Lack of fitness; deficiency in technique.

- Ruck falls over. Reason: Feet spread too far apart.

- Ruck not moving forward. Reasons: Poor foot positioning; lack of fitness; lack of push.

- Ruck too loose. Reason: Poor binding (sore ears and facial contusions are a symptom).

- Ruck continues though ball is gone. Reason: Failing to keep eyes on the ball.

- Giving away penalties. Reason: Failing to comply with the laws.

Forwards should always remember that they need a clear channel to hook or control the ball. Their body position on the tackled ball is very important in creating a clear channel in the early formation of a ruck. They can achieve this by being consciously aware that they must turn in the tackle as they are brought down.

In any ruck the role of the half-back is, of course, critical. His is the decision whether to hook quickly or to hold the ball in the ruck, and he must learn to make a quick assessment of the possibilities arising from each ruck and to call for the ball when the opposition is disorganised or at a disadvantage.

To perfect the 'hook' or 'hold' possession won from rucks is a drill requiring a great deal of practice, but it is absolutely vital to enlarge the opportunities for varying play and to create — if possible — demoralising uncertainty in the opposing team.

New Zealand rugby, both in the All Blacks and at provincial level, has always been blessed with strong, powerful forwards to whom the 3-4-1 formation in the ruck has become second nature. This has contributed greatly to the effectiveness of our forward play and the success of our teams. But it must be remembered that this rucking capability was gained only through constant drilling on the practice field and in the gymnasium. The key to this is the ability of the forwards to play every position in the ruck, and to turn on this drill in any area of the playing field.

Pattern and controlled rucked balls constitute gilt-edged possession.

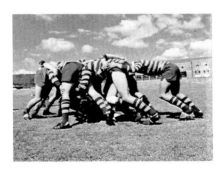

Forming the ruck.
Ruck if no further momentum possible.
Low body position — parallel to touchline.
Explode into opposition.
Form framework of loose scrum.
Maintain balance — bind tightly.
Feed on drive.

Laurie O'Reilly on

The Maul

- The ball-carrier greets an on-coming opponent with a shoulder charge, maintaining the momentum of the drive but turning his body away to screen the ball.
- Team-mates quickly come to the support of the ball-carrier. Their aim is to secure possession of the ball by forming wedges on each side of the ball-carrier or, if more support is lacking, by sealing off the ball.
- It is crucial to maintain firm binding.
- Players must stay on their feet, otherwise the maul will collapse.
- Drive! As with the ruck, it is important to maintain and develop the forward momentum.
- Communicate! Each man must know what is required of him.

Generally, in the maul, the ball is in the hand and it is worked, or fed back to a supporting player in the maul or to the backs. The ball can be put on the ground and the maul converted to a ruck — this sometimes has an advantage for an attacking side and prevents the ball from being tied up.

There is great dispute as to the correct method of forming a maul platform and the correct binding method in a maul. Much has been written about the Welsh method, the English method, the New Zealand method, and so on. As a coach I believe that there is no one correct way of setting up the maul platform and/or binding. There are advantages and disadvantages in all the methods. The strength of the team in possession, the number of supporting players in the maul and the strength and technique of the opposition will dictate the appropriate method.

Continuity of attack

Two important principles of play are support and continuity. The maul and the ruck are both continuity skills which enable the ball-carrier to maintain possession for his side and thus develop a number of attacking options.

The first decision the ball-carrier has to make is whether he should engage in contact or distribute the ball. Players must be encouraged to develop running and passing skills which may make contact in a particular situation unnecessary. Sometimes mauls are deliberately set up, but usually they develop as a result of physical contact with an opponent and particularly from a tackle situation. In modern play, apart from line-out mauls, backs are usually involved in the formation of the maul platform: accordingly backs must understand the basic techniques and must build confidence for contact in the maul structure.

Feeding from a maul. Australia v France, 1981.
Peter Bush

University of Canterbury senior player and coach 1960-81. NZ Regional Advisory Coach. Director of NZ National Coaching School, Lincoln 1980,81. Has coached extensively in the Pacific Islands, Japan and the United Kingdom.

The ball-carrier's body position

The key is to secure possession of the ball. The ball-carrier is all-important therefore, and the form and structure of the ensuing maul depend on what the ball-carrier does.

First, the ball-carrier's body position: the ball-carrier takes a low, driving position, maintaining momentum and balance; he must engage the opposition but must also protect or 'screen' the ball. I advocate a low body lean and impact with the shoulder. On impact the ball-carrier turns at least a quarter-turn but usually a half-circle, thereby presenting his back to the opponent. The elbows should be well out and braced, the player taking short steps (in reverse) with a swinging motion of the torso, using the elbows. The swing of the body helps transfer weight from foot to foot, thus helping the ball-carrier's balance and ability to drive in reverse.

Forming the maul platform

It is at this point that the great debate develops. Remember — the vital point is to secure possession of the ball. The attacking options will depend very much on the initial platform that is formed and the binding method used by the support players.

The appropriate technique in formation depends on the number of support players immediately available to support the ball-carrier.

If the ball-carrier has the immediate support of at least two players, then the first and second support players to arrive should go to alternate sides and bind on to and over the back of the ball-carrier. They form a protective wedge on each side and can drive into the opponent. By binding, they help keep the ball-carrier on his feet and help maintain their own stability. They form a broad and strong base on which to build a maul.

Other support players bind on with, say, two or three support players on each side of the ball-carrier forming an arrowhead or spearhead. The ball is usually released back through the clear channel to the half-back. From a wide frontal platform there is a straight feed back. This type of platform is sometimes developed from line-out play, but it tends to be somewhat static with no driving forces coming in behind the ball-carrier and the first two support players.

When the first two support players wedge on to the ball-carrier on alternate sides I prefer the third and fourth support players to drive in between the ball-carrier and the first support player on one side and the ball-carrier and the second support player on the other side as if locks in a scrum. This establishes a strong driving force. The ball can either be fed to the locks or put on the ground. If the ball is handled by the locks they can smuggle it back to another support player on the side of the maul or at the back of the maul.

The key factor is to develop the drive forward so the maul is dynamic and not static.

The Lions in control of a maul. All Blacks v Lions, 1966.
Auckland Star

Setting up a maul to advantage from a standing tackle

The third player drives into the maul, drags the ball from the opposition and (bound) keeps the impetus going forward. No. 3 also has the option of taking the ball forward and setting up a new maul on the drive, or feeding it.

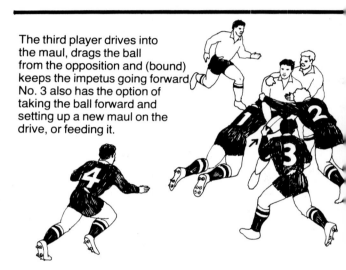

The first player tackles
and turns the ball-carrier.

The second player comes in
on the opposite side and
pins the opponent, preventing
him from releasing the ball
to his supporting players.

Other players drive in
on the wedge.

No. 3 then turns and
presents the ball ready
for the half-back's call.

Setting up a maul to advantage from your own possession

The ball-carrier drives as far as possible. Ball held away from the opposition, hand ready for fending or shoulder changing.

No. 4 also has the option to take a pass and drive in a different direction, or drive into the maul and take the ball to secure it in his part of the maul.

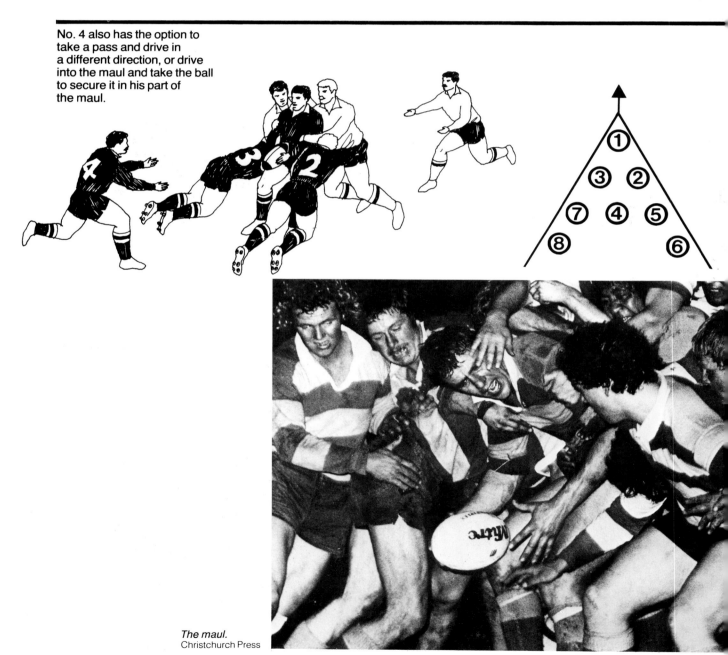

The maul.
Christchurch Press

As the ball-carrier is tackled (on his own terms), he half-turns, keeping the drive going and the ball away from the opposition. The second player (No. 2) has the option to take the ball and continue the drive or commit himself to creating a maul.

The No. 1 completes the turn only when support arrives. The No. 1 may pass to No. 3, or the No. 3 may drive in, creating a three-man platform for the maul.

Others enter, to create the now-familiar wedge drive.

The variations

Many coaches advocate the technique whereby the second player, that is, the first support player to reach the ball-carrier, drives on to the chest of the ball-carrier coming up and under and on to the chest, driving the ball-carrier on and at the same time ripping the ball from him. The next two support players then wedge or bind on to the first support player. The maul is built with the locks coming in on each side of the first two support players.

In this technique the ball-carrier turns his back to the opponent and then the first support player takes the ball and backs into the original ball-carrier. This technique has an advantage in moving the ball away from the opposition but it also has the disadvantage of limiting the ability to drive forward.

Some Australian teams prefer to have the ball-carrier assume a half turn (45°) with the first support player going in on the other side on a similar angle. The two shoulders lock in to each other, that is, left shoulder to left shoulder, or right shoulder to right shoulder. Other support players tend to build the platform on the sides of the first two players. So long as the transfer has not been made to the first support player, the second and third support players can bind or wedge on to the original ball-carrier. The advantage of this technique is the formation of a wide frontal arrowhead. It also allows a clear channel back to the half-back.

If the first support player senses that other support will be slow in coming, I advocate a technique whereby the support player drives on to the chest of the ball-carrier sealing off the ball and gripping the ball-carrier on the outside of the ball-carrier's arms. The ball-carrier needs to have his back to the opposition and needs to lift his head up slightly to enable the support player to drive over the top of the ball and on to the chest of the ball-carrier. The arms of both the ball-carrier and first support player seal off the ball. The first support player pile-drives the ball-carrier forward. Other support players can come to the side and wedge on to the original ball-carrier so long as the transfer has not been made.

The priority is to develop forward drive. Initially, no attempt is made to transfer the ball. The first support player will not be able to turn in this closely knit formation. Once momentum forward has been developed the ball can be squeezed down to the ground or can be smuggled back to a support player. The advantage of this technique is that it allows for a maximum forward drive, but the disadvantage is that it does not allow for a clean channel for a feedback by hand.

The rolling maul

The rolling maul is a recent development providing another attacking option. The ball-carrier drives into the opposition and sets up the ball by backing into the opponent. The first two support players bind over the ball-carrier creating a protective wedge on each side. A wide frontal platform is usually developed.

A support player takes the ball from the original ball-carrier but instead of feeding it back to the half-back, he rolls off the maul and, supported by another player, drives forward at the opposition. This explains the technique in its simplest form. Careful practice can develop a more effective concept.

Assume that the ball-carrier no. 1 makes contact with an opponent and turns and reverses into the opponent. The first two support players, no.s 2 and 3, go to alternate sides and bind on to and over the back of the ball-carrier. They face the opposition and bind on to their respective opponents with their outside arms. Support players no.s 4 and 5 come in between players 1 and 2 and 1 and 3 respectively as if locks in a scrum. As player no. 6 approaches the maul platform, he

assesses which side the attack should be developed. If he wishes to develop the roll to the left side, he binds on the left side lock with his left arm (the outside arm on the body of the left lock). He can then take the ball from ball-carrier no. 1 with his right arm (the inside arm) while applying force against the opposition. It is possible to wheel or screw the whole maul platform to the left with player no. 6 carrying the ball, but bound to the left side lock turning in a clockwise motion to present the opposition with their bodies driving in reverse but well bound together. As these two bound players shielding the ball make progress against the force of the opposition, support players come from the right side of the maul. The first support player binds with his left arm (the outside arm) and drives forward. The ball-carrier will still have his back to the opposition. The support player then rips the ball away by using the inside arm. He then backs into the opposition adding to the wall of players. The process is repeated maintaining at least two players bound together driving into the opposition. If the roll is to the right, players turn in an anti-clockwise motion. After the initial roll off or 'peel', it is important to develop some forward momentum. The roll off or 'peel' can be continued until a territorial advantage over the gain line has been achieved. There should then be a strong drive forward and the release of the ball as for a ruck. The direction of attack can then be switched by the supporting backs.

The advantage of this 'wheel and peel' technique is that the initial screw or wheel of the maul places defending opponents at a disadvantage, swinging them away from the areas of the ball-carrier and the direction of the drive. Players in the team with possession also have easy access to the flanks of the maul platform and can thus provide valuable support and momentum in the push against the opposition.

This technique has the added advantage of keeping the ball well shielded from the opposition. The protective wall of the maul can be used to launch a forward break once the opposition players have been outmanoeuvred.

Maintaining the maul platform

The following are the key factors for the maul:

- *Body position* The ball-carrier drives into the approaching opponent with a shoulder charge and drives, turning his body and screening the ball but maintaining momentum.

- *Support and secure possession* Players quickly come to a support position, assessing the situation as they arrive. Their aim is to secure possession of the ball by forming wedges on each side of the ball-carrier or, if extra support is lacking, by sealing off the ball held by the ball-carrier.

- *Balance formation* Players should approach and bind to provide a wide supporting wedge on each side of the ball-carrier and to drive through the centre of the formed maul. This provides the maximum protection and allows the team in possession a number of attacking options.

- *Binding* It is crucial to maintain firm binding; and even if the ball is being worked loose ready for transfer from the ball-carrier, it should be done by one hand whilst the other hand remains firmly bound on the supporting player.

- *Stay on your feet* If players don't stay on their feet, the maul will not drive forward — the maul will collapse and result in a pile-up.

- *Drive on* As with the ruck, it is important to drive on and maintain and develop the forward momentum. If a 'peel' is to be developed, a useful technique is to swing or 'screw' the maul whilst driving forward, and then have two players still bound to each other to peel away (inside-to-outside swing). This gives balance and protection.

- *Communication* Timing and communication are all-important and it is critical for each player in the maul to know what is required of him. Code calls are critical, to indicate the direction of any 'peel' or roll, the timing of a 'breakaway, or the release of the ball.

When the opposition has the ball

When the opposition has possession of the ball, it is essential that their ball-carrier be tackled, and turned bodily in the tackle, so that the ball he is holding will lie within your part of the maul as it is formed. Your next player to arrive will assist with the turning of the ball-carrier and will form the driving platform or wedge on the side opposite to the initial tackler. As the rest of your forwards arrive they will supply the drive through the normal maul platform formation.

A well-secured maul platform is difficult to counter and it is usually impossible to get at the ball itself. You can work on the system of ignoring the ball however, and maintaining the opposition's ball-carrier on his feet as well as the support players bound to the ball-carrier, and then endeavouring to drive the opposition's maul platform backwards. If all your players are bound together and are committed to the drive, then it is sometimes possible to gain the advantage of momentum over the team with possession while its players are concentrating on the transfer of the ball.

If the opposition ball-carrier cannot be turned to expose the ball, it may be possible to drive his feet from under him.

This requires a low driving impact on his legs at or below the back of the knees. As the ball-carrier falls to the ground into the opponents side of the maul, defenders can isolate his support by driving in and over the ball-carrier thus developing a ruck situation.

There are not many mauls that require more than five or six players to be effective. Hence, your team, as the defending team, may benefit from having your last one or two players arrive at the maul positioning themselves on either side of the maul ready to latch on to any opposition players who peel or break away from the maul. Players on the defending side who are stationed at the back of the maul should be encouraged to unbind and 'roll' to the direction of any 'wheel' or 'peel', thus achieving the same result as a defensive player who positions himself for a tackle without ever joining the maul.

As with a ruck, the more support players a defending side can get to the ball-carrier ahead of the team with possession, the better. It should be the aim of the first defender to endeavour to turn the ball-carrier and dislodge the ball, and certainly the aim of the second support player to rip away the ball once the possessor has been turned.

Again, the team without possession in a maul must endeavour to prevent the opposition from driving forward. The more it can force the team in possession to be static, the less effective will be the attack of the possessors.

All Black loose forwards break from the end of the line-out in cover defence. Left to right: Laurie Knight, Graham Mourie and Ian Kirkpatrick.
Peter Bush

Laws on the maul

The law book says:

'A maul, which can take place only in the field-of-play, is formed by one or more players from each team on their feet and in physical contact closing round a player who is carrying the ball.'

'A maul ends when the ball is on the ground or the ball or a player carrying it emerges from the maul or when a scrummage is ordered.'

'A maul ends a tackle.'

What you must do in law whilst in the maul is be in physical contact with the maul, that is, be caught in or bound to the maul, and not merely alongside it.

What you must not do in law whilst in the maul:
- Jump on top of other players in the maul.
- Join the maul from your opponents' side.
- Join the maul from in front of the ball.
- Drop the ball to the ground and then pick it up again.

What you must do in law whilst a maul is on and you are not part of it:
- Retire behind the off-side line, that is, behind the hindmost foot of your players in the maul, without delay.
- Stay behind the off-side line with both feet, unless you are joining the maul.
- If you leave the maul, you must immediately rejoin it behind the ball or retire behind the off-side line.

Comparing the ruck with the maul

Coaches debate at length the relative merits of ruck and maul. The team of today must be adept in both. It is poor coaching to suggest that the team will only ruck or will only maul. There will be ample opportunity for both during every game.

Teams may well have a preference and may well endeavour to create ruck situations in preference to mauls. The physique and technique of the players and the position of play in relation to the gain line will usually dictate the method to be used. Genuine rugby is applying the correct technique at the correct time and this is particularly important in the ruck and the maul.

'Attack' is converting possession, position and pressure into points. The object must be to develop a ruck or maul situation to gain the maximum number of attacking options. It is important to see both the ruck and the maul as part of the continuity of attack.

As a general rule, if the attack is developed quickly into the opposition territory and ahead of the attacker's gain line, then the quicker the possession the better. In a ruck the ball is left on the ground or is propelled back on the ground while the players in the ruck structure move forward over and ahead of the ball. Generally, this gives the advantage of quicker possession of the ball for the backs.

The ruck allows a more powerful drive forward thus committing more of the opponent's forward pack and causing the defensive back line to realign more hurriedly. Hence, some coaches advocate a ruck when play is going forward and quick ball is needed.

Conversely, if defenders have to track back to stop a driving attack behind their own gain line, they need time to regroup and their backs need time to form a new defence line. In such circumstances there are advantages in slowing down the momentum and feed by creating and developing a maul.

Accordingly, many New Zealand coaches advocate rucks going forward and mauls going back. It must not be forgotten, however, that some of the best attacking potential occurs in defensive situations when the ball is won quickly.

By varying the pattern of the maul structure, the speed with which the ball can be delivered from a maul can also be varied. If a maul forms across the gain line the ball can be ripped or transferred quickly from the original ball-carrier and passed through a clear channel to the half-back. Conversely, if players have to track back to a maul behind the gain line, it is more effective to wedge and drive thus slowing down the delivery of the ball.

If a team comprises fast mobile light forwards who are quick to support, it is likely to be more effective in the ruck than in the maul. The players would not wish to engage in grappling and struggling with much stronger opponents.

The maul has some advantages over the ruck: the ball can be screened from the opposition and usually it will be difficult for the opponents to see it. It offers safer possession with better control by hand and foot. The attacking options are greater. The ball can be worked back to the last man who can peel away, like the No. 8. It can be worked to the sides for a breakaway attack on the flank. The maul can be screwed like a scrum and the ball rolled away with players turning inside-out, binding in twos for maximum protection and drive. Finally, it can be easily converted into a ruck.

Because it has the advantage of better control, many teams set out to maul their own ball. If the opposition has the ball there is advantage in concentrating on the tackle and the ruck to rob the opposition of the ball or to deny it controlled ball.

The maul and the ruck must be used as attacking tools to exploit possession, position and pressure going forward to score tries. They are not ends in themselves, but are to be developed for their attacking potential. Once the attacking advantage has been obtained, the ball should then be presented to the team's backs to exploit that advantage.

I am a strong advocate of the driving maul. Therefore I emphasise the 'body before the ball' to ensure that emphasis is placed on physical commitment and momentum forward before the ball is transferred.

A maul situation. West Wales v All Blacks, 1978.
Peter Bush

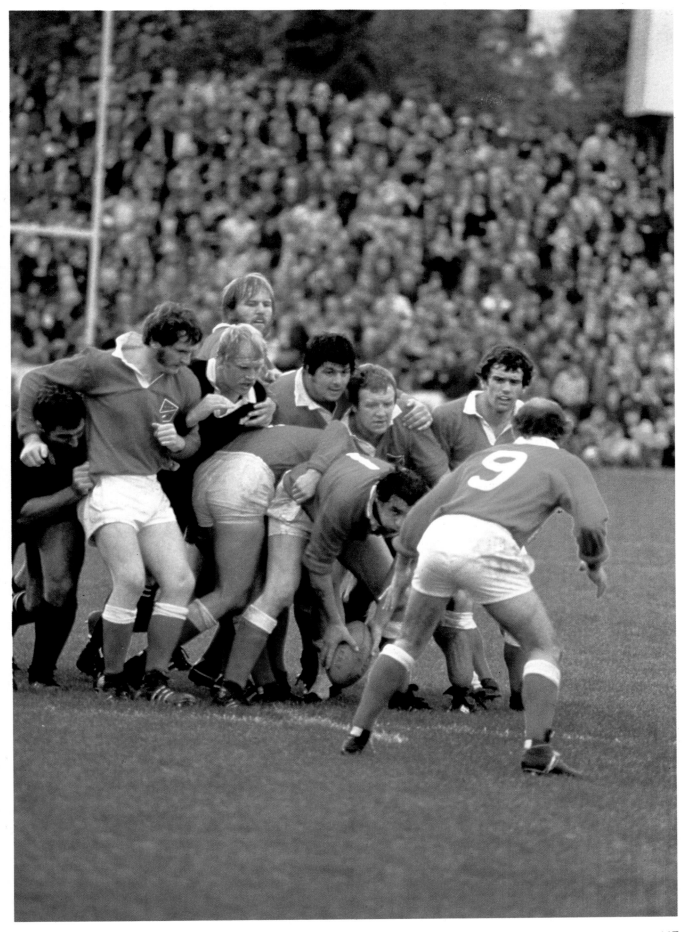

Back Play

- **Take the ball and run with it — be ball hungry.**
- **Take the shortest route to your opponents' goal line — run 'dead straight'.**
- **Get there as fast as you possibly can — work at top speed.**
- **Adopt an attitude that says: 'You won't stop me, not you, not anyone' — be aggressive in all that you do.**

My philosophy of back play is based on those four simple rules: Once you've won that ball you should keep it. There are all sorts of theories about the use of different kinds of kicks, and they are important. But unless you are particularly skilled at using them you give the ball away; so its best, once you've got it, to keep it and develop a way to pass it from person to person so you've always got control. With effective passing and catching you can therefore keep the initiative in the game at all times.

The well-made pass

To develop a good back line and the style of attacking rugby that I like to play with the teams I coach, I base my game on the old-fashioned hip-swinging pass. First, you position yourself to meet the ball, you never snatch at it in front of you or let it go past and take a swing at it. If it is coming from the left, you position your hands to take it on the left of you; from the right, you position your hands to take it on the right. Either way, all you have to do then is bring the ball across your body and pass it away. A dropping ball is a difficult ball to catch. It is easier to catch a ball on the rise, so aim up towards your team-mate's chest so the catcher can run on to it. Finally use the swing of the hip to straighten up play, and make your opposition hesitate. This exaggeration will also help in the development of a dummy and protect yourself in the tackle. Always accelerate into the pass.

Counties, winners of the 1979 New Zealand Provincial Championship, swing on to attack.
Counties Photo Den

Lions on the move. Barry John is supported by Mike Gibson.
Evening Post

As a provincial player has represented Manawatu 1951, Taranaki 1954, Auckland 1952, NZ Universities 1951, and NZ Maoris 1951, 54. Coached senior club teams in Okato, Kaeo, Hawera, Okaihau, and Ruanui. Assistant coach of Counties 1969-73; Counties coach 1976-79. Coached school teams at Okaihau, Wesley College and Tuakau College. Past member of the Management Committee Bay of Islands, Taranaki and Counties. Currently secretary Taranaki Maori RFU. Holds referee qualifications to senior B and has refereed in the Bay of Islands and Counties.

Developing the players' flexibility

Strict observation of the back line positions is not part of modern rugby. True, the programme puts the players at first five-eighth, second five-eighth, centre, wing or full-back, and often you get into these positions from set play from scrum or line-out — but once play starts and you begin to move towards your opponents try line, everyone in the team has to know how to pass, how to catch, and how to play in every back-line position. It's a real 15-man game and in practice it must be played as such. Every skill must be practised in slow motion until it is right; then it can be taken at pace. The first five-eighth has got to be able to play second five-eighth, the second five-eighth has got to be able to play first five-eighth. My wings have got to be able to come into the back line in any position and fit in there. What I ask of my backs is no different to what I ask of my forwards.

In order to get flexibility of position, the Counties teams practise what we call a '5,4,3,2,1'. (See diagrams p 121.)

The '5, 4, 3, 2, 1' has these objectives:

- Backs learn to slip into a supportive position, e.g. a centre may be at first five.

- Backs learn to react instantly to a call. When the centre calls 'two' he is at second five; the second five immediately moves out to the centre position, with the correct distance between.
  The blind side wing may call 'one'; he is taking over at first five; the rest of the backs move out.

- As the pressure goes on and exhaustion builds up, the demand is for greater concentration and more, and better, ball control — the requirement is for no dropped ball from start to finish.

- Backs learn to take up the correct position for support. Laziness will create a forward pass situation — this must not happen.

- Forwards must race to the position where the ball is placed by the wing on the ground.
  The demand is that all eight are at the ball by the time that the count reaches 5 or 4 or 3 etc. Not halfway to the ball, but right there and participating.

- The full team must think. Forwards must go into the maul behind the ball, especially when the direction of play has changed; backs must do likewise, and in very rapid time.

- By the time that the count is completed the forward with the ball must feed the ball to the half-back — and think about the quality of the feed; a maul or a ruck feed.
  The mechanics of the exercise: Start from a line-out or a scrum; there will be five men in each movement outside of the half — either a full-back or a blind-side wing. These usually alternate.

Diagram A

The ball is rolled to the half-back who passes to the first five-eighth, who passes to the second five-eighth then to the centre and to a wing — the full-back coming in every second run. (When moving in one direction the full-back comes in as the extra man; when moving in the other direction then the blind-side wing becomes the extra man. In other words, the aim is to have the extra man in every move in each direction.)

119

The ball passes through the full line with the full-back either outside the second or centre. The wing races across the line of advantage, at full pace, for 20 metres at least — and puts the ball down. A loose forward picks it up and sets up the maul but the maul will be such as to run in the opposite direction on the count of 5. Start the count as soon as the first player to the ball picks it up — Call: 1-2-3-4-5-feed.

Diagram B

As soon as the count reaches 5 (1, 2, 3, 4, 5, feed) the ball must go to the half-back and play is at full pace in the opposite direction. The left wing now races full pace at least 20 metres across the line of advantage — 30 or 40 metres — whatever the coach decides, and calls 'Ball down'. Again the first forward to the ball picks it up and sets himself for a maul — again in the opposite direction. On reaching the count of 4 (1, 2, 3, 4, feed) the ball is fed to the half-back and play swings in the opposite direction again.

Diagram C

The situation as in Diagram B is now recreated — and the count is now: 1-2-3-feed. On 3 the ball goes to the half-back, and the full 8-man scrum is expected to be in place, as is the full back line with either a wing or a full-back, or both, joining the line. The process is repeated as for Diagram C but the count is now: 1-2-feed; the demands remain the same — all eight get to the maul — a full scale 5-man back line-out is required — but the emphasis remains on a man being in the positions of 1, 2, 3, 4A or 4B with one extra man in. Repeat the situation as for Diagram B but the count is now: 1 — and the ball is fed off through the full line.

As my count lessens the players must get into positions that allow the routine to continue. A wing may become first, and a centre, half-back. This brings a tension into the practice session, making it similar to game conditions. Once the whole exercise is over, the team will need a short rest depending on the degree of fitness.

The ball is not to be dropped at any stage. The object is perfect handling and greater concentration on the ball as fatigue sets in. Greater concentration is also required by the forwards, firstly to get to the ball and secondly to take up a correct maul position. If you can go through one of these routines without a dropped ball, you're doing well.

During training sessions we practise three basic movements and involve everyone in them — backs and forwards. By practising the good pass and good catch and acceleration, we can control the pass that misses out a player, the scissors and dummy scissors, and the extra man. By practising these as a team, everyone can learn how best to combine. Our second five-eighth, Graham Taylor, prefers the full-back to come in inside him — then he can feed the ball back to him. In contrast, Bruce Robertson at centre likes the full-back outside him so that he can feed him into the gap. In these practices we try not to break up the half-back/first five-eighth combination, as successful play will depend on that combination working efficiently.

I prefer the first five-eighth position to be always occupied by the same first five-eighth unless he is trapped under a ruck or maul. I believe that a good half-back/first five-eighth combination depends on impulse and understanding so that the half-back builds up an understanding whereby the first five-eighth will always be where the half-back throws the ball. Similarly, the first five-eighth is able to sense where the half-back will throw the ball, from whatever position he may be in. The places where extra players appear, therefore, most often is outside of the first five-eighth.

As far as doubling is concerned, you are creating an extra man by action. You might double at first by the half-back being fed from the scrum by the No. 8 at the back of the scrum; the half-back feeds the ball to his first five-eighth and then doubles around the first five-eighth to receive the pass again. In the same way, the first five-eighth might run around the second five-eighth to get another pass. The important requirement in each of these situations is that the player who receives the ball and who knows that his own man is going to double around him, must run straight because by going straight he will make his opposition marker hesitate and create a gap outside of himself. Continual variation confuses the opposition. This is aggressive play, where everyone is looking for gaps for himself or his team-mates — no player is tied down to one position all the time.

The attributes required

The half-back has to be able to clear the ball well with a good, long pass. This player has to be able to run, back-up, be first to the ball; be able to rob the ball from opposition forwards often twice the size; be able to kick with both feet. Team tactics are not determined by the half-back — they are determined by a team talk before each game — but is is often the half-back who puts these tactics into action. The half-back must have a cool head, and during practice sessions must be exposed to every situation to learn to pass well from the most difficult positions.

The wings are the most mobile players. They can go anywhere they like as the full-back can. Actually, in some ways the full-back should be even faster than the wings, because the full-back has to attack and defend at top pace, particularly when chasing someone who has broken through your line on the outside, or when entering outside the centre on attack. The wings must look for work coming into the back line inside the second five-eighth or even further out.

All Black half-back Sid Going about to reverse pass.
Evening Post

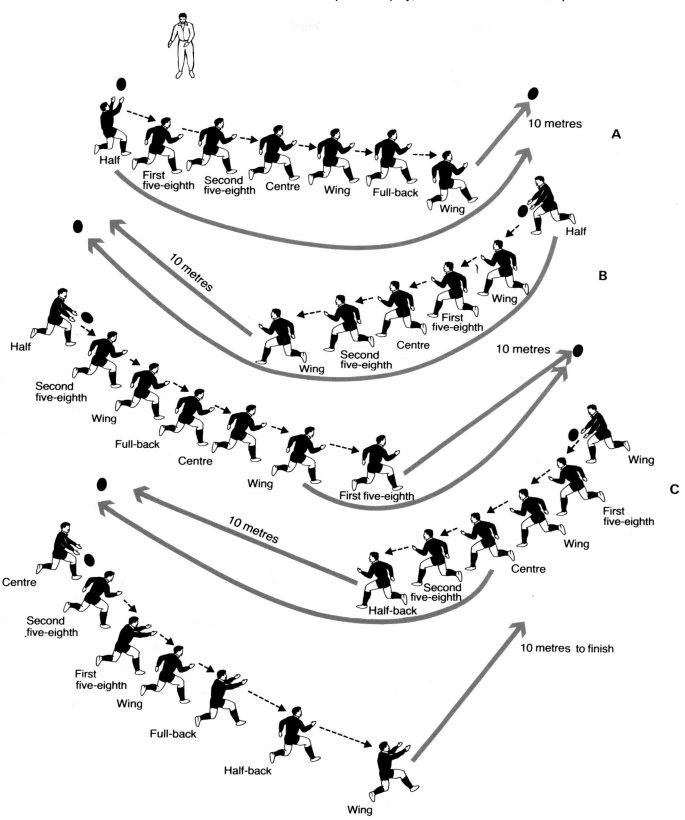

Developing the players' flexibility with a '5, 4, 3, 2, 1'. An important part of the Counties training programme under Hiwi Tauroa, this exercise increases passing skills, knowledge of positional play, and team awareness under pressure.

10 metres

A

Half

First five-eighth

Second five-eighth

Centre

Wing

Full-back

Wing

Half

B

10 metres

First five-eighth

Centre

Wing

Second five-eighth

Wing

Half

Second five-eighth

Wing

Full-back

Centre

Wing

First five-eighth

10 metres

Wing

First five-eighth

Centre

Second five-eighth

Half-back

C

Centre

Second five-eighth

First five-eighth

Wing

Full-back

Half-back

Wing

10 metres

10 metres to finish

121

Defence

To me, many teams spend too much time practising attack, on the assumption that they're going to get every ball from every line-out, scrum, ruck or maul. Time has to be spent on defence. With the teams I coach, we usually work on man-for-man defence: in other words, each player marks the opposition player, or the player who is filling the position opposite you — except from the line-out, where the attacking role of those at the end of the line will release the inside backs and allow them a covering role. If the opposition has possession of the ball, you must take the player with the ball as fast as you can. If an extra man is used, for instance when their full-back enters the line at centre, one of your wings must take the full-back, and your own full-back must not stay back but must come up and take their wing (now in the overlap position) as quickly as possible. The loose forward defence patterns and back support defence patterns take care of an overlap.

The half-back and first five-eighth are in a different position to many others in the back line. The loose forwards are committed to marking their opposites, so their job is to cover behind the back line, keeping inside the player with the ball so that he cannot cut inside. That, of course, applies to every other back: by positioning yourself inside your opponent, you not only prevent him from cutting inside you, but force him out towards the touch line and restrict the movement of the attack and the space the attack can be launched in.

Close marking can be upsetting to a back line. The first thing is to let the referee know when the opposition is creeping. (Creeping refers to the opposition back line moving further forward while attention is focused on the line-out or the scrum until, ultimately, they are off-side or very, very close to it. It is possible on the field to draw the referee's attention to people who are off-side and whilst there may be no immediate return there is every possibility that the referee will pay particular attention to the opposition backs from then on.) But perhaps more important is to line up properly. Not too deep — perhaps 15 to 20 metres behind the half-back — unless, of course, you want it deep. There are basically two approaches. You can deliberately drag your opponents as close as possible, then if you penetrate the advantage line all your opponents are behind you. On the other hand, you can have your back line organised to 'stand' and put the ball right out to one wing, then reverse the action when you've committed your opponents to running the maximum distance. Following a ball at speed can wear out the opposition's loose forwards quicker than anything.

The distance between players in the back line should not be regular and consistent. You must not establish a predictable pattern. That's why, when you're practising ordinary passing, you may stand 2 metres apart, or 3 or 4 or 10 metres apart. In a game it sometimes pays to run wide, so the person who has the ball must be able to throw a long pass to you. Then again, you may need merely to smuggle a pass — you're so close. Defensive patterns can easily be upset by changing relationships between the attacking players.

Lions player Phil Bennett spots the gap. Steve Fenwick in support. Lions v All Blacks.

Peter Bush

A man-for-man defensive screen

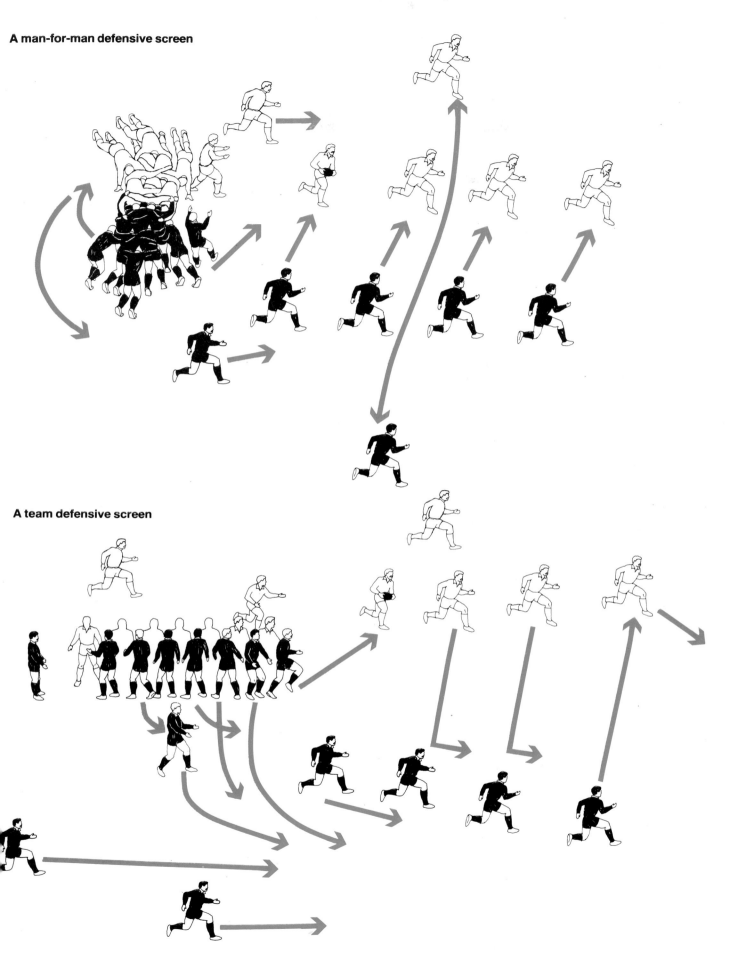

A team defensive screen

123

Varying styles of play

The coach must know the team well. Some people are naturally aggressive, some not. During practice sessions a more aggressive player in a tackle will teach a less aggressive one, if such things are practised on sawdust bags. In practice and in a game each player is communicating with and perhaps correcting another team-mate. Each must learn to give and take corrections and know it's for the good of the team. This does not mean arguing with one another.

In New Zealand, weather is often an important factor in the way a game is played. Under wet conditions you must concentrate that little bit extra. Remember the ground underfoot is not as firm as it could be; concentrate on your catch; concentrate on your pass — perhaps a slower pass, perhaps a more lobbed pass. This doesn't mean that you cannot play the passing game under wet or windy conditions.

Often our team has played better against the wind than with it. We choose to play against it quite a lot, because the first 20 minutes is a settling-down time for both teams. A referee may tend to 'blow up' the play frequently to establish control of the game. If you're playing into the wind the pass will be blown back to you, rather than away from you; it's easier then to take the ball. If you can kick with control and keep the ball low, you can often make better use of the kick than when you're playing with the wind, when overkicking can lose you possession of the ball and waste valuable time.

Perfecting the kick

When you kick, you kick to recover the ball, or to get it out and restart play. It's one or the other. You don't give ball away at all. A few years ago when Counties weren't able to get much ball from line-outs, we weren't kicking it out. It was easier to kick the ball down the sideline, put on the pressure and let our opponents kick it out and give us the throw-in. When you kick, you kick to attack and to regain possession. You must perfect your grubber kicks to deal with close marking as well as the little kick over your opponent's head. Robert Kururangi scored against Canterbury by putting a little kick over his opponent.

Positioning for kicking is another matter. If you've got the ball and you realise that it's no good pushing it out to somebody else . . . well, you've got to kick. To be totally flexible you must be able to kick with either foot accurately, and you've got to be able to put it out. If you are first five-eighth, most of the time you are kicking 'into the box' over attacking forwards coming at you. If you're second five-eighth, you rarely have forwards coming at you, so it could be a little kick over the heads of your opponents, or a grubber between them. If you're kicking down the line, you do have time to position yourself for it. If you have more than one opponent coming at you, a long, low kick into the gap they have created could gain more ground.

The thrill of the try

For me, it's the try that makes the game of rugby. It's this that you are aiming at when you are planning a philosophy of back play — a try such as Graham Taylor's for Counties against Wellington in 1977.

Wellington were on attack, inside our 22 metre line. Mark Codlin at half-back got it from a scrum and ran blind down the sideline. The ball went through three players to Robert Kururangi on the wing, he went as far as he could, then in-passed to our No. 8, Alan Dawson, who was backing up. As someone came in to take Alan, he passed the ball to Graham Taylor, and when he scored under the posts he had two players in support.

Another great try from the same game began between our 22 metre line and half-way. From a scrum the ball went out to Bruce Robertson who fed it to Robert Kururangi outside him on the wing, then Bruce doubled around Robert, took another pass, then kicked back in again. When we scored the try the whole eight of our pack were there — a real team try.

All Black half-back Mark Donaldson kicks for touch from a penalty.
Forwards in support: Andy Haden, left, and Gary Knight.
Peter Bush

Creating an extra man by doubling around

The moment of truth.
Peter Bush

Dave Henderson on

Half-Back Play

- **The half-back, the vital link between forwards and backs, must be agile, strong, mentally alert, and have the skill to deliver a variety of passes with speed, distance and accuracy.**
- **Different situations will dictate which type of pass should be used, but each pass should be controlled and without waste movement.**
- **Good understanding between the No. 8, half-back and first five-eighth is vital to the successful development of effective attacking play.**
- **The half-back's skills must include the mastery of a variety of kicks, the ability to break, and sound defensive ability.**
- **Practise all skills until they are mastered, making a special effort to polish any particular skill you have. It will develop confidence that will spill over into other aspects of your game.**

It could be argued that the half-back plays in the most challenging, stimulating and interesting position in rugby. After all, this player is the pivot of the whole team. This is the person who welds together the raw power and drive of the forwards with the special skills and speed work of the back line.

It has been said that you can cover up most weaknesses in a rugby team, but you can't cover the lack of a good half-back. So those of you who choose to play half-back, stick with it. You have some great times ahead.

Physical requirements of the position

When rugby teams up and down the grades are selected (especially those in the lower grades), the first player chosen is the half-back. The smallest player present is tossed the ball and told, 'Go and practise your passing'. Traditionally, a compact build has been considered the prime requirement for the position. While it is not essential, of course, there does appear to be evidence that as regards rugby half-backs, there is a reversal of the old adage — in this instance, a 'good small man' may very well always beat a 'good big man' — although that fine Welsh 188 cm (6 ft 2 in) half-back Terry Holmes would probably disagree.

Much more important than size, however, is agility and 'quickness'. Quickness is a physical *and* mental quality, giving a half-back the ability to decide in a split second how best to use ball delivered to him, at some pains, by his forwards. The quickness so beautifully demonstrated by Sid Going in the All Blacks' Third Test against South Africa in 1976, when he flicked an awkward ball swiftly between his legs directly behind him to Doug Bruce, giving Doug the vital extra second he needed to drop a goal — this from what started as an impossible situation. It was moments like that that made Sid 'Super'.

Capable hands are another essential. You can hide your hands in the front row, you can even bluff your way through on the wing, but ineffective hands can't be hidden at half-back. The half-back handles the ball so often that awkward fingers will strangle your team's attacking efforts before they begin.

The half-back pass

A half-back without an efficient pass can be likened to a gunfighter with one bullet in his gun; he can possibly stop an opposition team in their tracks with his running, but he'll rarely, if ever, finish them off. Only by passing the ball swiftly and often into the back line can a half-back activate all of his team's 'guns'. Then, having established a rhythm, he can use the break to bring his forwards into the game, varying play as match conditions dictate. To put it bluntly: the pass is the guts of the half-back's game.

Perhaps the most astute and thought-provoking summation of the half-back's pass was that attributed to Haydn Tanner, the great Welsh player of the 1940s, in Fred Allen's book *Fred Allen on Rugby*. Tanner described each pass as an inherent *contest* of speed versus length versus accuracy — adding that speed was by far the most important of all. Combine the three and you achieve the perfect pass.

The half-back whose passing came closest to perfection in recent time was 1960s All Black Chris Laidlaw, whose beautiful, sweeping left-handed spiral passes remain one of my vivid memories of rugby at that time. They were fast, they were long and they were impeccably accurate. I remember that as a schoolboy, I spent hours battering my parents' hedges and shrubs with what I hoped were Laidlaw-like passes.

For sheer speed of delivery two Australians, Ken Catchpole and, more recently, John Hipwell, probably have never been equalled. Not the most elegant of passers, they concentrated instead on whipping the ball away with absolute economy of movement. Both Laidlaw's spiral and the Australians' flick pass are examples of the standing pass.

All Black half-back Mark Donaldson reverse passes. All Blacks v Wallabies. Wallabies: W. A. McKidd, left, and Ken Wright.
Peter Bush

Played for Wellington Football Club 1965-79; Senior A team 1968-79. As a Wellington Provincial player, for: Under-21 Reps 1966; Senior 2nd and 3rd Div Reps 1968; Wellington B 1969-70; Wellington A 1971-79 — in total 100 first-class games for Wellington. All Black Trials reservist 1972. Wellington Province staff coach 1981. Wellington Regional Under-18 selector 1981. Executive Centurions RF Club 1979-81, and Club captain 1981. Member Wellington Provincial Promotions subcommittee 1981.

The standing pass

This is the bread-and-butter pass for virtually every half-back playing the game today. Its main advantage is, of course, that unlike the dive pass it leaves a half-back on his feet to back up quickly and remain in play. (A good half back *must* be on the spot whenever play breaks down).

The main points to aim for are:
- Foot placement behind the ball
- Your weight initially *over* the ball
- As you scoop the ball away — without a time-consuming backswing — take an exaggerated pace in the direction of your target (this contributes enormously to the accuracy of the pass).
- The hand behind the ball provides the thrust, the other is the 'guiding' hand.

To develop momentum, the pass should be built like a golf swing: using first the forward movement of legs and body as you take your pace. Then the sweep of the arms and finally a flick of the wrists to send the ball away.

This final flick of the wrists provides the main difference between the Laidlaw spiral and the Catchpole/Hipwell flick pass. The Australians tended to release the ball with a snap which shot the ball away at great velocity, usually over a short distance. (This fitted in with the Australian pattern of back play which features close positioning and short snappy transfers).

The spiral requires correct and particular placement of the hands, together around the 'meat' of the ball, and the distinctive backspin is then imparted to the ball with an upward flick of the hand behind the ball (the 'thrust' hand). Because this often requires a quick adjustment of hand positioning, the pass may take a fraction longer to release, but once away it travels at great pace, usually over a much longer distance and with considerable accuracy.

Which one should you use? I'd say both of them. As a general rule the spiral is ideal for passing from line-outs because the ball should come cleanly to hand and thus require little or no adjustment before delivery. Because scrum and ruck ball is delivered along the ground, often unpredictably, many half-backs use the dive pass to escape the attentions of their opposites. New Zealander Kevin Greene of Waikato was a particularly fine exponent of this — many's the time you would think you'd caught Kevin with bad scrum ball, when he'd whip the ball from under your nose and, with a dive, dispatch it beautifully into the back line.

However, if you have a good liaison with your No. 8, and you're satisfied the No. 8 can protect you from marauders around the scrum, either of the standing passes will serve you well — with the already-mentioned benefit of keeping you on your feet.

Aspects of the standing pass

Speed is of the essence. As Andy Milligan, that great character and scrum-half of Ireland and the 1959 Lions in New Zealand wrote: 'A huge pass requiring a countdown and liquid oxygen for fuel is useless.' Ask any first five-eighth who has received the ball and flanker simultaneously. As exercise practise bouncing the ball off the angle between wall and ground, and clearing it in one swift movement, ideally to your first five-eighth (though if your first five-eighth is unavailable, to anyone who will catch it).

Develop equal skill and confidence in both hands. Try these exercises:
- Make a mark on a wall and, using a tennis or squash ball, bounce and catch the ball underhand with your 'weak' hand.
- Use a weighted ball (for example, medicine ball or old football filled with sand) to strengthen your passing arm. Scoop the ball off the ground with no backswing. It's an exhilarating feeling rocketing out passes when you switch back to an ordinary ball. (Exactly this principle was used by Sid Going when feeding out the hay on his farm — by tossing out haybales underarm to left and right — with, of course, no backswing.)
- Team up with another half-back and practise tossing and catching the ball one-handed, using only the 'weak' hand. It may not sound impressive, but it's amazing how it improves your confidence. (Also try scooping the ball away one handed from the ground. This is an effective way to eliminate backswing).

Develop the habit at training of 'backing up' each pass immediately. Make it second nature — avoid the temptation to stand back admiring your handiwork.

One final point: take a tip from Joe Namath, star quarter-back of the New York Jets (roughly the gridiron equivalent of a rugby half-back), whose pinpoint passing made him a millionaire. At the beginning of each season he analysed each part of his pass, polishing and refining it to eliminate all waste movement, working hard until he had achieved what he called an 'instant throw'. Why not try for the same result? You may not make a million, but you'll earn a great deal of satisfaction and make your first five-eighth happy.

The dive pass

The three basic elements that are important in the standing pass are equally vital to the successful dive pass — that is, speed, length and accuracy. It is only the method of dispatch that differs.

The dive pass, however, has one major advantage over the standing pass in situations where you are under severe pressure from opposition flankers or half-back. It makes you a much more difficult target, diving as you are, away from trouble. In fact there is probably no finer feeling than scooping the ball away from the menacing toes of an opposition forward and sending it safely into the backline.

What makes up the dive pass?
- Foot placement behind the ball, weight over the ball and knees bent (think of yourself as a coiled spring).
- Grasp the ball lengthwise between your palms with, ideally, your forefingers along the middle seams of the ball and your hands slightly towards the near end of the ball. (With a heavy flanker breathing down your neck, it's impossible to be a purist about this.)

- From the balls of your feet, drive forward with legs and body in a *flat* dive, sweeping the ball away towards your first five in a *direct* line from the ground and releasing it with a final flick of the wrists.

The same basic 'golf swing' principle discussed in the standing pass applies: generate speed in your pass from your toes, through legs, body, and finally arms and wrists. Constant practice, again, is essential.

Avoid the temptation to hurl yourself high into the air in a spectacular dive. Although this looks dramatic, and photographs well, it tends to slow the pass into something of a lob with disastrous results for your first five-eighth. Remember Joe Namath — eliminate waste movement.

The major disadvantage of the dive pass is that it takes the half-back out of play momentarily — although Sid Going might disagree. In the All Blacks' Third Test against France at Eden Park, in 1968, he launched himself into a dive pass near the French line only to find his way blocked by retreating Frenchmen. Retaining the ball he crashed to the ground, bounced immediately to his feet and weaved his way through an astonished defence to score. A perfect example of 'thinking off your feet.'

The dive pass

All Black half-back Chris Laidlaw gets the ball away to his backs despite the close attentions of the Springbok half-back and captain, Dawie De Villiers. First Test, Pretoria, 1970.   Associated Press

The pivot pass

This is simply a pass, either standing or dive, in which a half-back half-turns and passes with his back to the opposition. For example, in a standing pass to the right from a line-out on the left side of the field, he receives the ball facing the touch line, pivots on his *right* foot and, leading with his left foot, sends the pass away.

This can be an effective and speedy pass, and it has the advantage that the half-back's passing arm (in the example above, the right arm) is moving forward *with* the back line,

which tends to send the ball well out in front of the first five-eighth. Because the pass begins with the ball well *behind* the body, there is a sort of catapult effect, like a discus release, which sends the ball further and faster — without that dreaded backswing.

The pivot dive pass is especially valuable when clearing fast or untidy scrum ball to the left. After feeding the scrum on the loose-head (left) side, you can swiftly follow the ball through the scrum and, pivoting off the right foot, whip the ball away without wasting a second.

Use the pivot pass with care, however, as with your back to the opposition you can be exposed to interceptions.

The pivot pass

The reverse pass

A speciality pass this, but one that can be invaluable in certain situations. Its sole purpose, of course, is to enable you to pass to one player, while giving every appearance of passing to another — fulfilling that most important function of the half-back, creating time and space for your outsides.

Two situations where you might try it:
- A field goal attempt from a midfield scrum. Facing left, you can reverse pass to an unmarked player on your right, instead of making the expected pass to the player on your left.

- You can relieve pressure from a tight defensive situation in exactly the same way.

Remember that the reverse pass should be practised in precisely the same manner as the standard pass, by breaking it down into its component parts. Go through it slowly step by step to your own satisfaction, then gradually speed it up as confidence develops. With practice a reverse spiral pass is not impossible. Initially though, you'll find it easier to scoop the ball back under your arm with a pushing motion — your right hand providing the thrust back under your left arm, and vice versa.

One warning. Don't throw it blind, or in desperation. It should be as controlled as a normal pass.

The reverse pass

Reverse pass by half-back Les Dickson.
Christchurch Press

Combinations

A half-back's two best friends on the rugby field are the No. 8 and the first five-eighth. These two players often literally hold the success of your game in their hands. They can make or break you, so for heaven's sake, spare no effort to establish cordial relationships with them both. It wouldn't hurt to cultivate an amicability with the whole forward pack — their combined efforts can make life on the field much more pleasant.

With the No. 8

This is the player who delivers scrum ball to the half-back, and how it's executed is vitally important. A good No. 8 can sense when to release the ball quickly, and when to hold it in the scrum … will know to toe the ball away from a wheeling scrum, or to detach and pass it to relieve severe pressure.

I have been lucky enough to play with three of the best: Ted Lines, a fine club and provincial player in Wellington in the 1960s and early 1970s; Andy Leslie, a superb international and provincial captain, and a brilliant ball player who played the 'sweeper' type of No. 8 game to perfection; and Murray Mexted, the current All Black No. 8, who is big, lightning fast around the field, and has excellent all-round rugby skills.

Each of these three had different strengths as players, but all had one thing in common — they gave superb service from the base of the scrum. On our scrum ball they would always pack between left-hand (loose-head) flanker and lock, eliminating the possibility of quickly hooked ball shooting unchecked from the side of the scrum, and at the same time placing a large and reassuring obstacle between me and my opposite number. The final touch was their expertise at moving the ball sideways to the right, further from the clutches of the other half, before releasing it. Surprisingly enough, even at senior level there are many No. 8s who haven't mastered these simple rules. In Wellington's match against England in 1973, the Lions No. 8, Roger Uttley (to be fair, he was usually a lock or flanker) persisted in rolling ball after ball back to a completely unprotected Steve Smith.

Many beautifully simple set moves can be pre-arranged between No. 8 and half-back. A quick pass from the No. 8 to the sprinting half-back can open up huge gaps on the blind side of a scrum, usually to the right, but perhaps even more effectively back to the left 'against the grain'. This can be devastating from a midfield scrum close to the opposition line, as it leaves you two to one against their winger. The main danger to watch for is an attempt at interception by the other half-back.

Other variations include either half-back or No. 8 picking up the ball, bursting forward close to the scrum and using a short hand-off pass to put the other into the clear.

Canterbury for years made use of Alex Wyllie's strength on the drive by having him detach before the ball was released and taking a pass from his half-back in a first five-eighth position. Very difficult to counter.

With the first five-eighth

The half-back's partner in crime. It's with the first five-eighth that the half-back should spend most of his spare time in practice sessions. The ideal first/half combination should be almost automatic, and this can be achieved only by hours of practice. Communication between the two players will establish where the half-back wants the first five-eighth to be, where the first five-eighth will want the half-back to place the ball, and how the rhythm between the two players can be developed.

One of my favourite partners was a University player named Dave Heather, a quiet, astute fellow who had the happy knack of being exactly where you wanted and, perhaps more importantly, *needed* him to be. When you were winning good clean ball he'd drift wider, knowing you'd have no trouble getting the ball to him at speed, but if the ball was scratchy and you were forced to clear under pressure he'd slip in close to the scrum or ruck, calling for a short, quick clearance.

Another favourite was not so quiet, but just as pleasant to work with: the one and only J.P. ('Darcy') Dougan, an early 1970s All Black noted for his enterprise and passing ability. He talked constantly on the field, which made him an easy target to find. He was also very precise about where he wanted the ball — usually exactly 'a yard and a half' in front. But he always made a point of acknowledging a good pass, even at training, which was genuinely satisfying. (In the same way I've always tried to thank my forwards for the good ball they've delivered to me over the years. Try it — I guarantee it will improve the quality of the ball you receive.)

The break

The half-back's break can be one of the most devastating in rugby. The key skill required is knowing the right moment to break. From a tight-head, for example, with opposition loose forwards in momentary confusion, there should be no hesitation. Sprint away with a low-slung body position — there is no time to straighten up and check out the options. Waste a second and your chance is lost.

Other ideal opportunities present themselves when opposition loose forwards are taken out of play — by a wheeling scrum perhaps, or a quick ruck going forward. Ironically some of the best chances may come from untidy ball that shoots back from scrum or line-out. If you manage to recover the ball with a second to spare, try a dummy pass — your pursuers, already moving at pace, may very well overrun you in their eagerness to get to your first five-eighth.

How effective a half-back is on the break depends upon his physical characteristics. Sid Going had almost the perfect build for it: low to the ground, strong in the hips and shoulders, with a powerful fend, slippery sidestep, and (as if all that wasn't enough), well-above-average pace in the open. Sid had it all. Both Jerome Gallion and Yves Laffarge of the 1979 French team are examples of a completely different type of running half. Smaller and not as physical as Sid, they relied on clever footwork to get them into the clear, and then used exceptional acceleration and pace to make immense ground gains. Welshman and 1971 Lions player Gareth Edwards was a combination of the two extremes — both physical and lightning fast, he scored some magnificient tries for Wales.

We can't all be Goings or Gallions, but by being aware of the opportunities the half-back can considerably strengthen your team's attacking potential. (A simple half-break can be enormously valuable to get your forwards moving forward — a short, sharp dash into the gap to commit one or two opposition loose forwards, then turn and hand the ball off to a team-mate driving forward into the clear with support.)

Exercise: to sharpen your breaking, practise sprint starts from a full sprinter's crouch. A dozen 20-metre sprints a day will make you a force to reckon with. If you really are keen you could place stakes at 5-10 metre intervals and work on sidesteps and swerves. The old rule prevails: the more you put into it, the more you'll get out of it.

Kicking

To round out his game an aspiring half-back should try to master a variety of kicks. Most importantly he should, as early as possible, develop the ability to kick with either foot. I played as a loose forward until my mid-teens without ever bothering to perfect a left-foot kick. This turned out to be a handicap in my first season as a half-back, so I set out to educate my left foot. This was slow, but with practice I developed an unorthodox but adequate clearing kick off the left foot — definitely not the most elegant kick you've ever seen but quick and confident, and that's what counts. You'll spot 'one-footed' inside backs at all levels of the game desperately trying to run the ball into touch on their wrong side. It can be disastrous when the pressure is on near your line.

The half-back will use mostly the towering up-and-under kicks into the box behind scrum or line-out, the long, rolling punt down the blind side to gain ground outside your 22 metre line and, on attack when the way is clear, a little chip-kick over the opposition back line. In tight defensive situations, the half-back will often be called upon to clear — and then speed of ball from hand to boot is vital. Sharpen it with practice.

Two other kicks worth trying are short punts to your wingers, left and right. From an attacking scrum on the left side of the field, gather the ball and sprint straight across the field to the right, drawing the defence to you; then — on the run — chip a kick back over your shoulder into the open space behind the scrum for your left wing. From a deep position this player can sprint forward on to the ball and, with a favourable bounce, has every chance to score. Gareth Edwards, playing for the 1971 Lions against Wellington, engineered a superb try for his fellow countryman John Bevan with such a kick-through. To their horror, Bevan was ruled off-side.

The other kick, from a scrum near the right-hand touch line, is simply a short chip over the scrum and behind the opposing blind-side winger for your right winger to run on to. At worst you'll gain valuable ground. At best there's a try in it.

One kick that very few half-backs attempt is a drop kick for goal from the base of scrum or line-out. Like all drop kick attempts, only success makes it justified, but that can be achieved with practice — and a powerful scrum.

I believe that in most instances, the first five-eighth is the player ideally placed to kick when required. This person usually has more time and room in the match to assess each situation and to use the ball accordingly. However, when the responsibility is yours as half-back, accept it with relish and turn it to your team's advantage.

The player who usually loves extra kicking and catching practice is the full-back. Before or after training this is the player to practice various kicks with. Both will appreciate it and the half-back's kicking and handling will certainly improve.

Defence

Rugby is an attacking game, but when one team attacks the other must defend. The half-back is a vital link in the team's defensive chain.

A half-back can start by bustling his opponent at scrum time. No half-back likes his opposite breathing down his neck with 'One slip and I've got you'. A dive for the ball as it's released from the scrum can be unsettling, and although a half-back may not catch his counterpart with the ball, there's every chance the rhythm of the pass will be disturbed.(If you, as half-back, can get to your opponent, don't tackle around the legs as this leaves your opponent's arms free to pass. Catch the arm instead and cut off the pass.)

If the opponents' No. 8 is channelling consistently well, your flankers should watch for any break by their half-back, while you, as half-back, switch your attention to their first five-eighth. You are 2 metres closer than your flankers and can get a flying start. In one memorable effort during the Second Test, France v New Zealand in 1979, Jerome Gallion of France not only tackled his opposite Mark Donaldson as he passed, but also bounced up and charged down first five-eighth Murray Taylor's clearing kick to score a superb solo try.

Another not so pleasant defensive duty of the half-back is the tying up of untidy ball behind the forwards, usually after a line-out or loose ruck. This calls for a dive in to 'kill' the ball, and perhaps the only advice worth giving is 'don't think about it, do it.' The more positive you are, and the more quickly you act, the less chance you have of getting hurt. If you find yourself in this situation too often though, give your forwards the message. Someone's not doing his job properly.

From defensive rucks and mauls you should make every effort to sight the ball and anticipate the direction of any threatened attack. Let your team-mates know what's going on. By simply calling, 'I've got the blind-side', for example, you'll discourage your opponents from attempting that avenue of attack.

Once opposition ball is cleared you should support your own back line as quickly as possible. By backing up you are ideally placed to make a saving tackle wide out, or field a centreing kick from an opposition wing. You should be deep enough to drop back and support your full-back if required but not so deep that you can't be immediately on the spot if play breaks down in midfield. It's a tragedy to see well-won ball lying idle while an out-of-position half-back sprints in from 50 metres away. Your forwards won't forgive you quickly.

Finally, don't neglect the chance to turn defence into attack — some of your very best attacking chances can come from deep in your own half. Don't take foolish risks, but be aware that the counter attack is a potent weapon.

Scottish half-back Roy Laidlaw breaks with the ball. Opposite half-back, Dave Loveridge in pursuit.
Peter Bush

Perfecting the skills

Fred Allen, in *Fred Allen on Rugby*, gave a piece of advice which I've never forgotten: any aspiring half-back should make one feature of his play a speciality. It might be the break, or his ability to harass his opponent. It might be the reverse pass or something unusual like the drop kick from behind the pack. Whatever you choose as your speciality, work on it and make it your strength. It will give you confidence that will overflow into the rest of your game. In fact, practice and more practice is the key to success. If you're fully fit and you've polished your skills to the best of your ability, you can guarantee you'll have the edge on 90 per cent of your opposition.

Two of the hardest trainers I've known in rugby were Grant Batty and Stu Wilson. To see them in action at Athletic Park or Twickenham you'd assume it was simply natural brilliance; but in fact there was much more to it than that. The brilliance was there all right, but they worked hard on it, developing their skills and fitness to the highest level. They were perfectionists.

Follow their example. You may not be the next All Black half-back but you'll be as good as you can possibly be. And that's all that matters.

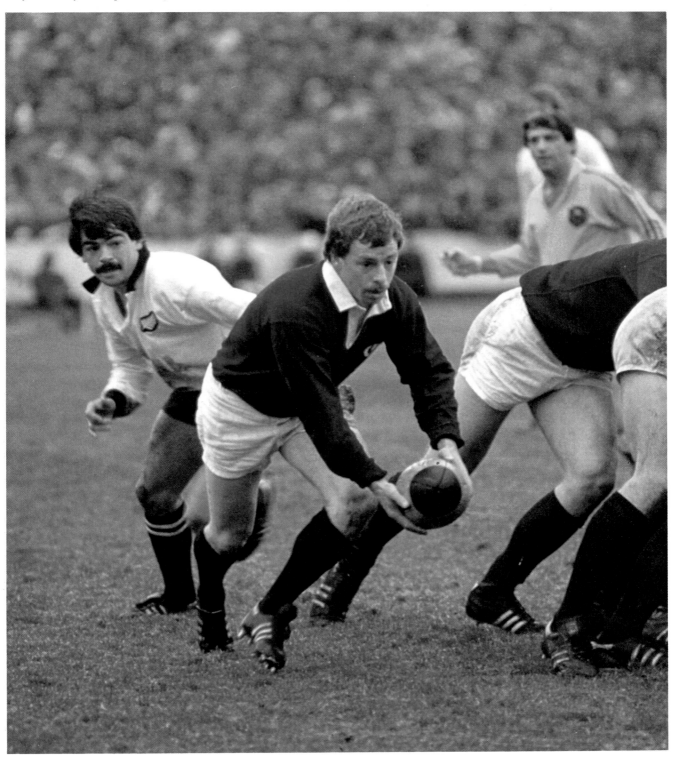

Doug Bruce on

Inside Backs

- **The skills of inside backs are to be able to catch, pass and kick with speed and accuracy, to tackle and be able to 'read' the game.**
- **Both the hip-swinging pass and the pass that allows the player to back up are used, according to the situation of the game.**
- **From set play the first five-eighth has three options: pass the ball, kick for territory or space, or link with the forwards. From the quick ruck or maul the first five-eighth almost always passes.**
- **A strong skilful kicker in first five-eighth position is essential, and all kicks are designed to regain possession, whether they be to gain territory, to find space or to put pressure on the opposition in front of the posts.**
- **Good communication is essential between the coach, half-back and inside backs. The half-back/first five-eighth link is vital, and some wonderful combinations have developed to add enjoyment and success to the game.**

The inside backs — the first five-eighth and the second five-eighth — are just two players in a team of 15, but as with the other players, they need certain skills in which they show mastery in order to fulfil their difficult roles in the team.

The skills of a first five-eighth:
- ability to kick accurately.
- passing with speed and accuracy.
- demonstrating sound catching techniques.
- ability to 'read' a game — that is, knowing when to pass, knowing when to kick, and sensing or discovering weaknesses in the opposition.

The skills of a second five-eighth:
- passing with speed and accuracy.
- having speed off the mark (not necessarily a skill, but it can be developed).
- demonstrating sound tackling.

The role of the first five-eighth

The first five-eighth's basic role, as I see it, is to make judicious use of a ball that has been won by the forwards for the backs to use — really a second distributor of the ball. The half-back clears it from the forward packs and the first five-eighth commits the loose forwards and clears the ball from them.

From set plays, the first five-eighth has three options: move the ball to the outside backs, kick for territory or to regain possession, or use the ball in such a way as to involve the forwards immediately in the play again. To involve the forwards, the first five-eighth can go for the inside break close to the scrum or line-out and link with the forwards, or may kick in such a way that the forwards can be close at hand when the ball comes to ground.

A first five-eighth need not be running fast when receiving the ball from the half-back following a scrum or line-outs. He need only be moving fast enough in order that he may be balanced to pass the ball on out to the backs. The loose forward(s) can be more easily drawn out of play by the first five-eighth not moving towards them, but rather allowing them to run at an almost stationary 'target'.

If a first five-eighth runs at pace on to the ball, he limits his options and is more often than not committed to trying to beat the loose forward; and in so doing, too, frequently neglects his outside backs.

Rucks and mauls pose a different situation, however. In these situations, the first five-eighth should take the ball flatter and be moving in an attacking manner. It is important to maintain the impetus of a well-won ruck or maul, and so by taking the ball almost in line with the half-back the first five-eighth takes the ball to the advantage line more quickly and hopefully gives a disorganised defence little time to regroup. Ideally, the forwards would have committed the opposition loose forwards as well.

While mentioning rucks, I would suggest that only on the very rare occasion should the ball, won from an attacking ruck, be kicked. By an attacking ruck, I mean a forward-moving ruck, not necessarily in opposition territory. In 80 minutes of rugby there are but few occasions when the opposition's defence is not totally organised. An attacking ruck is one such occasion, and it is folly not to try to take advantage of this.

First five-eighth Barry John scores under the posts.

Regarded as an outstanding first five-eighth possessing masterly control with the ball. Played 12 years of first-class rugby; represented Mid-Canterbury 1967-69 (Ashburton HSOB); Canterbury 1970 (Christchurch), 1971-75, 77, 78 (Oxford), 1976 (Ohaka); also South Island 1970, 73, 74, 77; played in the NZ Trials 1973-78; NZ Juniors 1970. Began his All Black career in 1974 but only in 1976 did he establish himself as a top first five-eighth. Toured Australia, Fiji and Ireland 1974, South Africa 1976, played against the 1977 Lions, toured France and Italy 1977, the British Isles 1978, and played against the Wallabies.

The hand action that creates the spiral pass

Passing

There are two basic methods by which a first five-eighth (or any back, for that matter) can pass the ball on. Both have different purposes.

Firstly, there is the hip-swinging pass where the ball-carrier props on the inside foot and moves the body 'inside' the defender when passing the ball on out to the backs. This pass is best used when committing the loose forward(s), and in so doing takes them out of play. It is a pass that puts a potential tackler in two minds — is the first five-eighth going to pass the ball, or sidestep inside me? By passing in this manner, however, it does not allow the first five-eighth to back up quickly.

The pass that allows a first five-eighth to immediately back up is the one where he follows his pass out to the second five-eighth. He virtually runs away from the loose forward as he passes, and then follows the passes along the backline. A backing up player (no matter which player) is the best loose forward if play breaks down, and should be prepared to be committed to the loose ball. After all, possession is what the game is all about.

The question then posed is: do you take a loose forward out of the play and allow your backs to move with less harassment, or do you allow this opposition player to follow the ball out among your backs and have the advantage of a player backing up each pass? I would suggest that it be varied, as all play should be. It is one of the first five-eighth's roles to vary play and keep the opposition guessing, and this is one aspect of play where this can be done.

Kicking

An important aspect of a first five-eighth's play is being able to kick. A game never goes by without the first five-eighth having to kick at some stage. Never kick, however, for the sake of kicking. Too often teams lose what advantage they might have had through thoughtless kicking. Conversely, a good kick can swing the advantage quite dramatically your way.

There should only be two kinds of kicks:
- The kick for territory.
- The kick to regain possession or at least dispute possession.

An important factor in kicking is knowing where the opposition players are positioned.

There are three types of kicks that should find space — that is, land where the opposition are not: the grubber kick, the kick to the blind side for the wing and the open-side diagonal kick.

The grubber kick

This is the kick that is put along the ground, not necessarily for a great distance. It is used to put the ball behind the opposition backs, who are then put out of play, and it also continues your own team's forward movement. The positioning of the opposition's open-side winger will determine the strength with which the ball is kicked. If the winger is close in it, it is important that the grubber kick be placed behind the second five-eighth. If that winger is positioned wider, the kick can be placed as far out as the centre. The whole point of this kick is to put the ball in a position where your team can regain possession and the

opposition, who have to turn around, cannot. It is an advantage if your outside backs are aware that the kick is going to be made, though this is not always possible.

A similar kick with the same purpose and result is the one that is put just over the heads of the opposition backs. I've usually called this one the 'pop' kick.

The kick to the blind side for the wing

This is commonly referred to as the 'box' kick. To increase the chances of success with this kick, the opposition (blind-side winger) must be drawn away from the area where the ball is to land. To do this, the ball can be moved on to the second five-eighth, suggesting that a passing movement is planned, and then this player kicks back to the blind-side or 'box'. The opposition winger should have made some movement to cover across field by this stage. The other alternative is for the first five-eighth to run wide to the open side and 'hook' kick the ball back. Once again, the effectiveness of this kick is determined by your own blind-side winger's alertness and speed to the ball.

The open-side diagonal kick

This kick should land behind the opposition's open-side winger and to make it easier this player must be drawn up on defence; the best way to achieve this is for the second five-eighth to make the kick. The fact that the ball has been moved to the second five-eighth will suggest again that it will probably be moved out further, thus bringing the winger forward, anticipating the need to tackle his opposite. Again, space must be found with this kick and your open-side winger must be alert. If, because of a badly placed kick, the opposition field the ball first, they then become the attackers and all advantage is lost.

The 'post' kick

This is the high kick, best done by the first five-eighth, which is aimed at centre-field near the opposition line. It should have plenty of height and I liked to try to have it land or at least come down in the vicinity of the opposition's goal post — hence the name 'post' kick.

The objectives of this kick are: to pressurise the opposition full-back; and to create confusion in the opposition defence.

It is a kick that does not necessarily need to find space, but because of its height it allows your team to dispute possession in a very critical area as far as the opposition is concerned. It is under this pressure that so many mistakes are made. It is a good idea to have one player (probably the centre) chase hard and dispute possession, with another hanging off to take full advantage of any spilt ball.

Key points on kicking

- Never kick for the sake of kicking.
- Kick to regain possession or kick for territory.
- Kick to find space.
- Chase kicks and pressurise the opposition. Often bad kicks become good kicks only because they have been chased enthusiastically.

If in two minds — Will I? Won't I? — well, don't! A bad kick is one of the quickest ways of losing territory and, more importantly, possession.

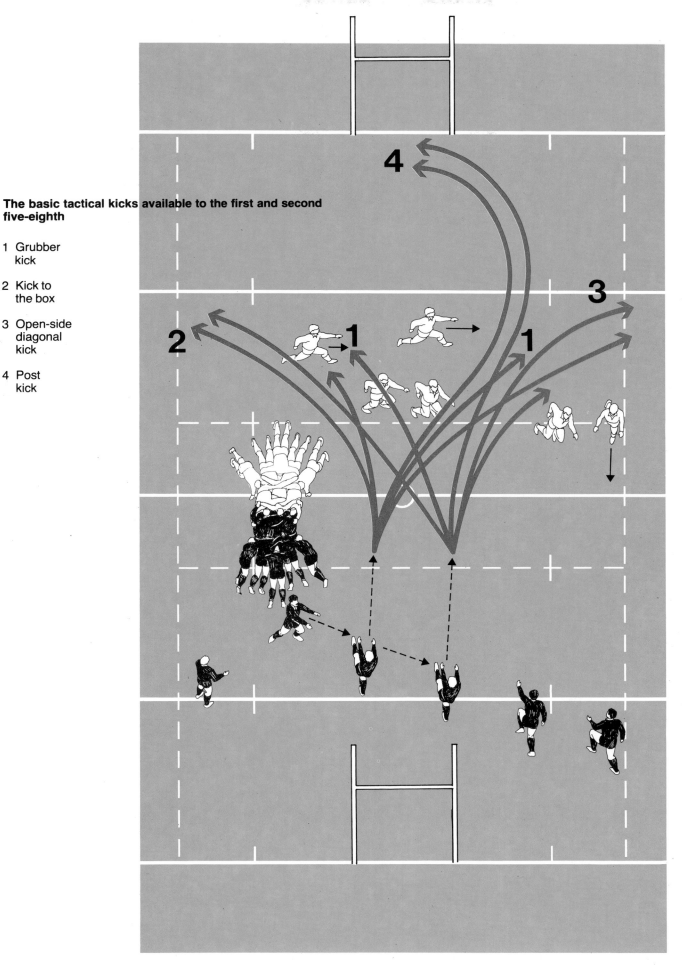

The basic tactical kicks available to the first and second five-eighth

1 Grubber kick

2 Kick to the box

3 Open-side diagonal kick

4 Post kick

Blind side

The blind side and short side is an area of play too often neglected by the first five-eighth. It is a very good area in which to attack and from which one can set up attacking moves. It could be called a 'safe' area, in that you have immediate close support from your forwards. I won't delve into blind side moves here, as the scope is quite large. I would mention, however, that a ball-carrier should take the most direct route to the advantage line when moving on the blind-side. The main advantage of doing this is that he is giving the opposition loose forwards less time to sight him and line him up, as well as putting himself in the position of having immediate support from his forwards, should anything go wrong.

The second five-eighth's role

Many aspects of first five-eighth play already mentioned also apply to the second five-eighth.

The positioning of the second five-eighth is a key factor in the effectiveness of any back line. If a second five-eighth is too flat, the impetus that he and the centre gives to the back line becomes limited; and if he is too deep, his outside backs will more than likely be confronted by the opposition defence before any ground has been made. The coach should have worked out the attacking potential of the back line before the game and position them accordingly.

The second five-eighth defensive positioning is also vitally important. The first five-eighth, second five-eighth and centre should approach the attacking opposition back line in a straight line, thus making it more difficult for the opposition's ball-carrier to break through. If, for example, the second five-eighth advances ahead of the first five-eighth, the opposition's first five-eighth can easily run in behind him.

Communications

Communciation plays a big part in all back play, particularly when on defence. It is important that each player has an idea of what the other is going to do.

The vital link in the back line is that of half-back and first five-eighth, and it is very important that these two players have an understanding of each other's play. To do this, they must be continually communicating with each other. Verbal communications are essential from broken play, but from set pieces a set of visual signs is all that is required. The more games the two play together, the less obvious their communication system becomes and the more effective they will become as a combination.

'Reading' a game

Perhaps the most important aspect of a first five-eighth's play, as far as the success of the team is concerned, is that of 'reading' the game. The first five-eighth's judgments often determine the outcome of a match — more so the misjudgments, I feel, than the correct ones. It is something that cannot be solely taught, but by coaches giving encouragement to and showing confidence in their chosen player, they will be well on the way to having a good tactical first five-eighth.

Doug Bruce (right) flick-passes. Lions v All Blacks Christchurch, 1977.
Christchurch Press

Murray Taylor (right), All Black five-eighth 1979, captured in evasive mood.
Evening Post

Earle Kirton shows a sound kicking style.

Bryan Craies on

Second Five-eighth & Centres

- Too much emphasis has been placed on creating a crunching second five-eighth who develops second-phase play.
- The midfield back should be nimble, quick and a good handler and passer, with the ability to make an outside break or half-break.
- The centre should avoid kicking — it's better done by the first five-eighth.
- In defence, midfield backs should keep inside their opponents and drive hard with the shoulders when tackling.
- When tackled, twist so that as support arrives the ball is available. Get on to your feet quickly and back into position.

In New Zealand we have developed a crunching, second-phase type of midfield player, which to my way of thinking is a mistake. We shouldn't be stereotyped, but instead should encourage any natural flair a player shows. And that little bit of flair will eclipse the stereotyped player every time.

What's required

The second five-eighth and the centre should be swift ball handlers, and be naturally fast and nimble. They should have naturally quick hands and the ability to pass in four or five different ways. They must be able to swing pass, but also must be able to execute the short, snappy pass, the long pass, and the lob pass over an opponent in between. Perhaps most importantly they should be able to make the half gap and be competent at the 'rolling' pass around their markers.

They must have a firm understanding with the player who's outside — at all times the wingers must be in the know about what is to be attempted, so that they will be ready to receive the ball.

Instead of the crunching, we should be endeavouring to develop our midfield players into making the outside break. With the current style of play, the inside break is not easy — there are usually too many cover defenders lurking around. On attack the greatest emphasis must be placed upon that outside break.

A try for All Black centre Grahame Thorne.

Played for Ponsonby, Waitemata Seniors and the Auckland A team 1963-65. Coached Waitemata Seniors 1967-70 and selector-coach for Auckland Second XV 1971-76. Auckland A coach 1978-81. During his time as selector-coach of Auckland A, 1978-81, the team won the Ranfurly Shield 1978-80.

Coaching tips

Fending Show the players just how the fend should be used. Don't let them run around 'telegraphing' it. It's not a matter of simply sticking your hand out.

Kicking Don't place too much emphasis on kicking. Of course, a player should be able to kick, but I prefer kicking to be done by the first five-eighth. The midfield backs should not have to kick to attack.

Tackling This is perhaps the most vital. Second five-eighth especially is the position from which to upset the opponents' back-line. It must be in with the shoulder — and hard. You must hit an opponent as he receives the ball. Knock him down, and you'll disrupt the opposition's entire back-line. But the priority is to always keep 'inside' your opponent and drive your opponent out.

The skills in attack

On attack, the second five-eighth and the centre shouldn't become stationary. Keep on the move — keeping in close, then moving out (that's where those skilful long and short passes are necessary). By doing this, each will leave the opposition marker guessing — in other words, don't let them settle down.

But once you've passed the ball on, that's not the end of it. If you are the first five-eighth move outside your centre or wing. In short, be there to carry on the attack. In the event that you are tackled, don't lose the ball. Twist, and present it for your loose forwards; and don't stay on the bottom of the ruck. Your job is to run back out to your position as quickly as possible.

When returning into position from any phase of play, never turn your back on the ball. Know what is going on at all times. Don't be caught flat when your side wins the ruck ball — keep your eye constantly on that ball.

Bruce Robertson, playing for Counties at centre, sets up his outside, Bob Lendrum (No. 15). The defender is in two minds about the attack.

Midfield players also have the option of making the outside break

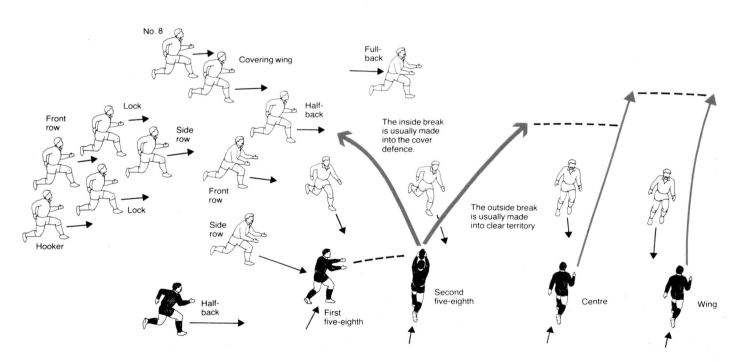

The perfect illustration of the crisp British type of passing . . . West Wales against the All Blacks at Swansea, 1978.
Peter Bush

144

Bryan Williams on

Three-quarter Play

- In New Zealand the centre three-quarter remains at centre. In the two-centre game in other countries the second five-eighth *may* go to centre.
- Wingers generally favour moving and kicking off one particular foot and should accordingly be placed on the left wing or right wing.
- Wingers need to be strong, aggressive and fast, have sound ball-handling skills and be able to swerve, side-step and fend.
- The winger in blind-side defence covers the 'box', moves across to cover the opposition's full-back and finally their open-side wing. On the open side he covers the kick through, or he moves quickly to the tackle.
- The skills required by centre or wing are sometimes different — dummying is often used by the centre, a winger may throw in at a line-out.

The New Zealand style

In basic terms I don't think there is much difference between New Zealand three-quarter play and overseas three-quarter play. The three-quarters are there mainly to finish off what the forwards and the inside backs have done for you. And that is to score tries; to that extent, there is no difference.

Getting down to specifics, the British have played two-centre game: a left centre three-quarter and a right centre three-quarter. The left centre stays on the left side of his partner for the whole game; the right centre stays on the right, regardless of which side of the field the play is situated. In contrast, in New Zealand the second five-eighth is always on the inside, and the centre on the outside.

In British rugby the centres aren't specialists, because they have to play two roles that we in New Zealand take as separate. The second five-eighth's role requires a lot of setting up of rucks — this player is generally the rock on which the back line is founded in New Zealand. In Britain there are two such players; in some instances they are setting up moves for the outside backs, they're setting up rucks, making tackles. Secondly — and this is in Britain — they are capitalising on what the inside centre has done for them in trying to put their winger away.

I think there are advantages in both styles of play — in the New Zealand way, I think it's what we're familiar with, we're always playing inside or outside the same player, whereas in the British system the fly-half is passing to a different player depending on the side of the field. Personally, I rather tend to favour the British style because you get a more complete centre — a person who not only sets up play but can also finish it off and make the break. So you have two people of almost the same skills. The one who is working on the right-hand side of the field, moving, might be more able to move out to the left or to the right.

In New Zealand the second five-eighth is not usually the one who makes the break. Perhaps the player might be a good passer or might be good at setting up rucks, but rarely does this player make the initial break. Generally that's left to the outside centre: the centre, as opposed to the second five-eighth. In Britain, both centres are expected to take either of the two different roles, and I think you get a more complete cover that way.

Bryan Williams on attack, cheered on by Ian Kirkpatrick.
Auckland Star

Bryan Williams kicking for touch. New Zealand v Australia Second Test, 1978.
Peter Bush

In 1980 named by sporting journalists as 'Rugby Player of the Decade'. A fast, dynamic footballer with a powerful kick. As a provincial player he established himself as a regular Auckland member at the age of 18, playing 1968-80 (Ponsonby); also North Island 1974, 75, 77 and in the NZ Trials 1970-72, 74-77. Represented NZ 1970-78 — toured South Africa as the youngest member of the 1970 All Blacks; played against the 1971 Lions, the 1972 Wallabies, toured Britain 1972-73. Toured Australia and Ireland 1974. At home played against England and Australia 1973, Scotland and Ireland 1975. Toured Ireland 1974, South Africa 1976, France and Britain 1978. Currently player-coach of the Ponsonby club.

Left wing or right wing

Taking myself as an example, players generally favour stepping off one foot or the other, although they can develop the ability to step off either foot. We all tend to favour one — and that makes a big difference when it comes to which side of the field you're going to play on. The other factor is the ability to kick with your left or right foot (and which is the better), or equally well with either foot. If someone playing on the left wing can't kick with the left foot, he shouldn't be playing there. The same applies to the right wing.

The player moving on the left wing would probably tend to favour the left foot. But I don't think you can have any hard-and-fast rules about which foot the player will move off. Whichever foot you move off depends on the positioning of the opposition, and a coach (or anyone else) should not make hard-and-fast rules. If a player can move well off the right foot and go on the outside — or come inside, for that matter — depending on how the opposition is grouped, it makes no difference.

Occasionally you will see a team that seems to have two different types of wing — say, a very hard, strong wing on the right wing, and a very nippy wing on the left. But I'm sure this is purely a matter of the skills available on the team.

The three-quarters' skills

These four players, the two centres and the two wings primarily should have a fair amount of speed. Allied to that, they must have good ball skills and be capable in their abilities to beat opposing players. These abilities include the swerve — a player 'straightens' an opponent up by running straight at him, but suddenly swerving on the outside of him; and the side-step — the runner (who has the ball) angles an opponent out, as if going to the outside, but then executing a side-step and coming inside him. They should have the ability to control their kicks, so that if they have to kick ahead they can follow up and pick up a bounce. They should be able to fend, and if they can bump as well, it's an asset.

Gerald Davies, the brilliant Welsh wing three-quarter, had a wonderful side-step and great pace — though he couldn't be classified as a hard, bruising runner. Pat Yates, from Counties, was a player who probably didn't know how to side-step, but he had a marvellous bump and he was a very hard man to tackle. A chap like David Duckham, the outstanding 1971 British Lions wing three-quarter, was big and strong and he had both things going for him; he could side-step beautifully, and he had enough strength to run through tackles.

There are ways these skills can be practised — although some would say that they're instinctive. Put it this way, I don't practise my side-step now, because I know that when I'm called on to do it, it seems to come instinctively. Side-stepping is a rather rhythmical movement. What I do, as I'm coming up to beat a man, is to angle out towards the sideline to give the opponent the suggestion that I am going on the outside — my eyes are in the direction I'm going — and then I do a reasonably large hop on the same foot, and throw the inside leg to the direction I want to head in. So it's a hop, throw your inside leg in the direction you want to go, and then off in that direction.

As I say, I don't practise it; it's something that comes instinctively, it's timing. But if you do want to practise it, do exactly what I've described: angle out towards the sideline, hop on the same foot, and then throw your inside leg in the new direction. The best way to practise anything is to try to recreate the situation as it happens on the field. I don't think practising side-stepping along a series of posts has much merit, because posts don't move and tacklers do.

Nor do I use any devices to practise swerving. Here again, you have to have moving opposition, otherwise it doesn't work. You can swerve away from any stationary object but really you're not getting any benefit out of it. Touch rugby is as good a way as any to practise these arts.

You can practise fending. A fend has to be done quickly — there's delicate timing involved. It has to be done powerfully. Too many players make the mistake of holding their arm out as a tackler comes to them, and that arm is actually then easy to grab hold of. You have to flex your elbow, bend it, and as the tackler comes in you let go with all you've got with an open hand. If you've timed it well, the tackler will go sprawling. Some players might actually have two systems of fending; the actual fend, putting a tackler off balance; and fending-off, using a tackler for leverage to shift themselves.

About the business of using the body in the bump. I've never been a great exponent of the bump myself, but I think that the main point about it is to use either your shoulders or your hips, and once again it's a matter of timing and using a bit of a swerve. I think the basis of it is that you catch the tackler off guard; instead of a tackler running to you, you suddenly veer into him when he's not expecting it. And he suddenly has to confront you with a hurried tackle; of course, you've got your shoulder into him and you're away from him before he knows what has happened. When you're running with the ball in a certain direction and a tackler is bearing down on you from another direction, you abruptly change direction and initiate bodily contact with the tackler when he's not expecting it — that is the bump, with your shoulders or hips.

Positional play in the centres — from the left touch

The British system

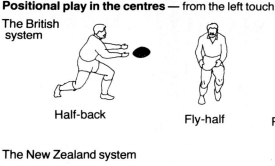

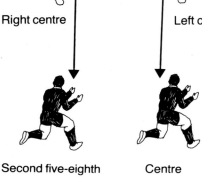

| Half-back | Fly-half | Right centre | Left centre | Wing |

The New Zealand system

| Half-back | First five-eighth | Second five-eighth | Centre | Wing |

Positional play in the centres — from the right touch

The British system

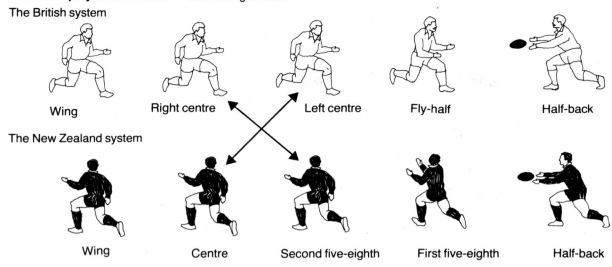

Wing   Right centre   Left centre   Fly-half   Half-back

The New Zealand system

Wing   Centre   Second five-eighth   First five-eighth   Half-back

The wing three-quarters' role

Whereas the centres, in a defensive sense, must move up quickly and knock the opposition over, the wingers' role is slightly more complex defensively, because primarily they have to wait to see whether the opposition kick — if so, they wait back to take a kick. If the opposition don't kick, they suddenly have to sprint to make sure they arrive on the spot where the opponent is getting the ball.

On the blind side (say, from scrums) the wingers need to use their discretion, because if a half-back runs blind, or a No. 8, a winger has to decide suddenly whether to go in and take the player with the ball or continue to mark the opponent winger. If it's close to the line, then more often than not you've got to go in and take the player with the ball if no one else is going to . If it's a little further out, you can use your discretion more.

And if the ball is going on the other side, away from the blind side, a winger must generally cover — if the play is not going towards his side.

I would use the pattern called corner flagging. You don't necessarily run towards the corner flag; you get in behind your backs and you slot in where you can — once again, it's a question of using your discretion. If someone goes through the middle, you're there to tackle.

On attack when you are supporting your own back line from a blind-side position, you'd cover, particularly if your full-back is part of your team's back line move.

A winger as the extra man

There's no hard-and-fast rule on the most effective position for a wing three-quarter to take to provide an extra man. It depends on how the opposition players are grouping themselves. If, for example, the opposition centre is running up quickly, but their second five-eighth is not getting up quickly, there's obviously a gap in the middle, so you'd go in outside your second five-eighth. If you can pin-point a weakness in the opposition second five-eighth tackling, obviously you'd come in outside your first five-eighth. If their backs aren't particularly fast on the outside, you'd get out — as far outside as centre. There's no hard-and-fast rule.

If the opposition brings in an extra man, then all your backs must move as one to take that extra man. Therefore if the opposition brings their full-back outside the centre, then that full-back should be tackled by your open-side wing. I think this is a sound rule for defensive positional play of the wing. The wings are so often caught in a position with overlaps and so on.

Wingers and the line-out

What about the wing's position at the throw-in at a line-out? There are two systems these days, the throwing in of the ball by one of the forwards, or by one of the backs.

If the hooker is throwing in the ball (which happens regularly in rugby outside New Zealand), one winger is usually back in a position to cover the box area if the opposition wins the ball. A winger is back there to cover any kicks into the box area. If his team wins the ball, then he's in a convenient position to enter any back-line move.

If the winger is throwing the ball in, it depends on what the team is planning to do — if the half-back puts up a high kick, for example, the winger is in a position to chase it. If the team loses the ball after the winger has thrown it in, then once again this player must get back to cover the box area.

As the winger throwing the ball in at a line-out, I throw it as a bowler in cricket bowls a cricket ball — that is, taking the ball up over my head in a cricket-bowling fashion, I bowl the ball into the line-out. (Other players, such as Grant Batty, throw the ball spiral fashion by holding the ball in one hand and spiralling it in American gridiron throwing style.) I hold the ball in the full palm of my hand with the forefinger at the end of the ball on the seam, and the forefinger seems to give me plenty of control as I throw. It also gives me perhaps a little more power, because it acts as a lever; and as I let the ball go, I use the finger to propel the ball as well.

There's not a great deal of difference between delivering a short throw and delivering a long (or extra long) throw, it's just that you throw the ball a little harder or higher. In this context, I would say that the gridiron throw is one that may give you a bit more power.

During general play

If a centre sees an outside break, obviously he has to run into the gap, and he shouldn't run his winger into the sideline. He should move into the gap, try to straighten it, and then feed his wing. Too many centres try to run around in an arc and, though the opposition aren't attacking them, they're running right towards the sideline eventually to leave their wingers no room at all. If they straightened up immediately, they wouldn't have run as far; they would have given their winger much more room and much more opportunity.

The timing of a pass to a winger can be made exact, depending on where the winger's marking opponent is placed. A winger can call for long passes, can call for short passes, but generally has to sum up just how the opponent is positioned. If the winger sees that the opponent is suddenly turning to follow a movement, it's possibly a good chance for the winger to take a short pass and go inside him because the opponent can't see where the winger has gone. Sometimes the centre may run to the opposing winger, and his winger would drift wide; the centre would then give him a long pass and he'd be away.

In terms of passing, dummying is used extensively in the centre positions. If the opposition are moving up very quickly on the outside on to the ball-carrier's team-mates, then the dummy is an effective ploy to throw them off the scent. But it shouldn't be used if the man is unmarked outside.

I would offer some advice on using the scissors move, between wing and centre, or centre and centre. I don't think the scissors should be overdone too much, because the ideal is for a winger to go around the outside away from cover defence. But from time to time, you do see teams with tremendous cover defences, everyone racing for the corner flag, and I think that's the time when a scissors move can be useful. The centre gets the ball and starts moving wide towards the sideline; the winger is a bit wider and a bit deeper and comes back on the tangent to take the ball from the centre three-quarter and, if the opposition's defence is caught off guard, sprints through a gap.

Centre kicking has gone out of the game to a fair extent, because of the advent of counter-attacking. Provided it's a good kick, a centre kick is all right — but if it goes a bit too far or not where you want it, it does present a golden opportunity for the opposition to counter-attack. So these days wingers tend to kick almost parallel to the goal line, and chase after it from there.

Generally I've found that a counter-attack doesn't often come from set play — where the opposition has won the ball, and kicked to you. More often it comes from broken play — where a kick has gone downfield from yourselves, the opposition has picked it up and kicked it back to you and, because your back line hasn't been in a rigid defensive pattern, the opponents haven't had to move up quickly. More often than not, they are back there in position to counter-attack. Usually you'll find that it's a full-back or one of the wingers who takes the ball after it has been kicked downfield, and, who must decide whether a counter-attack is on. If it is, this player would either run or throw a long pass to someone who is in a position to set up the counter-attack.

Creating personal advantage

A small player of any description is going to be confronted by big players and therefore must be able to 'foot it' defensively with the bigger player. If you are small, you have to be able to tackle — and I think Grant Batty was a great example of this. Despite his size, he built himself up and became strong, not by chance, but by weight-lifting, callisthenics, and so on. So if you're a winger and small, you must remember to play defensively as well as offensively, and you'll probably need to build up your body to take the knocks and particularly to improve your tackling.

The small player, however, is often more agile, can step off more quickly, can change direction quickly — and that's where Grant Batty was so effective. The big player, on the other hand, has the obvious asset of strength (and perhaps speed) but also has the ability to burst through tackles, which perhaps the smaller player hasn't. That's where the bump and just plain *strength* come into play.

When you go out on the field there are ways in which to implant in the opponent's mind that you're the superior player. I always like to look my opponent in the eye and give him the impression that he is in for a hard time. I think generally you can sum up fairly early in the game whether your opponent is fast, whether he's strong — those two things particularly. If he's fast you know you're going to

have trouble defensively, but you also know that you're going to have trouble getting around him on the outside. So you can use other means, such as a bump, or side-step, to beat him.

The great three-quarters

Gerald Davies was an impressive player. He had a marvellous side-step, off both feet, and tremendous pace. He was always a challenge. Grant Batty was always so unpredictable — you never quite knew what 'Batts' was going to do. David Duckham also had a wonderful side-step, but I don't think he had quite the flair of the other two. Unlike Davies and Batty he was relatively predictable.

I've seen Grant Batty score some marvellous tries. The try the two of us worked together against the Barbarians came from something we had developed over the years, helped a lot by John Stewart's attitude to training. J. J. Stewart let the backs do their own thing, and consequently on the field we did our own thing and knew exactly what the other was planning. I remember the day 'Batts' scored four tries against Cambridge University in 1972, he virtually had them running in circles — an exceptional performance.

Gerald Davies scored a couple of tries against me in the Second Test in 1971 — one of them was from a counter-attack, and he showed tremendous pace to get away from our cover defence. My best tries were the ones in South Africa in 1970. Possibly the reason they stick in my mind was because it was my first tour, and one or two of them came from a long way out, 60-65 metres, having to beat quite a few people. There were two in particular against Eastern Provinces in 1970.

To my mind the best centre three-quarter I've ever played with was Bruce Robertson. And the way he has played in recent years proves to me that he's as good as any I've seen. His main ability is that he sets his wings up so beautifully — he's not a greedy player. He has all the skills: he passes very well, he chip-kicks well, he's a marvellous attacking player, and an effective defensive player as well.

Rugby is not a predictable game. You can never go on to a field and know exactly what you are going to do. So my ideas about training for three-quarter backs is that while you can go through certain routines, set pieces, rucks and so on, I think you must have a period in training sessions when the backs are left to themselves, to practise scissor moves or whatever, to give them confidence. While you may have a coach who barks at players in the back line in practice sessions, telling them how to pass the ball, how to run, how to catch, what moves to do next, he can't be out on the field on Saturday and consequently the backs do need to know what to do next and how to do it, and how to do it well.

J. J. Williams, Lions, swerves past Ken Taylor, Hawkes Bay, 1977.
Evening Post

The value of the long pass

Here a centre
takes the play
to his winger's opposite.

The centre then
long-passes to
the winger
in the open.

The value of the short pass

If the centre's
opposite positions
himself badly . . .

It is often possible
to take a short pass
inside him as he turns
to reposition himself.

151

Mick Williment on

The Modern Full-Back

- **The full-back's role today is more an attacking one. Team-mates must now drop back to support the full-back in this role.**

- **Only if there is sufficient team support behind can a full-back avoid resorting to a kick for line or a kick up and under.**

- **Constant practice is required to master the skills required: kicking well with either foot, bounce kicking into touch, place and drop kicking.**

- **The full-back is in an ideal position to see the game as it develops, so both coach and team-mates should make good use of a full-back's observations.**

- **The ideal full-back is confident, has mastered the ball skills, shows a masterly tactical appreciation of the game, is controlled in all situations, fast, and aggressive on attack and on the tackle.**

Following the advent of the 'kick into touch' rules, it became obvious that a new breed of full-back was required, and that coaches should pick the fastest and most skilful runner and best ball player for this position. Players must adapt to the changed circumstances caused by rule changes — not attempt to play to old laws.

The modern full-back should be the first line of attack, not the last line of defence. This player should be able to capitalise on the increase in loose kicking that has followed the kicking rule changes, and be aware of the possibilities that now exist.

What does the average full-back do when in possession of a loose ball? Nine times out of ten he runs forward, kicks on up and under. The result: nine out of ten he loses possession, or a mark allows the opponent to relieve the situation. The alternative is to run the ball back at your opponents, using your wingers or any available players to support. This means that your team keeps the initiative and the ball (you can't score tries by kicking it away to the opposition). Coaches should demand that wingers race back every time the ball goes behind them, in order to support the full-back and start an attack.

Using the good player

Many good teams have been made great by revolving almost all their attacking plays around their full-back. Witness the impact made on modern teams by such players as Andy Irvine and Casey Pinaar. Full-backs need more individual practice than most other positions, and need a wide range of skills, most of which can be developed. Remember how well Joe Karam, the reliable New Zealand full-back with an impressive kick, developed the bounce kick into touch — this was as a result of constant practice, helped of course by his ability to think quickly.

Full-backs should not have a weak foot — both feet should be equally strong, in both drop kicking and punting. Impossible, you say? Try not allowing your full-back to use the 'good' foot for one month at practice sessions — the improvement will be phenomenal. 'Other'-foot kicking is just a matter of confidence and practice. (When New Zealand cricket captain Barry Sinclair broke his right arm, he took to bowling with his left, and after a few weeks could bowl a medium-pace delivery accurately and consistently — proof indeed that practice can perfect a seemingly difficult skill.)

A full-back should vary his entry into the back line. Nothing is harder to combat than an unexpected attack using the full-back in an unorthodox way. Has he tried coming in outside the winger? Does he use the blind side to give his wings a run? A good thing this, even for safety-first coaches, as your sideline is so handy in case of pressure. Does he use himself as a dummy regularly? Does he come into the line from every good ruck? If not, he should.

Developing the full-back's skill

What qualities are necessary to make up an ideal player? Perhaps start with the balance of New Zealand full-back Bob Scott — always totally in control of his movements, never hurried or careless, always assured and confident; add a touch of 1960s full-back Fergie McCormick — aggression personified, ruthless on the tackle and strong running on attack; combine the kicking skills of Don Clarke — practised by the hour, supremely confident in his ability; a large slice of Andy Irvine for his brilliant speed, and counter-attacking. What a player this combination would make!

If your club full-back doesn't have these qualities, what can you do to develop the player to the best of his ability?

First, realise that some mistakes will be made on the way to developing skills and developing a new approach to the position. Don't criticise your full-back — criticise (if you must) the players who didn't help him if a mistake was made. Encourage him at practice to use all the attacking options, and then after the game discuss how many were used during the match — the message will get through soon enough. Give him time to practise some skills on his own or with spare players. Encourage your full-back to help analyse your team's back play; after all the full-back can see the most, and should make the most suggestions. Above all, pick a good ball player for this position, and watch your results improve.

French full-back Paul Aguirre, place kicking.
Evening Post

All Black full-back Mick Williment, tackler regardless, touches down over the line.
Auckland Star

A versatile full-back and proficient goal kicker. Played for Rongotai College 1st XV 1956, 57; Wellington 1958-68 (University); also North Island 1965, 66; NZ Trials 1961-63, 65-68; New Zealand XV 1966; NZ Universities 1962-67. Represented NZ 1964-67 — against the Wallabies 1964, against South Africa 1965, against the 1966 Lions. North Island Under-18 selector, and club captain of the Centurions.

153

All Black Stu Wilson attempts to break the tackle of Wallaby Greg Cornelsen while Murray Mexted calls for the ball.

Peter Bush

Pat Walsh on

The Extra Man

- **The rationale behind the extra man is to gain an advantage in numbers, usually in attack though sometimes in defence.**
- **The best player to use as the extra man is usually the full-back or a winger. A five-eighth doubling round or a loose forward can be used.**
- **The pace of the extra man decides where he comes into the line and the pass to him must be controlled and soft. He should run hard until tackled, maintaining good position with his immediate players.**
- **In defence against the extra man, take the man with the ball.**
- **Practise attacking and defensive situations slowly at first, until working at top speed in a confined spaces.**

To explain what is meant by the 'extra man', we must look at what we consider the 'normal' positions. From a scrum we line out with a winger on what we call the blind side and the rest of the back line — half-back, first five-eighth, second five-eighth, centre, and winger — on the other, with the full-back positioned behind the ball. The extra man situation exists when we bring a player — say, the blind-side winger or the full-back — into the back line to give an advantage in numbers, which, if combined with the unexpected and with speed, could give us an advantage to score points.

It's all a matter of numbers. The moment that you have the ball and more players near it than your opponents do, you have an advantage. But you have to learn to capitalize on it. You must be convinced that three should beat two, and as a part of the practice session you should plan activities that prove that this can be done in a confined space without resorting to brute strength. Believe it or not, it takes time to develop the skills of timing a pass or running somebody into position to take advantage of an extra man in a confined space.

The full-back as the extra man

In the normal back line, set out as it usually is, the obvious place to obtain an extra man is the full-back's position. The full-back can adjust position easily without it being too obvious to the opposition and can come in anywhere into that back line.

From a line-out I would say that the best place for the full-back to come in would be outside the centre. Whether he takes it there, or the ball comes back in from the winger, or he runs inside the centre, it would depend upon the situation. Still another possibility is outside the winger. The ball comes out quickly and the thrust is usually made at centre. You see, if an extra man is coming in, someone will either have to make a gap for him or put him into a gap. So the player coming in as the extra man must really break through your opponents' line.

J.P.R. Williams taught us the advantages of a running full-back. He came in outside the centre with thrust, and ran and either scored himself, put a kick through or ran his winger into position. Of course, in a later tour Andy Irvine was even more flexible — he was faster and lighter on his feet and could come in anywhere into the back line.

Around the scrum, the full-back could most certainly come in as an extra man on the blind side. It doesn't matter whether he comes in inside or outside the winger; but referring back to his movements into the back line on the open side, it is better further out, because it is easier for him to penetrate the cover defence out there.

Using other players

Another player to use as the extra man is the blind-side winger, who can also come in anywhere; a blind-side winger with good pace can stand deeper and this will allow him to come in anywhere at all into that back line. The No. 8 is picking up the ball and the whole back line drifting out one position so that there is an extra man outside the winger. But I think that the extra man running in at full pace to penetrate the opposition backs can give you a substantial advantage.

In earlier days, the blind-side wing three-quarter would come in outside the first five-eighth or inside the first five-eighth. He used to run more or less in a line outside the first five-eighth and then take his pass close to him on the outside or on the inside. You could make a lot of breaks in that way when the first five stood a little 'flatter' than is usual today. They used to call it 'Boots and Socks' — 'Boots' if you were coming in outside, and 'Socks' if you were coming in inside. The late Ron Jarden and 1950s All Black Morrie Dixon used it as a favourite move. I've seen some other wingers of pace come in outside the second five-eighth and link up with the opposition winger — where you come in depends upon your pace. The greater the pace the further out a winger can come in.

From the forwards, use of the No. 8 to pass on the open or blind sides to the half-back is a good move. I've even seen the use of a strong, hard forward as a dummy five-eighth either to commit someone to a tackle and create secondary phase or to be missed out by the pass deliberately and so confuse the opposition. Perhaps the use of a hooker as a thrower-in of the ball at the line-out is a system that releases the winger to be used more frequently as an extra man.

Using the tactic

Firstly, I don't think there is much need for an extra man after rucks and mauls. You know that from a quick ruck — as all New Zealand rugby players should have learnt from Fred Allen — you spin it quickly on the inside. Gaps will close very quickly from a ruck or maul, so the idea is to the spin it quickly and create your gaps further out. You don't want to be caught down 'Mugs Gully', as we used to call it.

All Black full-back Allan Hewson moving as the extra man. All Blacks v Springboks, Third Test Eden Park (Auckland) 1981 Peter Bush

An enterprising and intelligent utility back. Played for Auckland 1954 (Ardmore) 1961, 62 (Otahuhu), South Auckland Counties 1955 (Ardmore); Counties 1956, 57 (Papakura) 1958-60 (Waiuku), 1963 (Manurewa); also North Island 1955, 59; NZ Trials 1956, 57, 59, 63; NZ Maoris 1955, 56, 58, 59, 61; New Zealand XV 1955; NZ Under-23 1958; Bay of Plenty-Thames Valley-Counties 1959; King Country-Counties 1959. Represented NZ 1955-59, 63, 64 — 1955 against the Wallabies, 1956 South Africa, 1957 Australia, 1958 Wallabies, 1959 Lions, 1963 Lions, 1963 England, 1964 Britain and France. Served as a NZ selector 1969-71; North Island selector 1980.

The system of doubling round — where you create an extra man by passing and then running quickly around the player to whom you passed to collect a pass from him on the outside — was a favourite move of Adrian Clarke, the 'first five-eighth double'. Under close marking situations, when it's man-for-man marking early in the game, you can often create gaps in this manner. It's certainly a beautiful move. Or even the second five-eighth doubling around the centre. Both are beautiful moves, though not seen enough in New Zealand.

As an extra man, the decision to penetrate the opposition line or to pass must be yours. You are the person who calls for the ball. You must assess the situation, based upon the defence patterns of the opposition. If their policy is to take the man with the ball, you could use the tactic of an extra man and put your extra man on the outside. If their policy is to stick to man-to-man marking, you could use your full-back as extra man to make the thrust. The player who's inside the player coming in could be your extra man; when the player comes into the gap, he must make the thrust and break the line. The extra man can then run up to the last line of defence and either pass another player into the gap or else get your pass away while the opposition outside you is still on the turn and your players are storming through. Bruce Robertson would be the best modern exponent of this type of play in New Zealand. Whether he is being tackled or not, he always gets that pass away.

Defence against the extra man

As a basic rule, you take the player with the ball. You come in quickly and you try to upset their timing. If you do this — man-to-man — you have done something. I think this is how you can tell the class of a player — merely another club player, or destined for higher levels — whether the player goes for the intercept or continues man-to-man marking or goes for the tackle, and whether what the player does is correct for that situation. My basic rule would be to tackle the man with the ball.

As a full-back, I'd like my back line to move in to take the extra man if he came in, and leave the opponent on the outside for me. The golden rule for a full-back is: 'No one gets past me on the outside.' So if only one fellow is coming at you and you're both on the sideline, that would be the situation I'd like if I was the last line of defence. (Likewise, if I had the ball under the old 'man-for-man' system, I'd be through the gap with just the one full-back to beat. It would be a matter of kicking over the top or putting on a swerve, and I'd be through while he was flat-footed in centre-field). Every time, tackle the player with the ball.

Practising set moves

Begin with small group practices amongst the nine or so backs of the side — including the emergency players — in small areas such as the space between the try line and the dead ball line. Place the players in all positions: three against two, and four against three. It's all timing then, passing the ball so that by timing and the use of the extra man three can beat two. On the other hand, two players may be more adept at defending against the overlap. How often does one see the situation where two players are approaching the try line with only the full-back to beat, and the player with the ball passes too early, the full-back takes him, and the full-back receives the applause? You could, on the other hand, pass too late, and the ball is knocked out of your hands or screwed away from the player who is up in support. It's really simple timing that we're practising.

In so far as set moves are concerned, I used to practise between the 22 metre line and the goal line, so that the players were doing everything at pace in a limited area. Everything was sharpened up. Everyone would be in his normal position and the full-back would be given a slight advantage, to time his movement into the line, by rolling the ball to the half-back. After the call, the full-back would be able to practise timing in coming into the back line. (Actually, anybody coming into the back line should call, not only to let team-mates know of this intention but also to set up a situation so that later in the game a dummy move can be used). If a full-back is timing his move into the back line too early, he must learn to slow up while still on his toes rather than wait flat-footed for the ball to come out into the centre. This will allow him greater acceleration to top pace when the ball does reach him.

The coach should provide the incentive for greater speed and precision, by timing and keeping a record of each player's progress in this and all other practices. The players involved should be encouraged to contribute to the development of the moves and techniques — and if someone has a point to discuss, a contribution to make or something to contradict — these things should be resolved straight away.

You can stand the team in a line — forwards and backs — and get them to sprint, and in 10 metres or so there might be only half a metre separating them, whether there is a sprint champion amongst them or not. You can give everyone confidence that they don't have to start early to move up into position. A full-back who does start to move too early will, by his movement, let the opposition know where he plans to go in. You have to remember that while all you are doing is running up there into position, the other backs have to take a pass and redistribute it. If you are coming in, you must come in at the last minute, and not telegraph your intention to the opposition and allow them time to combat it. The extra man is a surprise move.

Too many players fire a pass like a bullet. I think they forget that the extra man usually comes in closer than the normal outside player and that to a degree the extra man is unsighted. A lobbed pass is necessary, to allow the extra man to take the ball where he wants to at full pace. The player coming in should help by calling 'wide' or 'close', thus giving the person holding the ball some idea of where it's to be thrown. I remember years ago, when I was playing for Counties, Father Laurie Curtain always used to say, 'I'm with you — close' or 'I'm with you — wide', and this helped me to time and place a suitable pass.

There are so many ideas, though if I were coaching I would keep it simple for a start. I would say that from set play from line-outs you get the ball out quickly from the inside and you have your extra man out wide. From the scrum situation where your opposition is up flat with the No.8 you need to be a bit deeper - and that advantage line is still to me a very important aim in rugby — you would look for your ploy with the extra man on the blind side. From rucks you would not bother so much with the extra man, but it would be on the outside if you did.

The extra man on the inside is just a variation — for instance, by missing the full-back out as the ball is passed outwards, then whipping it back in again as the full-back runs into the inside gap. In this case, the extra man is coming in, in the second stage of the movement.

Grant Batty. His great try against the Barbarians in 1973 came as a result of an entry between the centres.
Auckland Star

Examples of play

I recall a try scored at New Plymouth in a trial that helped me into the All Blacks. I was playing full-back and Mick Bremner was playing first five-eighth. Mick Bremner went on the blind side, and the marking was very close — as all trial matches are. Ross Brown went across to mark him, I came in at first five-eighth as a full-back, ran through because everyone had stayed to mark their own men, ran up to Don Clarke, kicked it over his head, picked it up and passed it to somebody else who scored. That was an example of yet another use of the extra man. In that case it was a false run in one direction by one player whose position was filled by the extra man.

Good examples of the extra man can be taken from the play of J.P.R. Williams. He always impressed me by the way, when he came in, that he ran hard, very hard. Of course, when Don Clarke was playing, one of the effective ploys was to miss him out because, recognising him as a danger, the opposition would pay more attention to what they thought he would do than what was actually happening. That was a system of dummying, in the same way that a blind-side winger can rush in for a pass while the half-back runs the blind, or the winger coming in from the blind side and the full-back taking his place for a pass on the blind. In all these, the idea is that you may use an extra man as a dummy to catch the opposition wrong-footed.

J. P. R. Williams — his play showed good examples of the use of the extra man. Here he scores for Wales, while an elated Charlie Faulkner leaps over him.
Christchurch Press

Bryan Williams as extra man makes a burst upfield in 1971. Lions players moving to defence are flanker John Taylor, No. 8 Mervyn Davies (with head strap) and replacement half back Ray Hopkins.
Auckland Star

Bill Freeman on

Blind-side Attack

- The switch of play to the blind side brings enterprise into play, it will catch the opponent off balance and it can result in well-earned points.
- The advantage line is crossed easily and is ideal for setting up a ruck or maul.
- Blind-side moves must be practised in a 'live' situation, so that when a situation develops on the field for such a move the players have the confidence and the skill to use it.
- Care must be taken to avoid excessive use of the blind side, as players on the open side are too often out of the game.
- The key factors are surprise, good possession, good passing and running, a pre-arranged code call and a 'roomy' blind side.

If the game of rugby is to retain its vital characteristics of flair, sparkle, and enterprise, the coach, captain and players should be constantly endeavouring to initiate tactical moves of evasion and deception — those 'foxy' moves that bring tries and a little magic to what can sometimes be a dull event.

All Blacks v Australia, 1967. All Black forwards move to support blind-side play as Sid Going passes.
Peter Bush

160

Represented Wellington as a five-eighth 1942-44, 48 from the Petone and Athletic clubs. President of the Athletic Club 1976, 77 and life member of the same. Wellington RFU management committee 1961-73; selector 1964-70. NZRFU executive 1973-80. Coaching director of the NZRFU since 1976.

It is incredible just how many scoring movements can result from switching the attack from the expected — the anticipated and generally well-covered open side — to the near touch line. This is an incentive to probe and explore the blind-side possibilities. All Blacks Chris Laidlaw and Earle Kirton were great exponents of blind-side play, but it has until recently been a neglected area of attack. In recent test matches, the All Blacks have exploited the blind side — Stuart Wilson's try against France is an example, and Eddie Dunn's try against Scotland. The law now calls for a scrum to be called 15 metres from the touch line after a line-out infringement. It is both an invitation and an encouragement to launch the attack to the shorter side of the field.

Conditions for blind-side play

Firstly, the use of the blind side rarely, if ever means a loss of ground. If your attacker is halted, your forwards are poised to form a driving ruck or maul from which the movement can be continued to the open side, while the opposition backs are caught flat-footed awaiting developments.

By rehearsing tactical movements to the blind side and devising code signals, a team can be assured of numerical superiority over the opposition. No captain should subject the backs to unnecessary tackling against a flat defence — the team should switch to the blind side for penetration, or if stemmed, retain possession and then strike on the open side. In wet and windy conditions, when handling is difficult, persistent passing to the open side can prove disastrous, whereas the blind side brings positive action. The blind-side attack is perhaps the only sure way of crossing the advantage line — player moving from open to blind side should run hard and straight to achieve this.

The key factors

In set play:
- Good possession
- Good understanding between the players involved
- Good passing and precise directional running

- A pre-arranged code call known by all members of the team
- A 'roomy' blind side

In broken play:
- Quick possession
- Good understanding between players
- Good passing and precise directional running

Because blind-side movements can spring from scrum, line-out, ruck or maul, it is important to practise the moves in situations that are as 'live' as possible, so that the players learn to sense when they are appropriate and become confident at executing them. This is particularly important in rucks and mauls, as 'reading' the situation and timing the run and feed of the ball is vital.

The use of too many players in these movements can crowd the space available or slow down the ball's delivery to the player with advantage. In such situations, the 'miss out' pass can be used. Combinations or planned forward drives can also be used on the blind side, initiated by the half-back, to drag into the ruck or maul the opposition forwards and so create more space on the open side for back movement.

Overuse of the blind side, however, can be bad for the morale of the players on the open side of the field, as they become spectators rather than players.

The objectives in summary

- To effect a deceptive movement on the blind side from set play
- To tie up opposition loose forwards by creating a ruck or maul from which to launch an attacking back movement
- To further extend the opposition defence from a ruck or maul situation

Surprise is the key, and successful blind-side moves are not usually planned but spring from sudden developments in play.

Graham Mourie scores after a blind-side move. All Blacks v Brigend.
Peter Bush

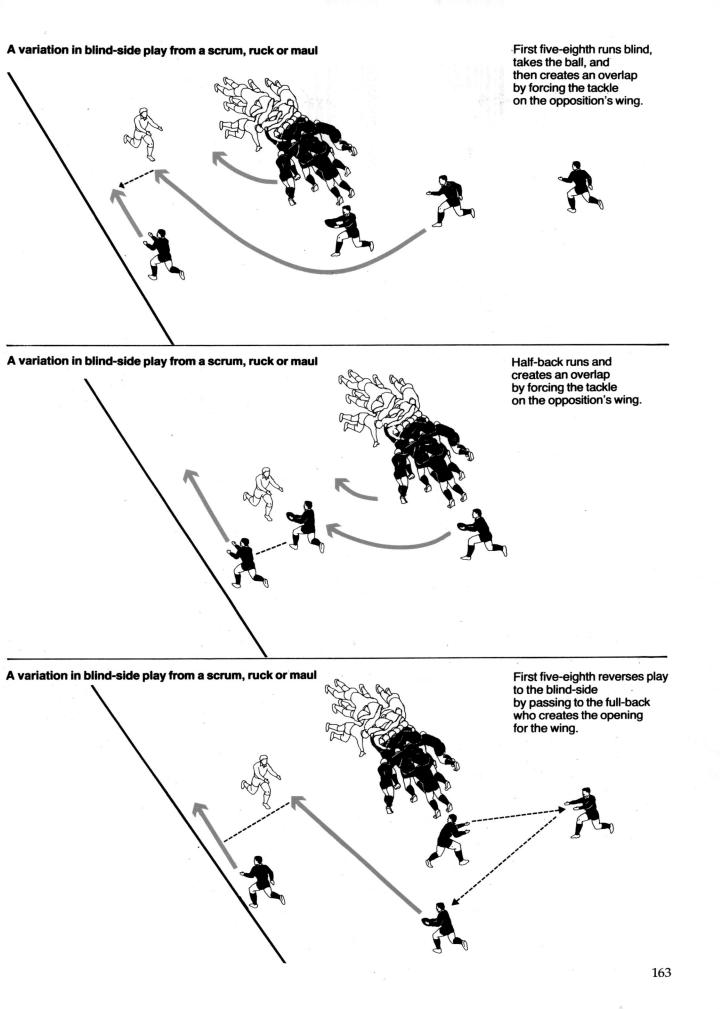

A variation in blind-side play from a scrum, ruck or maul

First five-eighth runs blind, takes the ball, and then creates an overlap by forcing the tackle on the opposition's wing.

A variation in blind-side play from a scrum, ruck or maul

Half-back runs and creates an overlap by forcing the tackle on the opposition's wing.

A variation in blind-side play from a scrum, ruck or maul

First five-eighth reverses play to the blind-side by passing to the full-back who creates the opening for the wing.

163

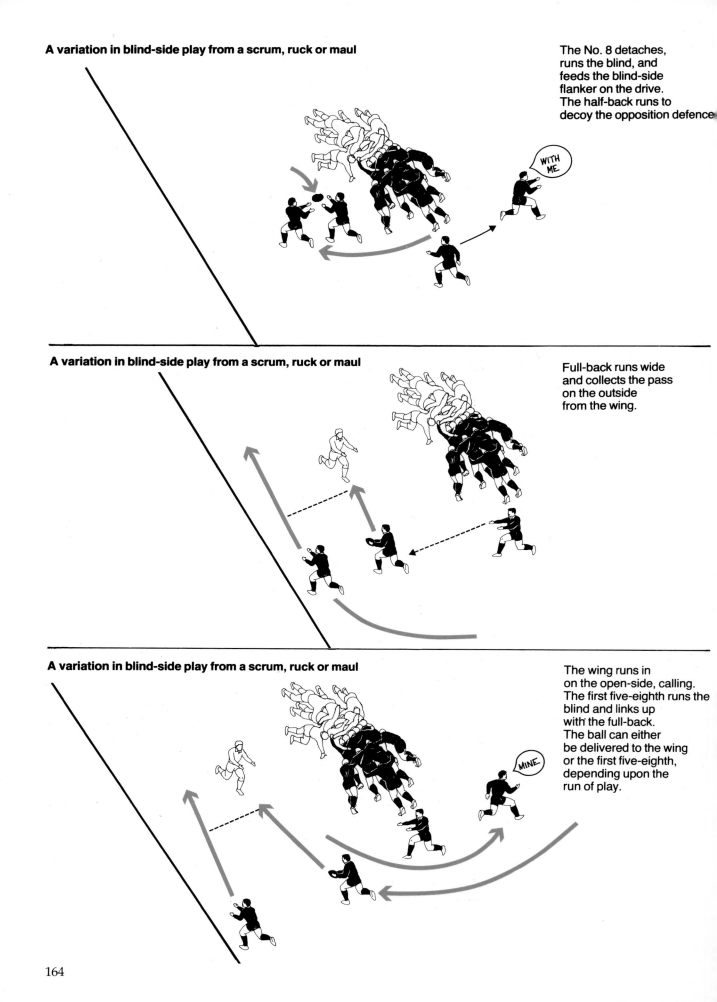

A variation in blind-side play from a scrum, ruck or maul

The No. 8 detaches, runs the blind, and feeds the blind-side flanker on the drive. The half-back runs to decoy the opposition defence

WITH ME

A variation in blind-side play from a scrum, ruck or maul

Full-back runs wide and collects the pass on the outside from the wing.

A variation in blind-side play from a scrum, ruck or maul

The wing runs in on the open-side, calling. The first five-eighth runs the blind and links up with the full-back. The ball can either be delivered to the wing or the first five-eighth, depending upon the run of play.

MINE

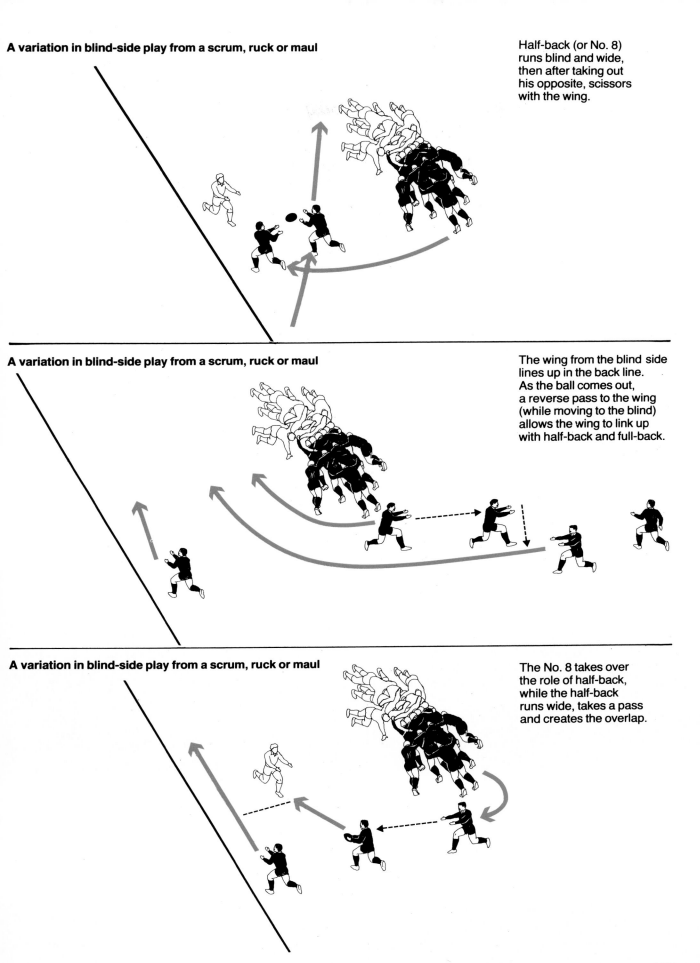

A variation in blind-side play from a scrum, ruck or maul

Half-back (or No. 8) runs blind and wide, then after taking out his opposite, scissors with the wing.

A variation in blind-side play from a scrum, ruck or maul

The wing from the blind side lines up in the back line. As the ball comes out, a reverse pass to the wing (while moving to the blind) allows the wing to link up with half-back and full-back.

A variation in blind-side play from a scrum, ruck or maul

The No. 8 takes over the role of half-back, while the half-back runs wide, takes a pass and creates the overlap.

A variation in blind-side play from a scrum, ruck or maul

Wing runs in from blind, calling. Full-back runs the blind, calling. Half-back passes to either player.

A variation in blind-side play from a scrum, ruck or maul

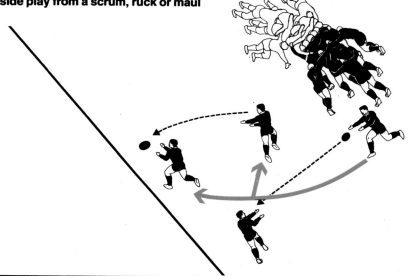

Half-back passes to wing. Wing runs to scrum and scissors with the half-back running around.

A variation in blind-side play from a scrum, ruck or maul

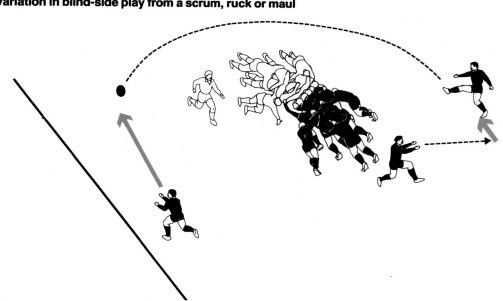

Half-back passes to first five-eighth, who kicks it into the 'box' on the blind (behind the blind-side wing) to allow his wing to run on to the ball.

A variation in blind-side play from a line-out

From a long throw the ball is reversed to the first five-eight running blind, who passes to the wing or who links up with the forwards.

A variation in blind-side play from a line-out

From a short line-out the side row (or half-back) gets the ball running wide and then passes to the wing on the blind side.

A variation in blind-side play from a line-out

The No. 5 taps to a No. 7 running the blind, who sets up a maul or drive or who passes to the half-back or wing.

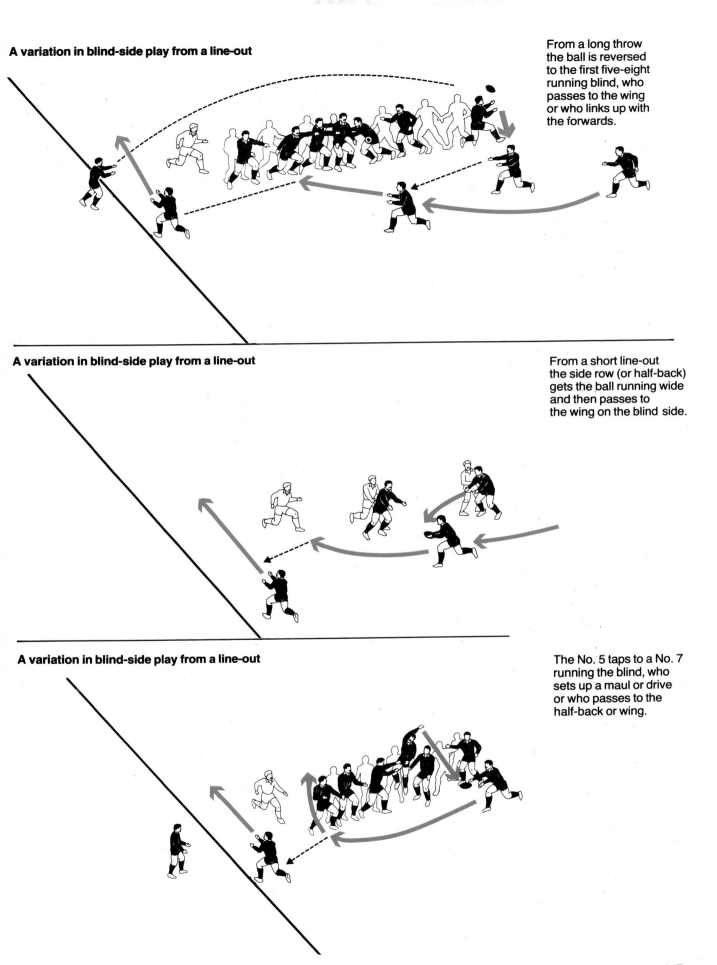

All Black half-back Sid Going, having received the ball from the line-out, about to kick over his forwards — left to right, Andy Leslie, Ken Stewart, Ian Kirkpatrick, Frank Oliver and Bill Bush. All Blacks v Springboks.
Peter Bush

169

Jim Wallace on

Improving your Rugby

- **The two aspects to improve your rugby are *mental* and *practical*.**
- **Mental — for example, by watching matches live or on television, by reading about the game, by talking with and listening to coaches and other players.**
- **Physical — for example, by becoming fit, by consistent practice to improve skills and by good quality and well-maintained rugby gear which does not limit your playing.**
- **After each match, free and open discussion between the coach and players will lead to improvement in the team's play.**
- **Accept the responsibility of attending team meetings and practices.**

We play rugby for enjoyment. The better rugby we play the more we enjoy it. To improve our game we cannot be permanently passive players, mentally dead as doornails, for our skills are dependent upon the ability of one good (or bad) coach. There are thus two main aspects for you to consider if you wish to improve your rugby. The first is the mental aspect, the second is the practical or physical aspect.

The mental aspect

Although you may be a player who is big, strong, naturally fast, enduring and capable, to be a successful player you need to be an intelligent player. So how do you learn to *think* about the game?

Watching matches intelligently

Firstly, and perhaps most importantly, watch rugby and discipline yourself to watch it intelligently. We can watch games 'live' and we can watch them on television, even games played long ago. But how do you watch intelligently?
- Watch a good player, perhaps an international player, who is playing in your favoured position. Try not to follow the magnet of the ball (this is difficult), but concentrate on the movements of your selected player. If he is a scrummager you can usually watch him quite easily at set scrums. Don't look at the scrum-half putting in the ball. Study your man's binding, his feet position, his body position, and so on. Observe how a skilful No. 8, such as Andy Leslie, Mervyn Davies or Murray Mexted, heels the ball so that it is well served, so that the scrum-half is not put under pressure by an opponent. If your selected player is a line-out jumper, such as Andy Haden, watch your player (not the ball) and note the variations of method he or others use during a single game. At maul-time, ask yourself why a certain player, although enclosed by the opposition, always seems to secure the ball for his team (as did the legendary Kel Tremain or as does Leicester Rutledge) — while, on the other hand, another even quite famous forward will lose it.
- The television replay of a match is valuable. At first sight we usually glue our eyes to the central action. On the replay of the match, however, we can focus on vital defenders (or attackers) and their movements and attempt to evaluate the worth of each attacking or defensive method. To give an example: we saw quite a few replays of the brilliant Sid Going try in the match against the Lions at Wellington in 1977. The try seemed so simple at first. Can the television replay tell you why and how a try was scored in spite of such a strong defence?
- It is very important — though on television often difficult — to observe the alignment and positioning of back lines and on attack and defence. If you aim to be a good full-back or three-quarter, your observation and thinking are essential. If, for example, one team has a great kicking five-eighth such as a player of the calibre of Mac Herewini or Barry John, how does the defending team align its full-back and three-quarters and operate its loose forwards? Is there any co-ordinated plan? Do some players — even international players — wander out of their usual position? Do they perhaps wander deliberately like crafty foxes and then suddenly dart explosively across the field? Watch the field as a whole, therefore, especially as the set scrum or line-out is forming.
- When you watch intelligently, you can compile your own statistics of a match. This is easier when there are television replays of the whole match, so that one can enjoy the first viewing but collect figures during the second. A few years ago during the first half of an international match, I noted that team A had 'won' nine line-outs and team B four. Then loud and clear came the TV commentator: 'line-out count is six to team A, seven to team B'. There is a lesson here.

Accurately compiled statistics on possession, for example, can provide a basis for intelligent analysis — impressions of spectators are unreliable and often erroneous. In the Fourth Test between the All Blacks and the Lions at Auckland in 1971, the result was a 14-all draw. During the second half, All Black half-back Sid Going received the ball (from all sources: set scrum, line-out, ruck-maul) 28 times, including once under real pressure (and thus valueless possession). His opponent, the Lions scrum-half Gareth Edwards, received the ball ten times, (once under real pressure). From this portion the Lions fly-half Barry John received the ball on only seven occasions. I did not record how many times John punted the ball on these seven situations, but it was, I think, about four, possibly five. So effective were these few Barry John punts, however, that the overriding impression gained by spectators and recorded by critics was (a) that the Lions gained a large share of possession, and (b) that John was kicking endlessly, almost mindlessly, throughout the match. (The overall reception of half-back ball was 45 to Going and 24 to Edwards.)

Phil Bennett's swerving and side-stepping genius was not acquired by 'being born on a Welsh mountain slope with one leg shorter than the other'.
Scott A. G. M. Crawford

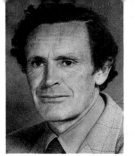

Representative five-eighth: Wanganui 1956, 59; Wanganui-King Country 1956. County player in England: Middlesex 1952, 53. All Black trialist 1956. Coach Trinity Grammar School 1st XV Middlesex, England, 1951-55; Wanganui Collegiate School 1st XV 1961-78; various Wanganui secondary school representative XVs. Selector-coach Wanganui Rugby Union Senior Representative team 1976-81. Member Wanganui Rugby Union's Junior Management Board 1961-75; lower grade fixtures subcommittee, largely as chairman or sole organiser 1961-75. Member NZRFU Coaching School Panel 1972; various other coaching schools.

Now what conclusions can you reach from your statistics? Have you ever recorded the origins of the tries gained by your own team? One often hears a standard view that tries seldom result directly from set play. But what proportions really do result from (a) set play (set scrum and line out), (b) ruck/maul, (c) opponents' mistakes, (d) counter-attack, (e) tap penalty, and other play? It is important to you and your team, if you discover that you have scored no tries from counter-attack, say, or from exploiting opponents' errors. Why not? Can you score in only a limited number of ways?

● Watching another game it may be interesting to observe the players' signals of various kinds: line-out signals, signals for 'moves', five-eighth and half-back liaison, direction of the attack, and so on.

● It is important to watch the game not only intelligently but also with enjoyment. You will learn more if you try to avoid being biased against certain individuals or certain teams, and thus learn from the good (and bad) play of both teams. Firstly, don't be too critical — you haven't had much rugby experience if you haven't at some stage played in a weak team or, if you're a coach, had a poor season. Quite often we read or hear the criticism that a certain game was a dull, scrappy affair with few redeeming features. But how drab and unexciting was this match for the players, the coaches and the genuine supporters involved?

This reminds me of a representative match which was won by the home team by a very narrow margin. There were some interesting aspects to the game (it was a divisional championship match), but at the after-match function the discontented host chairman expressed his disappointment in the match — he had been hoping for a handsome victory. The visiting captain cheerfully countered that, though defeated, he had found it a thoroughly enjoyable and stimulating contest, with the result desperately in balance till the final whistle. Any lesson here?

Some matches may appear scrappy, boring affairs to the grandstand or television-armchair critics. But ask yourself some questions. Why was a certain game 'scrappy'? Was it because the two teams were too tense? Was there, on the other hand, perhaps an absence of tension which caused sloppiness at set-scrum or in passing or punting or tackling? If so, why were the teams not geared-up? No doubt each had been given the psycho team-talk. But perhaps the team-talk was on the 'model' game, whereas breakdowns were the result of strength (or weakness) in a certain region — for example, a half-back who couldn't pass one way or a devastatingly aggressive-on-the-tackle loose forward. Did the referee bore in legalistically on every minute error but mindlessly ignore the advantage law? Most of these questions can be asked about play at any level. We have something to learn from every kind of game, from test-match level to the grass-roots at Wollongong or Whangarei, Pontypridd or Potchefstroom. We can watch with enjoyment and learn more.

The value of reading

● The first reading must be of the most up-to-date edition of the *Laws of the Game of Rugby Union*, both to read and to understand. There are just too many examples to illustrate the value of this. Take just one. In the Fourth Test between the Lions and the All Blacks at Eden Park, Auckland, in 1966, the Lions full-back, Scotsman Stewart Wilson, could not gather a ball that was rolling awkwardly to his left, towards the touch line and his own goal line. So he gave up the ghost and soccer-tapped the ball gently into touch 5 metres or more from his line and, with other retreating Lions, turned his back on the touch line and moved towards his appointed station for the inevitable line-out. All Black Colin Meads arrived. He grabbed the ball and moved smartly to where the ball had crossed the touch line. Colleague Waka Nathan

stood 5 yards (not metres, in 1966) from touch. He received Meads' sharp, straight throw-in. Nathan thereupon scored a try casually and literally behind the Lions' backs. To make one of several points, if Wilson had appreciated the law governing quick throw-ins, he would have slammed that ball into the crowd — for no quick throw-in can be made after a spectator or ballboy has handled the ball; Meads and Nathan, on the other hand, understood all the legal requirements.

Here is another example. The 1962 Wallabies touring New Zealand kept a greater control on the massive punting and drop-kicking of All Black full-back Don Clarke by a total appreciation of the 10yard (now 10metre) law in regard to off-side. Very few players understand the 10metre law, practically no spectators, not even all referees. Yet it must be one of the oldest laws in the book. To understand and learn from your watching you must know the laws of the game. You will also enjoy better personal relationships with your referees.

Still being published are the revised editions of the amusingly illustrated ' *Why the Whistle Went* ' by Fougasse, the former editor of Punch magazine. I recommend this as the second volume in your rugby library.

● Books on rugby history and on major tours by rugby teams provide valuable reading. When read without prejudice, the best of these books promote your interest and enthusiasm, and the right kind of pride in the achievements of your national or regional team. Furthermore, many of the writers attempt to analyse the reasons for the success or failure of a touring team, though the books may suffer to some extent from bias.

● More importantly, there are books on coaching. These are not usually such popular reading as the books on rugby heroes or those on rugby tours enlivened with the spice of rugby politics, but it is a rare coaching book that doesn't offer useful ideas. Unfortunately, problems arise from periodic law changes. A method that worked admirably in 1960, for example, may be unwise in the 1980s. This does not prevent you from thinking about the method, however, and devising a workable adaptation.

● Finally, there are books on athletics, sports medicine and physical fitness. There is much more emphasis in physical education nowadays upon 'skill-related fitness'. (What a wonderful expression that is.) You could be an international 400metre runner but still puff like a grampus alongside a B-grade cricketer at that first match of the season. Why? Many of these texts attempt to analyse the skills of various sports and their problems.

(A recommended reading list is given at the back of this book.)

Talking and listening

Now that we have watched and read, we can learn by talking and listening. Knowledge comes from reading and watching, but it also comes from experience. Therefore, to test the knowledge you have acquired in your limited mental playground, bounce it against the hardened wall of the mind of the experienced coach and of the experienced player. Get yourself to coaching schools, listen, ask your questions, and *listen* to the answers. It is important not only to learn to improve your individual contribution to the game but also to be able to suggest team patterns or amendments to your team patterns to suit its overall speed (or lack of it), or its strength in one area and weakness in another. It is very rare for a team to be powerful in every aspect of play.

Every now and again a truly great coach develops a plan or tactical technique of great significance. One example was the

All Black Doug Rollerson steadies himself for a simple conversion straight out in front.
Peter Bush

172

scientific rucking technique of the Otago coach of the late 1940s, Vic Cavanagh. His basic rucking methods have stood the test of time, though they have recently been challenged by the British mauling methods of the 1970s — mauling methods rather different from those of the All Blacks of the 1960s.

I doubt, too, whether anyone had ever heard the expression 'second phase' before the mid-1950s. Law changes often belatedly promote new ideas. So every time there is a law change, put on your thinking cap. Coaches are eternally, year by year, week by week, trying to think up new codes and signals for player intercommunication on the field of play, or novel tap penalty moves, surprise kick-offs and drop-outs, short line-outs, and so on. You must play your part. Don't be put off if your more experienced coach and captain reject your first one hundred suggestions.

Lastly, talk with your fellow players after each match and try to analyse why your opponents scored points, but without apportioning blame to your team-mates. Start watching, reading, listening, thinking *now*.

The physical aspect

The Roman philosopher Seneca was one of the first but not the only thinker to express the thought that 'there is no genius without some touch of madness'. The bee in your bonnet buzzes a love of rugby football.

Improving skills

Get on to the known local expert in a skill you wish to improve, or get your coach to arrange this through the Union's coaching committee. From your expert — and I mean 'expert as proven by performance' — learn the technique, the theory of the skill. Write down all the main points. Now, a skill — as defined by some physical education specialists — is 'applied technique'. The rest is absolutely up to *you*.

A second aspect of 'genius' was said a hundred years ago to be 'the capacity for taking trouble first of all'; or, as we mostly say now, 'an infinite capacity for taking pains'. That is

what is required of a young, aspiring rugby footballer. Too many youngsters of more than adequate ability (and their parents) believe that the talent of a Jack Nicklaus or a Don Bradman, of a great hurdler or discus thrower, of a Borg or Batty, is born and not made. But in fact to reach the top and then stay there, these people practise their skills for hours and hours. I remember reading when I was a boy of how the young Don Bradman improved the accuracy of his throwing into the wicket. In his country home town of Bowral, New South Wales, young Donald used to snap up a golf ball and hurl it at a tubular iron railing of narrow diameter. If he missed, he had to go and collect the ball. A tiresome way to practise? Bradman certainly put the pressure on himself to hit the rail.

Do you really think that Phil Bennett and Gerald Davies, the Welshmen, acquired their side-stepping 'genius' by being born on a Welsh mountain slope with one leg shorter than the other? And how did that amazing All Black full-back, Bob Scott, collect such a wide range of evasive skills that charging enemy forwards could never guess what he would do next? Why can All Black half-back Mark Donaldson pass so well? It is because he practises and practises — not only in the easier direction for a standard right-hander (to his left) but also, even more assiduously, to his right. Don't be a foolishly self-conscious teenager who is too embarrassed to spend hours on a skill. The clowns who ridicule you are the no-hopers of your generation.

Practising skills

What do you need to practise skills? Obviously you need a good football, and often having several balls is more convenient. A good coach will make these available to you, and perhaps you should buy a precious one of your own. For many skills, you can be helped by an amateur assistant. I have known a good mum on a farm kick the ball back to her

The young player must practise skills assiduously. Top players do, like Leicester Rutledge getting the better of a tackling bag.
Christchurch Press

place-kicking son. A line-out jumper can usually encourage a friend to throw the ball accurately. A scrum-half passer can either throw a succession of balls at a stake or pass one ball to a friend who immediately sends it back.

Devise your own practice drills. You need to organise your weekly routine to provide for a regular period of personal practice. Of course, there will be problems. You will need *patience* and *faith*. When you adopt a new or even slightly different technique, your performance of that skill will probably deteriorate for a time. This is especially true when you are older and you are trying to get rid of a long-established bad habit. If, however, after a while you are not improving, then you must get hold of your expert to make a reappraisal, to have another look at you. There may be only one small detail to repair — the position of one foot, for example — which is frustrating your progress. Videotape is the great help in this respect; some players cannot otherwise be convinced that they are making a fundamental error. They *know* they are exercising the skill as instructed — until they see the indisputable evidence of the videotape. Who has access to video-apparatus in your town? Chase your coaching committee again.

Furthermore, in any area where you have once been skilful, your skills may begin to fade. Do some hard revisionary brushing up. Don't be afraid to experiment. Neither John Hipwell nor Ken Catchpole, the great Australian half-backs, seemed to me to pass in an orthodox way (like All Black Lyn Davis or Welshman Gareth Edwards) but they certainly got the ball out quickly and accurately.

Only you can practise your skills. Only you can get yourself really fit. You must motivate yourself, not rely on others. Individual skills are your concern.

Playing with the team

Individual skills are your concern, but you are also part of a unit group of your team. The various groupings could be listed as:

- Wing three-quarters
- Midfield players
- Half-back and first five-eighth (fly-half)
- Flankers, No. 8 and half-back
- The set scrum
- Part of the set scrum, e.g. the front row
- The line-out
- Part of the line-out, e.g. one jumper and two supports, etc.

If you are a first five-eighth, then you and your half-back ought to get together for your private practices. Wingers and full-back can discuss and practise how to combine and counter-attack under various circumstances. And so on.

Finally, as a member of a *team* make sure that you are on time for practice sessions and matches. Let your coach or manager or captain (whoever is responsible) know when you cannot (for very good reasons) be on time, or when you will be unavailable. Play your part in the team discipline on and off the field, support your skipper and attend to your personal preparations such as thorough, effective warm-ups before practice sessions and match. Attend scrupulously to your equipment, boots, garters, down to the smallest detail.

Get advice from others, but remember that the *final responsibility* is your own. Then you will improve your rugby.

Bob Scott's evasive skills were so great that charging enemy forwards never knew what he would do next. Auckland v Lions, 1950 Jack Kyle (on the right) is running up to intercept.
N.Z. Herald

Bob Scott on

Handling

- **Passing should be rhythmic, controlled, and directed to allow the receiver to run on to the ball.**
- **The ball-receiver's hands should be still while running to receive the ball. Balance and body position are vital.**
- **Picking up a ball requires a low body position, relaxed hands, balance and, above all, the need to watch the ball.**
- **Coaches should keep an open mind on players' suggestions and should be prepared to use them.**
- **Players should be encouraged to improve their skills, and coaches must be generous in their praise for skills well performed.**

The good footballer always knows, senses, or has a special feeling for what is required in every situation. The good footballer translates this feeling into action only by a knowledge of the skills of the game — skills so constantly rehearsed that they become instinctive. Like the good golfer who can really hit a ball, the great player in rugby is not a freak — skills are known off-pat, and so their execution is automatically correct.

I think it would be true to say that in the amateur game of rugby in New Zealand, there has often been insufficient concentration on skills. Rather we have tended to rely on the gifted players for our teams' successes — conveniently, gifted players have emerged often enough for us to get away with it, but this doesn't mean it can go on for ever.

Also, when we coached we were too regimented to positional play — though somehow a player had to get the ball out to score a try. It's surely no coincidence that some of New Zealand's best players have been half-backs — they seem to have been able to initiate things, perhaps because they're a law to themselves with no-one marking them. But we need to instil the same sort of attitude and initiative in all the players of the team. The only way to do this, as I see it, is to recognise that the game can be played to its fullest only by players who have developed their techniques to the fullest. This means going back to the drawing-board, back to scratch — to the fundamental skills and their assiduous practice. And one of the most important skills of the game is ball-handling.

The first rule

Possession, you might say, is nine points of the game — but what point is there in getting a ball if you are only going to drop it, if you can't pass properly or catch correctly, or if you feed the ball out to a player whose positioning is such that he cannot possibly catch it? For instance, if you are going to regiment the half-back to stand *on* the position where the ball is going to be taken from, it is simply not going to work; the half-back has to be *inside* the position to have latitude to catch up with the ball — that way he can take it early or late, and

can also adjust position in preparation for passing the ball on. But if the half-back is placed at the extremity of the position, his options are taken away from him and he cannot move. And if he can't move with the proper rhythm that catching and passing require, the dynamic has gone out of the game.

So my first rule for ball handling would be:

- Learn to allow the ball to do the work for you. Your body should be part of the rhythm of where the ball is coming from and where you want it to go. *Use the flight of the ball to determine the position of your body.*

When one looks at the skill of such players as Lions first five-eighths Jack Kyle and Barry John — at their ability in receiving and disposal of the ball — it's obvious that their positional awareness is such that they allow the ball to do the work for them.

The reason why good players have time to move and change their mind is that they use the whole of the rhythm of the body. They have complete co-ordination — of their feet, hands, body, eyes and brain. Because no player was ever born with a complete mastery of the skills, it is obvious that they have acquired their expertise the hard way, by constant practice and a full understanding of the fundamentals. Not all players can or will apply themselves to this degree, but nevertheless it is this application and involvement that will produce the better player, the better team, and a better game. After all, what greater frustration can anyone have than to play a game when one has only limited ability in its skills?

Andy Haden gathers in a high-flying ball.
Auckland Star

The ball-carrier should pass the ball so that the ball-receiver can catch it with as little effort as possible. To do this, both players should be properly positioned. France v New Zealand.
Peter Bush

Admired as a skilful and well-balanced full-back. Played rugby league for the Ponsonby club reaching senior grade 1939. While in the army in the 1940s he played rugby union for the Motor Transport Pool and the Divisional Ammunition Coy in the Middle East. Played for Auckland 1946-48, 50-53 (Ponsonby); also North Island 1946, 48, 51, 53; NZ Trials 1947, 48, 50, 53; 2nd NZEF 1945, 46; NZ Services (UK) 1945. Played for the Petone club in Wellington 1954. Represented NZ 1946, 47, 49, 50, 53, 54 making his debut for NZ in the 1946 series against Australia. Retired 1954. Served on the Petone club committee 1966-70.

Basic passing

Balance is the key to all good ball handling, especially where the running player is concerned. The ball-carrier should run in a balanced fashion, almost knock-kneed, with the weight on the inside of the feet, shifting all the time in readiness to pass the ball, carrying it in a low, relaxed position. This balancing run, transferring the weight from foot to foot, allows for a quick change in direction. The run should be directed so that a support player can easily and quickly position himself on the ball carried.

When the pass is made, the ball-carrier's job is to put the ball where the ball-receiver can in turn pass it on simply, cleanly and swiftly, or the ball-carrier should pass it to the point where the ball-receiver is in a gap ready for attack. If the ball is passed towards a reasonable position, the receiver should be able to catch it without dropping it (as too often happens) — and if he does drop it, the chances are that he is 'using his hands' to run. Fast runners are notorious for dropping the ball for this reason. Players should practise running while keeping their hands virtually still. This ensures a steady platform to take the ball. Don't grab; the ball should be stopped with one hand, with the other hand coming in to hold it so that it doesn't fall to the ground.

As mentioned earlier, the ball-carrier should be balanced by keeping the weight on the inside of the feet. A group of three players can practise this exercise: the ball-carrier runs along holding the ball low with both hands, shifting balance from one foot to the other. This develops body and feet positioning for a pass. While the ball-carrier practises this shifting position, the two ball-receivers also run, changing their balance constantly and ready to adapt their position — deep, shallow or wide, as required. When one of them takes the ball — say, straight in front, or slightly inside; (which will happen, of course) — the ball-receiver must be prepared to reposition the feet in readiness for passing on the ball. A common fault is that a player catches the ball and only then starts to position himself to pass. But the platform for receiving and passing the ball on to a team-mate should be beginning to be formed *before* the action of taking the ball is completed — without the player taking his eye off the ball, of course.

In good passing it is important that the ball come to the outside hand of the receiver. This will allow the receiver to begin the correct positioning for the pass just before getting control of the ball. So the ball-receiver should always be at such a distance as to allow the pass to be taken beyond his outside shoulder, just above waist height. The turning of the head, hands and body should be an uninterrupted rhythmic flow over the constantly repositioned, balanced feet.

Dummy pass The aim of this is to trick the defender into thinking you've passed the ball, and it is used when a defender is moving towards the player he expects you to pass to. Extend the arms to full length and get the eye of the defender — the dummy pass must look like a real pass in every way, except that the ball is not released.

Scissor pass The scissor pass is used to change the direction of attack. The ball-carrier makes a sudden break to the gap between his opponents and his outside player, then turns his body to screen the ball, while the outside player scissors in to take the pass going on the inside. The opposition can be further confused if the inside player continues on the outside break.

Dummy scissor pass As above, except that the ball-carrier retains possession while the outside player carries on as though he has taken the ball.

Option pass 'Option' passes involve various types of pass, and the key to all of them is of course position on the ball.

Doug Bruce executes the swing pass.
Christchurch Press

The scissors pass

The dummy scissors

The soft pass

The option pass

In the option pass,
the ball-receiver has
the option to run on to
the ball and catch it
where he wants to, thus
giving greater flexibility
to his play.

The overhead pass

Here the ball is lobbed
over an opponent running
between the ball-carrier
and the supporting team-mate.

*Welsh backs move against the All Blacks, 1963. D. R. R. Morgan
passes as he is tackled by Kel Tremain.*
Sports & General Press Agency

Taking and passing the ball — the flick pass

Once the pass has been placed
so that the ball-receiver can
take it at his left foot as
it hits the ground, the player
can not only have peripheral
vision (to ascertain the
opposition's position) but
also put the ball out
in one stride if he wants to.

Hip presented
to your opposition

The smuggle pass

The smuggle pass is a hand-to-hand pass used particularly by forwards charging with the ball in close contact.

The lob pass

An opponent running between two players is preventing a pass. The ball-carrier runs in a way suggesting he will not pass, drawing in the opponent. Then the ball-carrier lobs the ball to the obstructed team-mate — into a spot where the ball-receiver can run on to it at maximum pace.

Half-back passing

Before talking about specific half-back passes, I'd like to outline what I consider is the ideal stance for a half-back who is about to receive the ball. In the 'open stance' the half-back is facing the direction he (in turn) will be passing the ball. The half-back is inside the ball-carrier or at the point where the ball will appear. Feet are almost together, balance slightly on the foot opposite the one that will be moved forward to the point where the ball will be received. As the hands move to take the ball, what I call the 'swinging' foot is already being moved out in the direction of the pass. That, in my opinion, is how the half-back should be positioned.

Feed pass Remember the positioning of the feet. If passing a ball won at scrum or line-out direct to the five-eighth from left to right, trap the ball when on the left foot and pass the ball on in one movement, the left hand providing the impetus and the right hand the direction.

Pivot pass This is used when the first five-eighth will be taking the ball on the same side as the half-back puts it in. At the start of the pass, the half-back will of course have his back to the first five-eighth. Passing from right to left, the ball is trapped when on the left foot and it is delivered to the first five-eighth with one continuous sweeping movement of the hands while pivoting on the right foot.

Reverse pass As above, but instead of pivoting the body the half-back projects the ball under the arms.

Ball-handling skills

Wet weather or fine, the secret of picking up good, clean ball depends on a low body position. With a *high ball* the hands and arms should form a cradle, with the feet balanced ready to move in any direction; the hands should move as a final extension of the movement. With a *ground ball* the feet should be apart and the hands relaxed. With the *ball coming straight on* the feet should be well apart, weight on the inside of the feet (as always), knees relaxed and turned inwards (so that you look like a crab), hands low and near the ground, forming a cradle ready for the ball to more or less roll into them before they close around it to grasp it. The side-on pick-up can be accomplished by keeping the feet away from the ball, and allowing the same low body position and placement of hands to scoop up the ball.

Wet ball on ground Keep the feet well apart and the knees bent, relaxed. This brings the body and hands close to the ground. Let the ball roll into the hands. If the ball is wet, try not to use a grabbing action.

Retrieved ball Whenever possible, overtake the ball to reach a position facing the oncoming opposition before attempting to pick up the ball. On a wet day, when the opposition is close, the obvious thing is to go down on the ball first.

For head-on *rush stopping*, the body position should be the same as for the normal pick-up, but the hands should be well back towards the feet and low to the ground. As the ball comes under control of the hands, the right shoulder turns around and down, so that in a prone position you present your back to any oncoming opponents.

If you are *going back for the ball*, you've no time to spare: shift a metre or so to the side, drop your body to the ground, your ground arm cradled ready to control the ball. As your momentum slides you into it, your other hand comes in to complete your control of the ball. Your back, of course, is to the opposition as you slide, and eventual control of the ball is completed. Practise turning your body over with the aid of your feet — so that you can get to your feet facing towards your opponents.

In *going down on the ball* (for example, when rush stopping), the more quickly you can have your feet nearer your goal line than your head is, the better control you can have over the

situation. Keep your head tucked in and your shoulders well-hunched, and quickly shift your feet back for bracing. It may sound complicated, but with practice it isn't. Think about it. Just diving on a ball doesn't necessarily stop a rush — the ball can still be kicked away — so always use your hands in conjunction with your body actions.

Coaching handling skills

There is no one recipe for coaching. The only basic rule for a coach is to be receptive to all ideas — you never know when one idea may turn out to be helpful, if only to one player. And players vary so much, not only in size, but in capacity for assimilating skills, in quickness, reflexes, and flair and flamboyancy. But the coach should be able to define the vital points of position and balance, and know precisely what should happen to a player's feet, hands and body in executing each particular skill. The coach needs to be much more specific than merely saying to a young player, 'Keep your eyes on the ball.' or 'Pass in front of your team-mate.'

Only with sound technique can a young player develop the confidence of a Johnny Smith, or an Aguirre (a player who was always able to anticipate a blossoming situation) or an Andy Irvine (whose speed and positional awareness gave him the advantage in numerous situations). Sid Going is perhaps the classic example — a tremendous player who used strength and timing to whip the ball away. Though he may not have had fellow All Black Chris Laidlaw's skill in passing, he had the guts and also the three prime requirements for ball handling: speed, alertness and, above all, balance.

J. P. R. Williams makes a good catch under strong pressure.
Auckland Star

Catching a high ball

Present the side of your body to the oncoming opposition, take the ball across your body and into you, turning so that any supporting team-mate will come from behind and be able to take the ball.
For a mark, you must have both feet on the ground and call out the word 'mark' as the ball is taken. This qualifies you for a free kick if you take the mark inside your defensive 22 metre mark.

Taking a ball along the ground to the side

Get low and to the side of the ball. The hand nearest to the ball goes under and behind the ball, the other comes across the body and gets under the front of the ball.

Stopping a ball skittering towards you

Get low to the ground behind the ball. Keep your knees together to prevent it slipping through. If the ball is on the ground, to stop it push down on the ball with both hands.

Alternative position

183

Ralph Caulton on

Running

- The natural ability to sprint is a great asset but rugby running also requires additional abilities to enable the player to deal with the various situations that occur during a match. These can be coached and developed.
- Rugby running usually involves short sharp bursts of 10-15 metres, and the coach's programme should be designed to quicken the players' reflexes and produce greater speed in all situations. Stamina is all-important.
- Ball drill work is essential. Competitive games to develop speed of thought and movement can be fun for the players and at the same time achieve the required results.
- Boots must be well maintained, and the sprigs placed to assist the player's balance and ability to change direction suddenly.
- The best running position is with the body slightly hunched forward, providing control to change direction suddenly, to ride a tackle and to fall without injury.

The ability to run is obviously one of the basic requirements for the game of rugby. Natural ability gives some players an advantage, but others can develop this skill through concentrated effort during the summer months on the athletic track, practising short sprinting and acceleration and also sharpening their reflexes. Rugby running, however, is different in many respects from track sprinting.

What is required in rugby

Firstly, the player has to be able to run comfortably and at speed carrying the ball under either arm, or in both hands. The player also has to be able, at top speed, to pass the ball across the body to either side but not lose any momentum. Furthermore he has to be able to run with the ball, and run at pace, when the body is well balanced, and be able to change direction quickly without losing momentum. Examples of this are the rapid side-step or propping of either foot. Acceleration is a very important feature of running — speed off the mark from a stationary start is essential. Sharp reflexes play a vital role here. And acceleration when the player is already running — that is, a change of pace to a top speed — is a great attribute. The rugby player needs to be able to run on the diagonal without losing balance. An example of this is fielding a high kick which has been kicked behind you. The player must be able to run in a curve at

Evasive running is a key skill of rugby, as demonstrated in this Trial at Auckland.
Peter Bush

A fast, proficient wing three-quarter always aware of scoring opportunities. Played for Wellington 1957-65 (Poneke); also North Island 1962-64 and NZ Trials 1958-60, 62, 63, 65. Attained All Black status in 1959, making a dramatic debut by scoring two tries in each of his first two matches, and represented NZ 1959-61, 63, 64: 50 occasions including 16 tests in which he scored eight tries. Coached Poneke club 1967, 68; co-coach of the successful Marlborough Ranfurly Shield side 1973. Marlborough selector 1970-75. Served on Wellington RFU committee 1977-79, NZRFU coaching committee 1978-80 and Junior Coaching committee 1977-80.

speed, like an athlete running around the curve of a 200 metre track. Examples of this are running through a gap or running around an opposing player. He must also be able to run and maintain balance, even though the runner is being buffeted by would-be tacklers.

What emerges from these observations is that the player must have basic speed, plus particularly good balance, acceleration, strength, quick reflexes and a good top speed. The latter are all bonus advantages, and can be achieved by good training methods. Most running required in a rugby game is in short, sharp bursts of up to 10-15 metres — and in every match there are plenty of these. Stamina therefore has to be developed, as does short-sprinting ability.

A tackler's view of Australian lock Dick Thornett, 103 kg (16st 2lb), advancing at full speed.
Christchurch Press

Elements of the training programme

Coaches must design a programme which encompasses all these features, and insist that a high level of fitness is achieved and maintained. The game of rugby lasts at least 80 minutes, and many games are won or lost during the last 20 minutes when the fitness and effectiveness of a team start to wilt, giving the opposition a decided advantage.

There are many drills that can be used to develop these qualities in players, and they fall into two distinct groups. The first one is just hard, uninteresting drill work, which includes sprints: repeatedly sprinting and jogging 10-15 metres up and down the rugby field.

The squad jogs around the perimeter of the field, one player after the other in close single file. The person at the back sprints forward past the rest of the team to the front and, once more, reverts to jogging; the next person at the rear goes through the same procedure, and so on. The team can jog for some considerable time, but it is advisable to keep this drill reasonably short, maybe until each player has made three or four sprints then finish. To make these exercises more interesting, a competitive element can be introduced — say, where the backs compete against the forwards in running drills, or players of approximate speed compete against each other. Unfortunately, though this drill training is uninteresting, it is essential. It develops discipline and teamwork, and all players need to strive for greater speed and fitness.

The second category uses more creative methods of achieving the same results. It is amazing the effort that players will put into running, dodging, side-stepping and swerving when they are involved in competitive games with one another. Such competitive outdoor games include touch-rugby, soccer, rugby league and Australian rules, plus variations or combinations of two or more of these. Indoor games that prove worthwhile, particularly when practice outside is impossible — are indoor basketball, volleyball and handball, and again when these games are varied or combined, the desired results can be achieved. Divide the players into different team combinations for these games and drills, using age groups, colours of practice gear, and so on, so that the natural division of the squad into forwards and backs is avoided most of the time. Make all games of short duration, say 5-10 minutes each way, and insist that they are played non-stop at top speed. Strict refereeing by the coach is usually necessary, in fact, essential.

When an individual player wishes to improve his speed outside the rugby season, and not on the athletic track, he can devise a schedule for himself and record and compare the results achieved week by week. Three or four different courses should be selected for this programme, with terrain as varied as a beach, at the water's edge, sand dunes, undulating and low-lying country, a racecourse or park and short steep slopes for repetition work. Distances must be measured carefully, so that times taken can be accurate and therefore results can indicate any improvement. This is hard work at first and improvement will usually be slow, but if the player keeps to the programme and uses various courses, he will achieve better results.

The gear required

I do feel that gear plays an important part in the ability to perform in top-class rugby — particularly boots. I think that today a player who is trying to reach the top must own at least two pairs of rugby boots, one pair with long sprigs and one pair with short sprigs, which can be used according to the weather and the ground conditions.

Also I feel that the placement of sprigs on the boot should be given more consideration, and that players should experiment to establish the most comfortable combination to maintain balance when running. Particularly if a player has the habit of propping or side-stepping off one particular foot, careful placement of the sprigs on the boots can give that player an advantage.

Finally, on this question of gear, it is essential that players keep their gear well maintained. Again I refer to the boots, to the sprigs: if the sprigs are wearing down in a particular place, they should be replaced. Sometimes when I see top players playing in worn-out gear, or boots, when they are striving for top-class performance, it amazes me how they ever get through the game.

New theories on running

There is an increasing awareness of injury prevention in rugby play, and it is interesting that some recent publications advocate quite significant ways of running. One excerpt from one publication is headed 'Close Running'; 'close running' is described as, 'with the ball in hand, the ideal body position for protection is the slightly hunched-over, rather the old-fashioned position advocated in the days when short passing amongst forwards was the fashion. When tackled in this position, the muscles are more rigid and in tone and therefore protective of vital structures such as the head, or the neck. You are also predisposed to rolling and striking the ground thus dissipating the impact.'

In this category is another section on running in the open. It advocates that when running at full speed in the open it is a bad habit to hold the head high and the back arched, as an unexpected tackle from the back will exaggerate this hyperflexion. The ideal running position — when a tackle is imminent — is with the body forward so that the muscles are in a more flexed position, and if the tackle does occur the body is at least prepared to cope with the force of the tackle.

Ken Stewart (on tour in South Africa) shows an ideal running position.
Auckland Star

Fergie McCormick on

Kicking

- **Successful punt kicks require the correct grip of the ball, good balance and timing, head down and leg following through after the kick.**
- **With all kicks except the place kick, the ball drops on the instep — the angle of the instep depends on the type of kick.**
- **Three different methods of place kicking are the 'torpedo', up-and-down, and round-the-corner kick. The success of each method depends on sound placement of the ball, watching the ball, head down, careful run-up and timing, good balance, and power in the kick itself. Follow through after the kick.**
- **Practise with good balls, but also with all types of balls. Kickers should wear the best, most comfortable boots to get the best results. Positioning of the sprigs on the soles is important.**
- **The kick into touch rule requires great skill and has brought a new dimension to the game. Practice is essential.**

Bruce Robertson shows fine balance while punting. Barry Wolmarans, Orange Free State, looks on.
NZ Herald

The punt kick

The phase of play will always dictate how a player approaches the punt — the punt, of course, is kicking a dropped football before it touches the ground. If you're under severe pressure, you should try to come over (or under) your opponent — the angle of the ball on your foot will depend on which you plan to do. For all kicks, you must try to keep your head down and follow the kick through. Try to get a spiral with the ball swinging out at the last second. There are many kickers in New Zealand who can kick the ball a long way, but they don't necessarily get the ball out into touch. Not enough practice. Or they kick it a long way but don't gain any ground.

Too many kickers do not hold the ball correctly and on the correct side of their body — especially if they are aiming for the right-hand touch with the left foot or the left-hand touch with the right foot. Kicking for the right-hand touch with the left foot, you hold the ball on the left-hand side of the body. For the kick with the right foot, you hold the left hand forward and under the ball and the right hand on the back of the ball on its right side. The lacing on the ball is always upwards. For the kick with the left foot, the right hand goes to the front and under the ball, the left hand goes to the left side rear section of the ball. It's just a case of changing hands.

To be a reasonably good kicker you must have your balance right at all times. Tall people seem to have better balance than short people. Mick Williment was a very good example, especially with his follow-through. You don't just

All Black Bevan Wilson kicks for touch.
Peter Bush

A powerful, determined and reliable full-back, devastating in his tackling and accurate in his kicking. Played for Canterbury 1958-75 (Linwood); also South Island 1960-69; NZ Trials 1961-63, 65-73; New Zealand XV 1960, 65; Rest of NZ 1960, 66. Began All Black career in 1965 against the Springboks. Represented NZ again 1967-71 — 43 matches, 16 internationals. In 1969 against the Welsh tourists he created an individual record in international rugby by scoring 24 points. In 16 tests he totalled 121 points and his first-class tally from 310 games was 2065 points. Continued to play for Canterbury until 1975 and toured Europe 1979 with the Cantabrians.

bash at the ball; you 'stalk' it, and let everything flow through your body. It's timing that gets you distance. You must always keep your head down and follow through the line of the kick. As you release the ball, your arms tend to go with your body — as I said, everything flows together.

To achieve the spiral, the broad top of your foot is angled slightly inwards. You don't actually kick *across* the ball as much as *'through'* the ball, which gives the spiral to your kick.

If you are going to kick a high up-and-under, you would rarely spiral it. You would probably lean back a bit on one foot and lift your head slightly, and this tends to put the ball up higher. But it must be practised. The position of the ball on the foot is probably slightly further up the instep of the foot. There again, you keep your head down and follow through; you know where the ball will go, so you don't need to watch where it's going.

You don't throw the ball up — you drop it on to the foot. Most of the action comes from the foot coming up to meet the ball rather than the ball being forced down on to the foot.

The punt kick

Flight path of the spiral punt

The action of the punt kick

Holding the ball for the right foot kick

Holding the ball for the left foot kick

Foot movement for the spiral punt

The drop kick

With a drop kick you need to hold the ball a little further back from its leading end. Again, it's a matter of timing. If you are having a real 'slam' at goal . . . right, then, you let go. But if you are making a drop kick from the 22 metre line or a kick-off at the half-way line, you do tend to lean back slightly and place your kick a bit more — so long as the ball goes past, say, the 10 metre line. From the 22 metre line, you can give it a good slam, for instance, or put it up into the air so that your forwards can get to it.

Some players when kicking point their toe and get it under the ball. Others use their toe. I consider that there is more margin for error when you use the straight toe instead of the instep. In all my kicking I aim to put the instep into the curve of the ball — except for goal kicking.

There is a similarity between the drop kick and the grubber kick, in that you tend to push the ball onto the foot and guide it through. Your aim is to make the ball bounce end over end so that any team-mates following on to the ball will catch it on the bounce — it will either come up to them or it will bounce along a path that they can predict. Again it is kicked from the instep while you are pointing your toe.

One important factor is using your hands, moving your hands to where you will be kicking the ball. If you can get the ball out in front of you — if your team-mate can direct the pass to the front of you — you can see as you receive the ball what opponents are coming at you and where they are coming from. In other words, you can place yourself so that when you receive the ball you can see what options you have. If one of the opposition's big loose forwards is charging down on you, you will have to kick the ball low. If you are being approached from below, you'll probably try to kick it over your opponent. Under severe pressure most kickers tend to lean back as they kick. You've got to get rid of the ball in the best and easiest way possible. No spiral kick or anything. Get it around your opponent or over your opponent. That's the time you do tend to lean back a bit and thus lose balance. (Tilt your toe back a bit so that it does go up and over). At times like this, how you hold the ball is instinctive, really, but most certainly you spread your fingers to maintain good control of the ball.

For a drop kick from the 22 metre line you stand back from the line so that the opposition can't come charging through on you. You judge this and drag your own players back with you. Generally you kick to the side where your forwards are lined up.

What about the other side? There again, if your opponents have dropped their guard, a little push kick through a gap might prove useful, or even a long kick to a gap where a player is out of position way up the field — there you are keeping it away from all of your opposition. The other times you are kicking to your forwards. Obviously you are watching very closely the positions of your own players and your opponents. This is what every kicker should do — before making the kick.

The drop kick

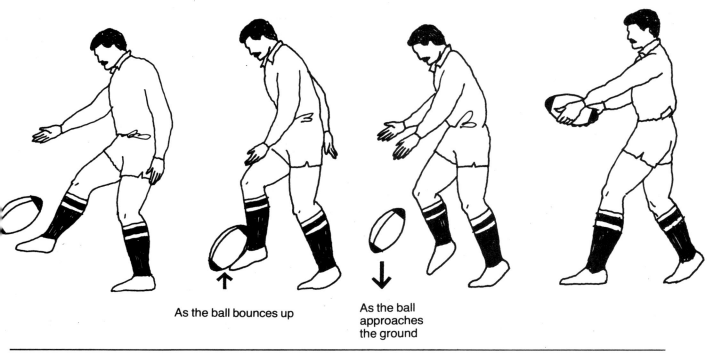

As the ball bounces up

As the ball approaches the ground

Accuracy in kicking

In my time we used the term chip kick to describe a kick that made the ball 'hang' in the air. It's the sort of kick made by a first five-eighth or second five-eighth who runs into a hole and pushes the ball up a bit, not too hard and not too far. This is a kick every player must practise. Unfortunately too many players at training sessions kick a ball around without thinking for 10-15 seconds before they kick how they will kick and what they will be kicking for. But that is the time to practise these things: the grubber kick, the chip kick, kicking for the spot, kicking to each other and trying to land the ball in each other's arms. This is something I used to do, and even now I aim my kick and can put the ball on the spot almost every time.

In many games I played in there were times when accuracy with kicking really paid off — when I was able to push the ball through for my winger. Terry Mitchell had the benefit many times when I grubber kicked through or put the ball round or over his opponent. Terry got the ball and took off, over to the corner for a try. These are the kicks that can really put the pressure on your opponents.

Grant Batty was a wonderful exponent of this. He also had the advantage of being very fast off the mark. A lot of wingers today attempt a centre kick, but the ball goes off the edge of their foot. Here again, it comes back to practice. Ron Jarden used to be able to aim a centre kick at a handkerchief, he was so accurate. Perhaps the rules have changed but I'm still an advocate for the centre kick under the posts.

Ron Jarden was a left-footer. It was a great asset for a team to have a player like him who could return the ball so accurately from the outside of the field. One kick he developed was a high spiral centre kick. He put hours and hours of practice into developing it.

Bruce Watt was the absolute master of putting the opposition's full-back under pressure. He could put the ball on the spot. Adrian Clarke was another. Mac Herewini was another on his day. As a full-back I coped with such kickers by trying to outfox them. There was some luck involved, but it was usually a matter of trying to anticipate the way they would play.

Occasionally I'm asked to give an opinion on the three place-kicking methods that have been advocated over the past 20 years or so. There was the 'torpedo kick' (employed by Bob Scott), the straight up-and-down method (Don Clarke), and the round-the-corner kick (say, Barry John). All have been successful in their own way. I used to use the straight up-and-down method or leaning them over. When I was having a bad patch with a straight up-and-down kick I'd sometimes try the 'torpedo'. But I don't really think the 'torpedo' is more accurate. Buddy Henderson, who was a great kicker, kicked 'torpedoes' and was very accurate, but he did plenty of practice.

Practice is the key to making yourself into a goalkicker. Just practice. Kicking and kicking. But when you're really kicking well, you don't seem to need practice that much. The ball just seems to go over.

The grubber kick

When the grubber kick is useful

The action of the grubber kick

If kicked with the toe pointed, the ball will bounce end over end and in a straight line. It can then be picked up by an attacking team-mate who's on the run.

192

The 'chip' kick

Kick the ball only
just hard enough
and with great accuracy
to ensure it will clear
your opposite and can be
caught by you following up
or caught by a team-mate.

The ball is almost placed
on the foot, higher up
on the instep than for
the usual punt kick.
This will ensure a higher
trajectory, and if the
backlift of the kicking
foot is less, a short
high accurate kick results.

For a grubber kick,
hold the ball
across the body.

The centre kick

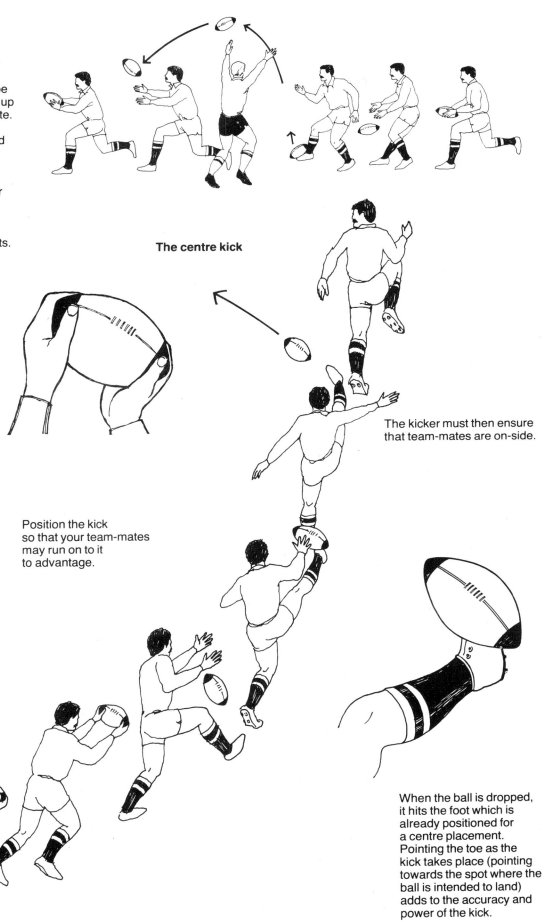

The kicker must then ensure
that team-mates are on-side.

Position the kick
so that your team-mates
may run on to it
to advantage.

When the ball is dropped,
it hits the foot which is
already positioned for
a centre placement.
Pointing the toe as the
kick takes place (pointing
towards the spot where the
ball is intended to land)
adds to the accuracy and
power of the kick.

193

A variation of the tap kick —
the tap and drive. (The tap kick variations illustrated here must be done while your opposition is still regrouping after the giving of the 'penalty' or free kick.)

A useful surprise move near your opposition's line when you have a strong heavy forward pack

A variation of the tap kick —
the tap and scissor

Several supporting team-mates, each running in a different direction and each calling for the ball. The ball-carrier obscures the direction of the pass from the opposition by turning his back to them.

A variation of the tap kick —
the tap and spin

A move to get the ball quickly out to your back line, while the opposition's back line is regrouping for a penalty

A variation of the tap kick —
the tap to better position for a kick

When the opposition is slow to regroup

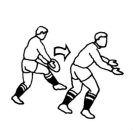

194

Dribbling — a skill of controlling the ball on the ground

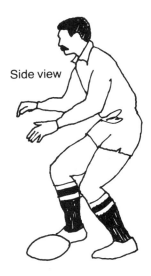
Side view

Although to many dribbling is a lost art, it is a very useful skill when the ball is difficult to handle, perhaps in poor weather conditions, when a fast rush from a loose ball or from a wheel of the scrum is tactically vital. The body is low over the ball, the head well over the ball. Feet are splayed, controlling the ball with the inside of the foot when it is passed (under control) from foot to foot in a zig-zag motion.

One of the great kickers — Barry John takes a conversion. British Isles v New Zealand Third Test, 1971.
National Publicity Studios, Wellington

The place kick

Firstly, you must always make the mark for the ball very sound. Too many players merely place the ball! — it's wobbling in the wind, it's not set properly. It means there will be a margin of error, and it only needs a slight error for you to miss. What about shaping the earth around the ball? With a straight up-and-down, you just dig a hole in the ground with your heel. In the past 'torpedo' kickers, in particular, dug trenches to tee the ball up so as to get the foot underneath the ball. When I used to 'torpedo' I also used to tee the ball up a bit. Different kickers use different methods. There's a story about a player in South Africa who used false teeth to tee the ball up. The grounds do tend to get a bit hard over there! Sand is often used.

Too many kickers place the ball while they're standing up. You must place the ball while you're crouched over the ball, either kneeling or squatting. It is no good just plonking the ball down. I'm a great advocate of knowing when I place the ball where it will be going.

When I stand up and address the ball, I don't take my eyes off it. (Too many kickers do — perhaps it's a nervous reaction.) Once you've seen the direction the ball will take, it's going to go in that direction. As soon as you let your eyes come up, you'll miss the kick — nine times out of ten, you'll miss the kick.

Several kickers place their foot up past the ball. But because of my shorter height, I didn't — I used to stand with both feet together behind the ball. Sometimes I used to stand back a bit from the ball, but this depended on the timing. This is something all kickers have to work out for themselves.

There is not really any difference between kicking against the wind and kicking with the wind. You might try to kick the ball a bit lower against the wind. When you hit the ball properly and judge things properly, the direction of the wind does make a bit of a difference but not a great deal.

You have to be prepared for watery and muddy conditions. In goal kicking you would change the style of your run-up, because on a wet day, your foot tends to slip forward. You would not actually shorten your run but rather take shorter steps, because each foot tends to slip in the mud and by the time you reach the ball you will have picked up 75 to 100 millimetres (3-4 in) and you will be too close to the ball. So therefore you've got to shorten your run and your steps in. You probably would take longer paces on the walk-back and shorter paces on the run-up.

Pick out the best ground surface for your run-up. Sometimes you might have difficulty, but always try to choose the best one you can.

You must have a balanced walk-back. I usually use four steps; some kickers take six; some take seven. So that you are able to use the same pattern coming forwards, you begin your movement forward to the ball with the foot that on the walk-back was put down last. Remember that your power does not come from the run-up — when you goal kick, you tend to 'stalk' the ball. As I come into the kick, I tend to lean forward a bit. It may throw the body off balance, but it does put the head over the ball. It's the last step that you get the power from. So many kickers charge into the ball and mis-time their kick. As an analogy, in a golf shot it's the last half-metre of the swing that you get the power from. In a goal kick it's the last metre, your last pace or, in some instances, the last two paces.

Your head must be down at all times — that is important — but the follow-through is just as important. Too many people miss goals because they stab at the ball. As you follow through, your left arm (if you are a right-foot kicker) goes straight up in the air. Mick Williment was about the most well-balanced goal kicker I've ever seen, because his leg and arm followed through and went up high. My arm used to go slightly out to the left. People have tried to change it, but that was my style and it worked. I kick goals as I see goals, so they go over. Follow-through is essential. Head down over the ball, balance in the run-up and the kick, and use your arm to balance yourself in the follow-through. Don't rush your kick.

The exponents of round-the-corner kicking bring tremendous power into their kicks. All the basics are still there, but they don't seem to concentrate as much; they just plonk the ball down and kick it. (I once gave some advice to a round-the-corner kicker and suggested that he should concentrate more. Then he did as I said and missed many kicks through concentrating too much!)

While you are concentrating, you do hear the crowd noise. But you shut it out. Booing never used to upset me — it used to make me more determined. You've got one thing in mind and that's getting a goal for your team. After all, a kicker is not trying to miss a goal, he's trying to do his best. But a lot of kicks are missed because of this lack of concentration.

Fergie McCormick in action (1969).
NZ Herald

The place kick straight up-and-down

Apart from the angle of the ball to the foot and the ground, there is little difference in the run-up and lining up to suggest that this is a different form of place kick.

The follow through (in this case, a two-armed follow through)

The moment of impact

The final stride

Footprints of a six-pace run-up

Feet together before beginning the run-up

1 2 3 4 5 6

The place kick — the torpedo kick

Line the ball up
with the goal posts.

To accommodate the ball
kick a small trench
with the heel,
then with the toe.

Direction of flight

After placing the ball,
concentrate on it
throughout the walk-back
the run-up and the kick.

Footprints of
a six-pace run-up

1   2   3   4   5   6

Round-the-corner kick (the technique as used by Pierre Villepreux, the great French kicker)

Line up the ball as for the other place kicks.

Pierre Villepreux steps back, then to the side, then moves forwards to the ball in an almost haphazard curve. As he hits the ball, his supporting foot is just behind the ball.

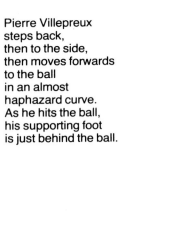

Address the ball from the side rather than from straight behind.

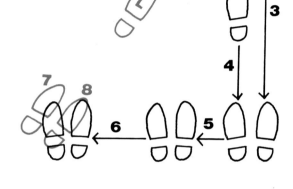

The ball is hit with the instep of the foot.

Because of the side approach to the ball, the leg is allowed to swing in a larger arc than the usual kick, thus giving it greater power. Eyes are on the ball.

Once the foot has kicked straight through the ball, the natural follow through is across the body.

Pause

The kick-off

There's a lot of difference between the technique of kicking a goal and that of kicking off. At the kick-off you aim high enough so that your forwards can get near it when they run after it — at the 10 metre mark. You will probably tend to lean back a bit and stab at the ball.

Your forwards will need a signal from you so that they know you are coming in for your kick. Always make it with your hand. Then the forwards will know when to expect the ball. (When you are training, you must practise signalling.)

For a kick-off you place the ball straight up and down. If you are going for a long one over the line, you might lean the ball back a bit. You try to kick the ball to the opposition's weakest position. (Under the goal posts is a long way to bring the ball back from!) If the opponent you are kicking towards is a strong right-foot kicker, you try to kick it near the right-hand touch so that he won't have a lot of room to clear his kick from. So in a long kick you would usually be trying to put the opposition's full-back under pressure.

The 'funny' kick-off, as a variation — where you look as though you are planning to kick one way but then kick the other — requires a lot of practice. If you are going to kick a 'funny' kick, you must kick it into an area that will put your opponents under pressure. Too many 'funny' kicks turn into good ball for your opposition if you are not careful.

Everything needs to be practised. What has crept into the game of rugby over the past few years has been a lack of basic skills: catching a high ball, kicking with the ball after you've caught it — things like that.

There is quite a lot of difference between a drop kick at half-way and a place kick. There is more room for error in a drop kick, because the ball is moving when you kick it. When you are place-kicking, the ball is on the ground and it's not going to move away.

Your kick is aimed to go fairly high and to come down at the 10 metre line, especially if you are kicking for your forwards. You try to bring it down on an opponent who has a weakness — perhaps a hooker who is not a good kicker of the ball. Not many forwards can kick the ball well. You aim the ball at that opponent because you know that as well as getting the ball he's going to get at least one of your own players! Or you put the ball high enough so that one of your own players will be able to get through on it and catch it, and get it back.

The kicker's training

All rugby players need a thorough warm-up before a match and at the start of a training session. I think a kicker must get the kicking muscles stretched (as should any rugby player), especially the hamstrings. The warm-up needs to concentrate on the muscles from the waist down: in the thigh, the backs of the legs, and the ankles.

To practise kicking during training sessions, we have a team game in which you are allowed two passes out, then one in. After that you must kick — kick for space. It's a bit like Australian rules football. Players learn to watch where they kick. Others learn to cut the gaps or take the ball under pressure. Too much practice in merely kicking to another player can get you into a bad habit for a game. These games take the boredom away from a practice session.

Sometimes I make the players kick only with the left foot. That's quite amusing actually. For any right footer trying to develop the left foot, or any left footer trying to develop the right, you've just got to practise. Don't feel awkward. If you're walking along a street and you've got a handful of stones, you can practise kicking the stones — or a tennis ball. Have it in mind that sometimes you've got to use your right foot and sometimes your left — keep reversing it. That's the way I learned. It's a matter of getting into your mind that

when you kick with the opposite foot you just reverse the action. You just change sides. Some kickers try to kick with their left foot across their body, whereas if you hold the ball on the left side the movement comes easily.

It helps if you can practise with fairly new balls, while they've still got their shape and the leather is in good condition. However, using many different balls will get you accustomed to kicking anything. In a match you cannot be certain what the condition of the ball will be. I know a lot of kickers who criticise the condition of the ball. I used to grumble myself — perhaps that's the easy way out.

Different types of balls are used in different countries. In England and France I had no trouble adjusting to the type of ball. In South Africa, on the other hand, the ball is made of a chrome leather, which is quite different from the natural leather used in New Zealand.

For individual practice you must begin with as many balls as you can beg, borrow or steal. You must start to practise right under the goal posts so that you get your rhythm right at the 25 metre line straight out in front. Then try kicking from a distance. No kicker should ever attempt a shot at the goal early in a match if there is any doubt about it being successful. The reason for this is that if it's a bit of a strain on him and he misses, he'll probably miss them all day. He'll be straining all day for kicks that he should never have to strain for.

Nowadays there is so much criticism of kickers who miss goals (and in my time playing test matches, I was the subject of criticism), but I don't think the standard of goal kickers is necessarily lower than it has been in the past. However, I do think that the basic skills the rugby player needs are often not practised sufficiently. That applies to running, catching, passing, kicking, tackling — you can't make it without practising.

The around-the-corner kickers, for example, need to practise as much as the 'torpedo' or straight up-and-down kickers to get their timing right. If you get your timing right, and your balance right, everything seems to fall into place.

The changing laws

The kick into touch rule, with its emphasis on bouncing the ball out, has made some changes in the way you kick the ball. Instead of merely 'popping' it out, when you kick it out you must kick it very hard with a grubber kick so that it can't be knocked down or spring up into a winger's arms. I must admit that getting the ball out never used to worry me. If there was any doubt I used to kick it out on the full. The new rule has made players more conscious of the way that they are going to kick the ball.

I've noticed Karam and a few other full-backs tend to put the ball far down the field; they try to get too much distance, but often they get one load of trouble. Slightly up and under balls that they could retrieve. Or one in front of their forwards would open the game up with an advantage for their side.

Even at a national level I've seen the kick for ground too long, giving the ball, and the advantage to the opposition. I think that the kick into touch rule has made all players very conscious of where they are when the ball goes back over their heads. If they don't get back and help a full-back or winger under pressure, then they're in a lot of trouble.

Following the introduction of the new rule with the direct and indirect free kick, there has developed the idea of doing a tap and then having a drop kick at goal. I haven't played in many matches where this has taken place, but here again you must practise it.

All Black front row, left to right: Gary Knight, Andy Dalton and John Ashworth.
Peter Bush

Boots and sprigs

Generally, I don't think that rugby players look after their feet on the rugby field. Your feet do a lot of running on the field. Top players are realising now how much pleasure they can get out of their rugby by wearing good comfortable boots. My boots were always well made — I made sure of that. You see boys who can't afford to buy good boots wearing hand-downs from their older brothers — this is negative.

I always use a hard toe-cap for kicking. On rare occasions I have gone out on the field with soft toes — and kicked the ball with soft toes — but I don't find it as comfortable. I recommend a hard-toed boot for kickers — a strong boot, and as light as possible. So many boots come out that are very light, but the strength in the basic boot is not good enough for kicking.

There is always argument about sprigs being too high or too low — we do have a size specified in the laws, of course. Forwards seem to like five or six sprigs in the front, so that they can get a good grip for pushing in the scrum. I've used only four studs on my boots — two on the front and two on the back — and that has been enough for me. All kickers have their own thing about boots. It depends upon what you get used to. There's no basic pattern.

The spectacular kick

One really phenomenal kick that impressed me was made by Pierre Villepreux, when France played the All Blacks at Lancaster Park, Christchurch, in 1968. He kicked a goal by hooking the ball out of the mud 5 metres inside his own half. In Wellington he kicked a goal from 10 metres inside his own half, and the ball seemed to be still going up when it went over the cross-bar.

The 'battle' for power up front. All Blacks v Springboks.
Peter Bush

Ron Jarden on

Beating the Man

- **Agility, body contact and kicking are three ways to beat an opponent; of the three, agility is the most important.**
- **An agile mind coupled with natural physical assets is the base for the development of skills to beat an opponent.**
- **Most skills used to beat an opponent depend on running at a controlled speed in short strides.**
- **Basic skills required to beat an opponent must be practised thoroughly, and the success on the field is usually in proportion to the time spent in practice.**
- **The physical size and speed of a rugby player usually dictates the most appropriate method to use to beat an opponent.**

The great paradox of rugby football is that on one hand it should be regarded as the pastime of the 'muddied oaf' and on the other hand require agility of mind and body as its foremost prerequisite. Today the 'oaf' finds a place on the sideline, while the quick thinker and agile runner, whether back or forward, dominates on the field of play. The characteristics that distinguish the international player from the club player narrow to two basic factors — the ability to make the right decision and the ability to put that decision into effect.

One can do very little to develop nimbleness of mind, but all rugby players can do a great deal towards developing those body skills which will enable them to beat their opposite numbers. There is no point in a player making a correct decision and then being incapable of carrying it out, and nothing creates more anguish during a game than to have a scoring opportunity wasted because a player cannot execute the basic move which will enable him to beat his opponent. There are, of course, several skills which a player can develop in order to beat his man. They fall into three main categories: agility, body contact and kicking.

Beating an opponent by agility

In this section I want to consider the skills that I consider to be the most important of all — agility skills — the skills that enable a player to carry out a move on the field of play by balance, speed and nimbleness. Agility has of course been the keynote of most great rugby backs, for by their agility they effect the rapid changes of pace and direction that result in the breaks being made. Agility is often synonymous with a short stride. The greatest backs, for example, have usually been those with short strides or at least those who can make use of a short stride when it is necessary. The long-legged, bowling runner often needs time in which to make the limbs obey the brain's instruction, and this player's swerve, side-step or dodge is rarely so effective. Agility can be developed. The ability to swerve and side-step can definitely be improved by practice and application, and while natural aptitude gives a player a great start in the attaining of these skills, there is no reason why any player, with correct application, should not become proficient at them. Similarly, while speed off the mark is mainly a natural characteristic, every player can improve in this respect with practice.

The most important thing to remember about any of the moves I discuss here is that none of them can be accomplished when the player is running at full speed. A player who is running 'flat out' appears to have no control whatsoever over his running. I have found that running at full speed produces a peculiar weakness in the legs, as if all the effort used in maintaining maximum speed cannot be spared for anything else. Even at 80 per cent of top speed a tremendous amount can be accomplished in comparison, and it would benefit each player to experiment and realise exactly what I mean by this difference.

Three-quarter running — Stu Wilson running with the ball. All Blacks v Australia
Peter Bush

Bevan Wilson uses a strong fend to evade the tackle of Lions player G. L. Evans in the Third Test, Dunedin, 1977.
Scott A. G. M. Crawford

The late Ron Jarden was one of New Zealand's most outstanding wing three-quarters and most prodigious scorers. Played for Wellington 1949-56 (University); also North Island 1950, 52-56; NZ Trials 1953, 55, 56; New Zealand XV 1952, 54-56; NZ Universities 1951-56. Selected for the All Blacks in 1951 and remained a NZ representative until 1956. Played total of 37 matches (16 internationals). Retired at 26 after 134 first-class games in which he scored 945 points, tallying a NZ try record of 145.

The side-step

The object of a side-step is to change direction abruptly at right angles to the line of running, and by so doing evade a would-be tackler. It is important to realise, however, that it also involves an equally abrupt change of pace. It is practically impossible to side-step at high speed, because of the tremendous strain that is thrown upon the ankle and knee joints when the change of direction is executed. The side-step, therefore, is the characteristic attacking move of an inside back or three-quarter who is not running at full speed, because the change of pace is just as important for success as the change of direction.

There are two types of side-step. One is a change of step followed by an immediate step at right angles; the other a mere push-off abruptly at a right angle to the direction of the run. (The difference can be seen in the illustration.) The side-step is almost invariably undertaken to evade an opponent coming from immediately in front or from the direction in which the side-step is made. Let us assume that the side-step is to be taken to the left . . . As the defender approaches, the attacking player calculates how far away the opponent is and decides to make that side-step at a certain point. A side-step to the left must obviously be taken off the right foot . . . As the diagram illustrates, instead of the left foot passing the right foot (as in a normal pace), it merely comes up to the right foot, and the right foot advances again to the ground to enable the step to the left to be made. This is nowhere near as difficult to achieve as it is to describe, and a little practice will make the point clear.

Maximum effort must be reserved for the actual step to the side. This step must be as wide as possible and must be at a right angle to the original line of running. If the player is running too quickly the momentum will carry the body on, over the right foot, and the player will not be able to make the necessary change of direction.

The body, arms and hands also play their part, and this is the aspect in which the skilled side-steppers shine. As (in our example) the right foot is coming forward, the right shoulder is dipped, and the arms carrying the ball in front of them move across to the right. All these movements combine to bring an opponent up short, imagining that the ball-carrier is going to pass him on his left-hand side. It is at this moment that the right foot of the attacking player is dug firmly into the ground and the whole body is launched to the left. With a burst of acceleration the attacker then passes completely by the right-hand side of the opponent, and through the gap that has been created.

In the alternative method of side-stepping — the push-off abruptly at a right angle to the direction of the run — the attacker realises that the right foot will come to the ground at the desired spot without necessitating a change of pace, so merely runs to the required spot and accomplishes exactly the same result. The side-step, of course, need not be a single action, but can be repeated immediately in order to beat a second opponent. But a note of warning here: the player at all costs must avoid the temptation to continue side-stepping across the field. The words of my club coach, Dr Uttley, are as true today as they have ever been: 'If you go in, go out.' In other words, once the side-step has been accomplished and the gap created, it is imperative for the play to be straightened up through the gap and contact made once again with the players outside.

Two basic side-steps

The first side-step involves a hop on one leg (here, the right) and a rapid side-step with the other foot to off-balance your opponent.

Hop

R foot

The other side-step involves a 'prop' from one foot and a side-step to carry you away from an off-balanced opponent.

R foot

L foot

R foot

R foot

The swerve

By running in on to the inside shoulder of your opponent . . .

You force your opponent to slow down and turn to prevent a break on the inside.

At the moment your opponent stops, your sudden movement outside again will catch your opponent off guard.

The swerve

The swerve differs from the side-step in that it is accomplished at speed and does not involve the same abrupt change of direction or change of pace. Sheer speed will rarely enable us to beat our opposite number unless we have enough room in which to move, and that very rarely happens on the field of play . . . So to beat one's opponent one must rely not only upon speed, but also upon change of speed and change of direction.

Look at it this way. The easiest opponent to beat on a field is one who is standing still while the ball-carrier is travelling at full speed. Obviously the difference in their speeds is as great as it possibly can be, and therefore the attacker has the easiest possible task. This situation rarely occurs on the field of play, but the theory of beating an opponent is still based on the fact that one should always attempt to create the greatest possible difference in speed between the attacker and the defender. This is why we swerve and side-step rather than merely try to run straight past an opponent.

The swerve is best executed when attacker and defender are approaching each other from a relatively large distance, say 15 metres or more. If the attacker merely runs around the arc of the circle, the defender has a simple task in cutting off the attacker's run. So the attacker must make the defender uncertain about which side the attacker is going to run, and must make his opponent come as near to stopping as possible, while still himself running at speed.

The simplest way to make an opponent stop is to run straight at him, and this is always the first move when the swerve is being accomplished. (Imagine yourself in the defender's position . . . You are coming nicely across the field towards an attacker heading straight for the goal line. All of a sudden the attacker turns and runs straight at you. The only thing you can do in this instance is to stop, for if you continued running across the field the attacker would simply run past behind you. So you are now in two frames of mind. You are not sure which side the attacker is going to attempt to pass you . . . The attacker has gained the initiative, by introducing an element of considerable doubt in the defender's mind.)

It is obviously necessary for the attacker to decide at the outset which side of the defender to pass on. Usually this is the outside nearest the sideline, for usually this part of the field is clear of the cover defence. Once the attacker has made the decision, then it is important that he should, when

207

running at the defender, aim at the defender's inside shoulder (assuming that he is ultimately going to swing outside his opponent). By running at that inside shoulder the attacker forces the defender into straightening up and slowing down. That hesitation may be all that is needed to enable the attacker to accomplish his change of direction around to the outside and get through to the goal line. A controlled, balanced run — not full speed — is absolutely necessary until the very last moment, when the attacker swings round outside his opponent. By running at less than top speed and even slowing down as he approaches, the attacker thereby introduces the other important part of the swerve — the change of pace. If the attacker runs at the same speed throughout the movement, it is much easier for the defender to gauge the point at which a tackle should be launched. It is far more difficult for the defender to accomplish this if the attacker, having approached at a certain speed, swings away with a change of direction accompanied by acceleration.

Once the attacker has turned towards the defender and is running at the defender's inside shoulder, the important thing is to decide when to make that dash to the outside and how to go about it. The decision is a matter of judgement depending on the distance the attacker is from the sideline, the speed of the opponent, and the ultimate speed of the attacker. The less room that is available for the attacker, the closer will he have to run towards his opponent before the swing outside is made . . .

The change of direction is abrupt, and for that crucial sway in and sudden burst of acceleration ouside, the attacker must actually slow down and be completely balanced at the moment the direction of running is changed. As with the side-step, the whole deception can be accentuated by the attacker's arms and body as he approaches the defender. I found it helpful to look at the defender's inside shoulder and move my hands across towards the inside to help the deception. When I had 20 metres or so to make my opponent straighten up, a few dips of the shoulder in-field every two or three strides reinforced the defender's belief that I planned to get through on the inside. The essence of the swerve is deception, and that deception should be carried out with every possible ruse the attacker can conjure up. At no stage should the attacker give the defender time to think or time to assess what is going to happen. A couple of players I have known have even talked at their opponent, or whistled at him in order to add to his state of confusion.

Once the change of direction has been accomplished — when the right foot (in our example) has been thrust down and the attacker wheels to the outside — it is then flat out for the corner flag. From that stage onwards the deception has gone. There is no point now in doing anything else but run at top speed.

The swerve is, of course, the great attacking weapon of the wing three-quarter, or the centre who is alone unmarked. Only rarely does an inside back have sufficient space to manipulate an opponent into the situation described above. Even the wing three-quarter rarely has a chance to make the opponent stop or slow down significantly. In many instances, particularly if the opponent is right on top of the winger, the only thing the winger can do is to receive the pass from a team-mate, swing in towards the opponent, then swing out again immediately, trusting that the defender has hesitated sufficiently to allow the attacker to get through on the outside. If an attacking winger who has the sideline near at hand can during his swerve make his opponent stop short by just 15 centimetres, then he may be able to get through a seemingly impossible gap.

The basic skills described above must be practised thoroughly in order that the player may meet the innumerable situations that arise on the field of play. Very rarely do you have the opportunity to execute a swerve or a side-step in what may be called the purest form. Most often players find themselves executing something that is half-way between the two because of the circumstances. Though it is impossible to lay down conditions for the use of either the side-step or the swerve, there are certain basic points to be remembered . . .

Lions back, David Duckham, swerves past two Wanganui defenders and heads towards the goal line. Lions v Wanganui, 1971.
Evening Post

It is essential that an attacking back make the fullest use of the space available between himself and his opponents. In no circumstances should he manoeuvre his opponent into position for a side-step when the same opponent could be effectively beaten by a swerve. The side-step involves loss of pace and loss of time. The swerve enables momentum to be achieved and maintained, allowing the team's whole back line to sweep through in a concerted drive to the goal line. A player who swerves is himself making ground, while the side-stepper is not and most often has to rely on team-mates to regain the forward impetus lost when the side-step was executed. While inside backs must of necessity rely upon an effective side-step, outside backs should use this move only as a last resort, and concentrate on maintaining their pace at all costs.

There is one final note I should like to add regarding beating one's opponent by agility. It is always difficult for a player to determine exactly when to make the break against an opponent. The player may already have decided to side-step, but the question is when is the best time to do it. A very good practice, which many competent players follow, is to watch the feet of an approaching defender, and if a break is to be made to the right then to make it when the defender's left foot is on the ground. When this happens the defender's weight will also be on the left side of the body, and before turning to grasp an attacker passing on that side the defender must take another step before pushing off to his left to make the tackle. This applies particularly to the side-step. If the attacker decides to make a straight diagonal run inside the opponent, it is again best to choose the moment when the defender's inside foot is forward.

The dummy

With the dummy, the element of deception is carried even further. The success and frequency of a dummy pass depend entirely on the wisdom of the defender. I say wisdom because this is a combination of intelligence and experience. There are some opponents, particularly in club matches, who will 'buy' a dummy on any occasion. In test matches a long period of orthodox passing by the five-eighth may be necessary before an opponent is lulled into thinking that this will continue indefinitely. Whether it takes five minutes or 50 minutes, it is necessary to establish this element of deception before the dummy can be effectively carried out.

The dummy pass is simply executed by following out every motion of a normal pass except that the ball is not let go, but is retained by the attacker at the last moment and followed by a side-step or swerve, depending on which side the opponent is to be beaten. Emphasising the passing motion helps the deception. It is surprising how often a defender will straighten up and not attempt to tackle when seeing an attacker in the middle of a pass: 'It is too late now. The ball is on its way and nothing I can do will prevent it.' These are the defenders who can be easily deceived by a dummy, for by straightening up and slackening off the momentum of their tackle, they intimate to an attacker that they are prepared to concede he is going to pass the ball.

There are many occasions during a match when the opposition can be 'sold' into thinking that something is going to happen, when the reverse is actually the case. The dummy pass can, of course, be given inside or outside. The former is a particularly effective way of creating a gap on the outside of an opponent, as the opponent almost inevitably straightens up when seeing the attacker preparing to reverse pass the ball infield. Before the defender can realise what is happening, the attacker can retain the ball and swing away to the outside without a hand being laid on him . . .

Dummy calls are an essential part of advanced team plays, and the widely advertised moves that are only a cover for an alternative provide a great source of satisfaction for the team initiating them. One dummy that should never be believed is when a tackled player, still on his feet, calls 'No ball' and continues with the ball in his hand when the opponent lets him go. It's surprising how often even this rudimentary deception succeeds against gullible opposition.

The fend — the push-off

In the push-off, a player with good strength and weight pushes on to the opponent at a critical point as the opponent is moving into tackle and forces the opponent away.

Beating an opponent by body contact

Before discussing the moves by which an opponent can be beaten by direct body contact, I'd like to make one point. Unless a player is so constricted that there is no alternative method of beating an opponent (which would be a very poor state of affairs), these moves should be used only as alternative rather than as the prime means of offence. Whenever a player comes into contact with another, he is slowed down and is more vulnerable to being caught from behind. In addition, each impact reduces his strength and stamina, and over 80 minutes of hard play must reduce his ability to participate fully in the game, particularly during the latter stages when it may be most necessary for him to give of his best.

Nevertheless, for a player of suitable build and strength these moves are an essential part of the repertoire, and the player who can combine them with the agility skills described above is indeed fortunate.

The fend

Often there is not sufficient room for an opponent to be avoided by any of the moves described above, and the attacker has no choice but to beat the opponent by body contact. The fend is a most useful form of offence, even for a relatively small player. Its purpose is to enable an attacker to push himself away from his opponent by bringing the heel of his hand into contact with part of his opponent's body. It can be accomplished in two ways: by an attacker actually pushing himself away from the defender; or by the attacker pushing the defender away from him. Only the strong player or player who is heavier than the opponent can succeed with the latter method. But all players should develop the ability to use the first method successfully, and often a lighter player is more successful with it than the heavier one.

The attacker should try to avoid having to fend off an opponent who is coming straight at him — the arm is seldom strong enough for this method to succeed. It is most effectively used against an opponent coming at an oblique angle or from right angles.

The attacker must approach the defender with the fending arm bent. (If the arm is stretched straight out, it could be grasped by an opponent and the attacker will finish up in an

aeroplane spin.) The defender must not have an opportunity to know when the fend is actually going to be delivered, and the arm must move so fast that it cannot be grabbed as the attacker approaches. As with hitting a golf ball or a tennis ball, the essence of the exercise is timing. If the attacker runs with the arm outstretched, the fend has no speed except that of the velocity of the run. The impact of the attacker's hand on the defender can be trebled if the arm is suddenly straightened and the hand shot out to push the defender in the desired place. We then have body velocity plus arm velocity, which is infinitely more devastating. The best contact points are the heel of the hand under the defender's chin or under the defender's nose, or on the point of defender's shoulder.

It is necessary to distinguish clearly between the fend and the push-off. With the fend an opponent is pushed away from the attacker, but with the push-off an opponent who has come in for a very low tackle is pushed down to the ground.

The push-off

With the push-off — used to evade a would-be tackler who is coming round the knees or the ankles — the same principles apply, except that the opponent is bending over and thus can be forced on to the ground by a well-directed shove from above. At the same time, the attacker can lever himself away from the outstretched arms of his opponent and force himself clear of the tackle. Normally, the tackler who approaches too low is simply grasped by the top of his head and pushed, nose first, on to the ground. A handful of hair can be a great help!

The bump

A player should think twice about the bump as a means of attack unless the opponent is at least 3 kg (7 lb) lighter. For the suitably built player, however, this is a method of offence that can be effective. I emphasise that one should never bump unless it is absolutely essential, for it does slow down the attacker. Even when deliberately bumping, it is best to try for contact that is more oblique than head-on. This will enable the attacker to bounce off at a tangent and thus keep going — more easily than if the contact jars the attacker almost to a standstill.

As with the fend, there is more to a bump than would seem at first sight. Quite often we see big forwards who, despite their weight, merely seem to run into their opponents rather than bump them; a really effective bumper even though he may be smaller than these big forwards, can achieve a devastating effect against them. One calls to mind Ted Woodward of England and Tom Katene, Eric Boggs and Jack MacLean of New Zealand, all of whom were most accomplished bumpers in their day. These men achieved with their hips what the good fender accomplishes with the hand. They didn't merely run into an opponent, but accompanied the velocity of their run with a swinging of the hips at the right moment which added considerable force to the contact they made with their opponents.

The bump is best effected by the attacker crouching over towards his opponents as he nears him, then straightening up and driving his hip or shoulder into the defender as the two players meet.

The fend — the push-away

Here a smaller player pushes off an incoming opponent to change direction

The bump

The tackle of an opponent is broken by a timed movement of the hips and thighs.

Breaking from the tackle

Though a good tackle will always accomplish its objective, a defender is seldom in a position to launch himself at the ball-carrier in exactly the desired manner. On many occasions the ball-carrier is moving away from, or has suddenly moved into the defender, and most tackles, although they may bring the player down, are rather imperfectly executed. It becomes important, therefore, to take full advantage of any opportunities to break free from an imperfect tackle. To my knowledge this is an aspect of the game that is rarely discussed, and to which attention should be paid. The ball-carrier must keep running at all costs, even when the defender's arms are actually around his thighs. The strong aggressive runner who keeps his legs moving will, on many occasions, break free, and one often sees opportunities lost because a player has given in to the tackle as soon as he feels the defender's arms around him.

When the tackle becomes inevitable, this is the time for the ball-carrier to use strength and every means to break free. I found that even though the tackle had actually forced me to the ground, I was often able to break clear sufficiently to regain my feet and continue play. Sometimes it was possible to jump out of the tackle by using a push-off as the tackler's arms came round my legs. The last thing a tackler expects is to have the ball-carrier try to raise his legs out of the tackle before he has reached the ground, and on many occasions the tackle is made without the arms being drawn tightly around the ball-carrier's legs. By bringing the knees sharply upwards and by pushing vigorously against the tackler's shoulder, you may not always succeed in jumping clear but will yet manage to land on the ground sufficiently out of the tackle to regain your feet. I suggest that the moment to start running after a tackle is not when the ground is reached, but as soon as the attacker feels himself falling towards it.

The hardest part about getting to your feet from a tackle is drawing the knees sufficiently under the body. I found that the easiest time to do this (particularly on hard grounds) was during the first bounce which one always makes when landing on the ground in a tackle. The human body, like almost everything else, has sufficient resilience to bounce a couple of centimetres off the ground, and this is the opportunity for the aggressively-minded player to draw the knees up and start moving again towards the goal line. Once that first fraction of a second is lost, the task is made considerably harder, for by this time the tackler is usually hanging on in a determined effort to make the attacker stay on the ground as long as the laws will allow.

When held

When held, bring up your knees so that you can spring up with the use of them and your spare arm, and move away before you have been prevented from passing the ball.

The art of beating a man.

RELAX WAL'—I'LL HAVE THE NIGGLY OLD BEGGAR IN ME POWER AS SOON AS I CATCH HIS EYE!

Murray Ball.

Robin O'Neill on

Tackling

- **Tackling requires determination, courage, confidence, timing and balance.**
- **There are three types of tackles: side-on, frontal and rear — frontal and rear can be smother tackles.**
- **Practising tackling should be carried out at a slow pace to develop techniques by both tackler and ball-carrier. Training aids include tackling bags and rubber tubes.**
- **Getting in close before the tackle is essential, and players should be up on their feet as soon as possible.**
- **It is a wise coach who sets time aside at training sessions to develop the players' skills in the art of tackling and being tackled. The results will show in fewer injuries and fewer points for the opposition.**

Tackling is and always has been one of the finest and most satisfying individual skills in the game. It is an art requiring many qualities — courage, concentration, confidence, timing and balance. Likewise, *being tackled* demands similar qualities.

When a tackle is properly executed, both parties can absorb the physical demands and pressures without injury and they can noticeably enjoy the experience — either as tackler or as ball-carrier. Tackling techniques and their execution are skills available to each and every player — more so than other eye-catching skills — and provide an excellent medium for all players to make a positive contribution to the team effort. Properly executed, the tackle is a joy to behold. Ill-conceived efforts such as head-high tackles, foot trips, still-arm tackles, scragging, and even ankle taps bring discredit to the skill itself, as well as to the player, team, coach and the game. The 'one-handed' tap in touch rugby is rather encouraging to a one-armed high tackle, but it should be banned and the two-handed touch used instead.

The statistics reveal that lack of skill and lack of fitness account for something like 80 per cent of all sports injuries; which means that most are preventable, and this is clearly the case in tackling.

In a week-long survey in new Zealand in July 1977, carried out by the Accident Compensation Commission, rugby contributed something like 43 per cent of all sports injuries. (Obviously with 190 000 active enthusiasts the rate could be expected to be high!) Of the 174 rugby injuries incurred during the week of the survey, 26 (or 15 per cent) related to tackling. Of these, 24 concerned the ball-carrier and only two the tackler — a rather surprising statistic.

Coaching the skills

Tackling provides a challenge to a player — even, in some instances, when that player is the ball-carrier! A player must ultimately have the motivation to make that vital tackling drive at the right time, but nevertheless, in the hands of a skilful, patient and helpful coach with a progressively balanced training programme, many a player will overcome any hesitation about tackling. Once the sweet taste of success is savoured, players respond well and become keener to retain the skill and repeat the effort.

It is interesting to observe the paucity of reference to tackles, either by photographs or by written accounts, in the numerous tour review books that appear these days. Tries, penalty kicks, etc, seem to be far more popular topics. Is it because the authors have never enjoyed the deep sense of satisfaction that skilful tackling gives? Or is it symptomatic of a decline in the art of tackling?

Coaches of teams of all grades can encourage the players to tackle well:
- by developing team-approved techniques for the skill of tackling and being tackled
- by building up the standard of physical all-round conditioning of the players' bodies

Training sessions must include a range of exercises aimed at 'hardening' the body.

For the tackler, a positive approach is vital, positioning equally so, eyes must be open at all times, and the arms, shoulders, hands and fingers need to be in tip-top physical condition.

For the ball-carrier, a positive approach is also necessary. The ball-carrier must be able to 'ride' the tackle and fall correctly. The player must be in top physical condition to be able to absorb the driving force of the tackler and the subsequent contact with the ground.

There are basically only three types of tackles: side on; frontal; and rear. On the field of play these are usually executed as: side on, low; frontal, low; frontal, high; frontal, smother; rear, low; rear, smother.

A strong back tackle, Hawkes Bay v Springboks, 1965.
Evening Post

Played for Manawatu 1961-65 and Waikato 1967 — both as a midfield back and loose forward. Following retirement in 1967 was involved in the selection and coaching of many clubs, subunion and union teams at various grades with great success. Member of NZRFU National Coaching College 1977-81. Describes himself as 'Just another mad rugby lover.'

The side-on tackle
— the tackler's role

- Do approach the ball-carrier at an angle to keep your opponent running one way.
- Do use your right shoulder if approaching from the left (use your left shoulder if approaching from the right).
- Do make the tackle as and where you want it.
- Do aim to strike the middle of your opponent's thigh (midway between waist and knees); with your head to the side behind.
- Do keep your eyes open at all times.
- Do tackle with a shoulder drive, getting both your feet off the ground to promote momentum.
- Do keep your head behind the ball-carrier as you take the tackle and as you fall on top of your opponent.
- Do make full use of your arms — hold tightly even as you are slipping down further over legs.

- Don't go too high and into a fend, nor too low and miss altogether.
- Don't forget to accelerate in the last couple of strides, otherwise you will fall on your opponent's knees and boots.
- Don't watch the ball-carrier's hands or body movements. Watch the ball-carrier's legs and feet.
- Don't be half-hearted in the effort — that's asking for trouble.
- Don't forget those techniques you practised so well.
- Don't dive like a swimmer — drive off one leg.
- Don't forget to be first up to play the ball.

The side-on tackle

The tackled player must release the ball once he hits the ground or once his knees touch the ground.

The side-on tackle
— the ball-carrier's role

- Do carry the ball away from an intending tackler.
- Do lean your body into the tackler — sometimes swing your hip or buttock into the tackling shoulder.
- Do consider use of a fend, swerve or side-step to avoid the tackle.
- Do relax your body as you fall if the tackle is successful.
- Do try to turn and present the ball (either on ground or on your body) to team-mates.
- Do use your free arm to help break the fall (if possible).

- Don't keep the ball in the stomach area as you fall.
- Don't forget to release the ball immediately when the ball touches the ground.
- Don't forget that you must be up and on both feet to play the ball.
- Don't forget to get up quickly and move to support team-mates.
- Don't forget to make a mental assessment of the power and tackling ability of that particular tackler — for future use.
- Don't throw a wild pass while involved in a tackle.

The frontal low tackle
— the tackler's role

- Do place your head to one side, adopt a crouched position, head well forward, legs well bent, and back rounded. Eyes open all the time.
- Do encourage a moving opponent to run into your shoulder.
- Do try to get both your knees and head on the same side of the ball-carrier.
- Do try to wrap the ball-carrier's knees tightly with your arms and allow the ball-carrier's momentum to carry both bodies back and down.
- Do retain a rounded back and perform backward roll (which can prevent the back of your head from hitting the ground with any great force).
- Do remember to twist in the tackle so as to get on top after tackle.
- Do be first up to play the ball.
- Do generate your own drive as the ball-carrier is static.

- Don't forget to keep your head to one side and away from the ball-carrier's knees.
- Don't lean back at all.
- Don't be half-hearted in the effort.
- Don't forget the techniques practised so well.

The frontal low tackle
— the ball-carrier's role

- Do try to drive in with your hip or lower shoulder, with the ball held away from the tackler.
- Do ensure that your body twists and that the ball is presented to your team-mates.
- Do drive your legs with power to break the tackler's arm-clasp.
- Do relax your body as you fall, keeping the ball away from your stomach area.

- Don't forget to release the ball as soon as it touches the ground.
- Don't forget you must be up on both feet to play the ball.
- Don't throw a wild pass when falling in a tackle.
- Don't forget to get up quickly and move to support team-mates.
- Don't forget to mentally record the effectiveness of this tackler's tackle — for future reference.

The frontal low tackle

The frontal high tackle
— the tackler's role

- Do try to make the tackle high, endeavouring to lock the ball-carrier's arms firmly against his body with the ball well locked between.
- Do hold on tightly with a strong grip.
- Do cushion your fall by spinning or turning the ball-carrier who will then take the impact on the ground.
- Do — if the situation doesn't allow drive or power by either ball-carrier or tackler — try to hold and turn the ball-carrier in an upright position for your team-mates to gain access to the ball.
- Do — if well away from goal line — try to aim for the ball-carrier's stomach area.
- Do — if attempting a crash tackle — lead in with your shoulder. The target area is anywhere between the chest and the knees of the ball-carrier.

- Don't turn your head too far aside, otherwise the tackle will be made with your neck.
- Don't forget to be first up and look for the ball (if not over the try line).
- Don't forget that the ball-carrier may side-step or swerve, which may turn the tackle into a 'side tackle'.
- Don't forget that if the ball-carrier is running at pace, round your back and neck to reduce the impact of the fall.

The frontal high tackle
— the ball-carrier's role

- Do drive with power through the tackle.
- Do use a low shoulder to effect penetration, with a possible 'lift' at the time of impact.
- Do twist and present the ball to team-mates.

- Don't forget to turn and keep the ball away from the tackler.
- Don't forget you must be up on the ground with both feet to play the ball.
- Don't forget to get up quickly and move to support team-mates.
- Don't forget to mentally record the general effectiveness of this tackle.

The frontal high tackle

The frontal smother tackle
— the tackler's role

A frontal smother tackle is required in open-field play when endeavouring to ensure that the ball is not passed on in a two to one situation.

- Do make the tackle at the precise moment the ball-carrier receives the ball.
- Do aim to lock the ball-carrier's arms firmly against his body with the ball well lodged in between.
- Do hold on strongly until help arrives, endeavouring to twist or turn the ball-carrier towards your team-mates or, if power allows, drive the ball-carrier into ground.

- Don't forget to keep your eyes open at all times.
- Don't let the ball-carrier smuggle the ball away.
- Don't let go with those arms.

The frontal smother tackle
— the ball-carrier's role

- Do endeavour to restrict the tackler's efforts to engulf the ball and your body in the tackle.
- Do try to keep the ball away from abdominal area.
- Don't forget to keep on your feet and maintain possession of the ball until help arrives.

The frontal smother tackle

Though tackled by New South Wales hooker Peter Johnson, Kel Tremain still manages to get his pass away. All Blacks v New South Wales, 1968.
Sydney Morning Herald

217

The rear smother tackle — the tackler's role

The rear smother tackle is for occasions when the ball-carrier has deliberately turned his back to the tackler to conceal the intended delivery path of a pass.

- Do strive to drive your chest onto the back (high) of the ball-carrier with your arms around the ball-carrier locking the ball and the body of the ball-carrier together.
- Do slide your arms down to the ball area to restrict any pass.
- Do — if the occasion allows — drive your tackle 'through' the ball-carrier, endeavouring to put him to ground with you finishing on top.

- Don't forget to keep your eyes open at all times.
- Don't let the ball-carrier get a flip pass or suchlike away.

The rear smother tackle — the ball-carrier's role

- Do try to get the ball down as low as possible, away from tackler's hands, so that you can distribute it to your team-mates.
- Do try to stay on your feet and so present the ball to team-mates.
- Do hold on strongly until help arrives — if possible work your body (elbows, hips, etc,) strongly into the tackler.
- Do be aware of any lessening of tackler's arm strength which might allow you to make a burst for freedom.

- Don't panic when the tackle is first made.
- Don't let the tackler put you to the ground.

The rear smother tackle

Winger John Morrissey, tongue protruding, speeds down the sideline as Australian five-eighth Phil Hawthorne hits the ground behind him.
Auckland Star

218

The rear low tackle
— the tackler's role

When the ball-carrier is running hard for the goal line and only a low tackle from behind will halt his progress, a rear low tackle is required.

- Do calculate the correct time to dive onto the ball-carrier's legs.
- Do aim to make impact on the ball-carrier's buttocks with your shoulder.
- Do use your left shoulder after a left-foot take-off, and your right shoulder after a right-foot take-off. Plan to tackle with your favourite shoulder.
- Do tuck your head to one side to ensure it makes no contact with the ball-carrier's boots.
- Do wrap both arms around the ball-carrier's thighs and slide down his legs.
- Do keep your eyes open.

- Don't miscalculate the timing of your dive.
- Don't dive on the ball-carrier's back and slide down — his boots and your chin will meet.
- Don't forget to keep your head on one side.

The rear low tackle
— the ball-carrier's role

- Do keep your thighs moving and the drive going full-tilt to break the tackle.
- Do use your free hand to break your fall.
- Do maintain possession of the ball where you want it for support.
- Do twist as you fall.
- Do endeavour to be up on your feet speedily and look for the ball.
- Do relax your body as you fall.

- Don't panic as the tackle is being made.
- Don't fall onto the ball — especially in your abdominal area.
- Don't play the ball until you are up on both feet.

The rear low tackle

Argentina v All Blacks, 1979. All Black flanker Mike Burgoyne well-held in a dual tackle by two Pumas.
Evening Post

Hints on practising tackling

There are varying opinions on the value of practising tackles when the players are moving at pace and with power. Coaches usually find it difficult to motivate team-mates into tackling one another at practice sessions. But there will certainly be the odd session during the season when it may be warranted and will be worthwhile.

Tackling can be practised and improved by a combination of two methods:

● Players actually tackle each other, but they are kneeling and either static or moving only slowly. This allows greater understanding of the actual techniques.

● Players work out hard on tackling bags or rubber tubes. This allows development of power, pace and, obviously, confidence.

Together the two seem to form a splendid combination which the Saturday match will confirm. In training sessions (whatever system is adopted for practising tackling), the players should give equal emphasis to tackling with left shoulder and with right, — as part of the overall effort to become balanced players. These tackling suggestions should be adopted in all grades (despite any suggestions to the contrary by the odd senior player!)

Kneeling tackles

In pairs, both players (ball-carrier and tackler) kneel. Ball-carrier to carry a ball. Tackler is at right angles to ball-carrier's line of movement. Tackler now falls gently into the side-on tackle. Repeat a few times, then reverse roles. Then reverse again, and again, to give both players the opportunity to tackle with the other shoulder. As knowledge and awareness of the mechanics progress, more drive can be generated by the tackling player.

The next stage is to have the ball-carrier moving — both players are still on their knees. This begins to provide more realism to the tackle. Repeat the changes in roles and shoulders. From the kneeling position, players can advance to a walking pace and then a jogging pace.

This practice technique can be used for many types of tackles — especially the side-on and the frontal high (with some modification in falling backwards). The frontal smother, the rear smother and the rear low should be practised with the ball-carrier moving at walking pace. The ball-carrier should always hold a ball and learn how to fall controlling both ball and body.

Tackling bags

Tackling bags and the inner rubber tubes of tractor tyres are valuable training aids which allow players to generate power, pace and confidence, once the mechanics of the tackle have been clearly understood. *Understand, practise, perfect.* Individual players can obviously practise alone with the tackling bags.

To encourage the players to use speed, effort, knowledge and fitness in a high-pressure situation, games can be devised for the training session. Here is one: a tackling bag relay.

Two teams line up. Ten metres in front of each team is a tackling bag held up by a player. Ten metres farther in front is a football, or marker (again, one for each team). The player at the head of each team's line sprints forward, tackles the bag (at this, the bag holder returns to become last in the team's line), the tackler then sprints on to the football (or marker), rounds it, and back to pick up tackling bag. Then the second tackler can move off, tackle the bag, up and around the football, and back to the bag. The spirit of competition between the two teams (under supervision from the coach) encourages greater effort and, obviously, familiarity. As a point of interest, other skills can be included in this relay, such as picking up, side-stepping and dribbling.

Using rubber tyres

The inner rubber tubes of tractor tyres offer an interesting and valuable variation, in that when they are bowled they are very similar to the movements of a ball-carrier and can be tackled from the front, from the side and from the rear. A blob of white paint on the side of the tyre can provide a focus for players to time their side-on tackles accurately. Work in pairs for all types of tackles. Make sure the tyre valves are safely covered.

Four players (A, B, C and D), each with a rubber tube, stand at the corners of a large square. A fifth player (E) is within the square. The object of this exercise is to see how many tackles player E can make in, say, 20 seconds. Player A bowls a tube to player E, who tackles it. B's tube is bowled and tackled, then C's tube, then D's tube. (A, B, C and D sprint to retrieve their tubes after each tackling and return to their positions ready to bowl again), and so on until the 20 seconds has elapsed. A and E swap places and it is A's turn to tackle the tubes. Techniques must always be watched carefully by the coach. This is obviously an exercise for frontal tackles; with slight alterations to the game, side-on tackles and rear low tackles can be the order of the day — not forgetting to work both shoulders.

The 'old-style' tackling bag and sawdust pit

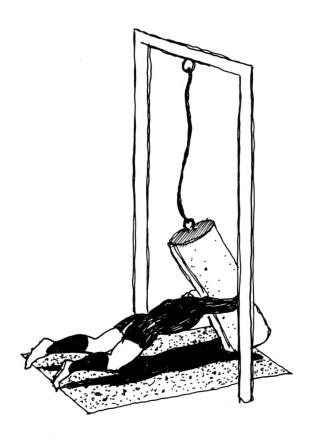

Practising tackling a rolling rubber tyre

A rolls his rubber tube to E, who tackles it. While B rolls his rubber tube to E (who tackles it), player A is retrieving the first tube.
And so on.
The aim is for E to tackle as many tubes as possible in, say, 20 seconds

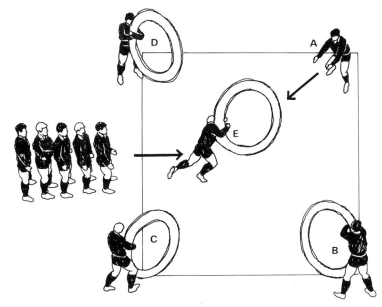

Tackling bag relay

The first player sprints forward to tackle a tackling bag, then sprints 10 metres further on to round a marker on the ground, then returns to the tackling bag to hold it up for the second player to tackle. After this, the first player will jog back to the end of the line.

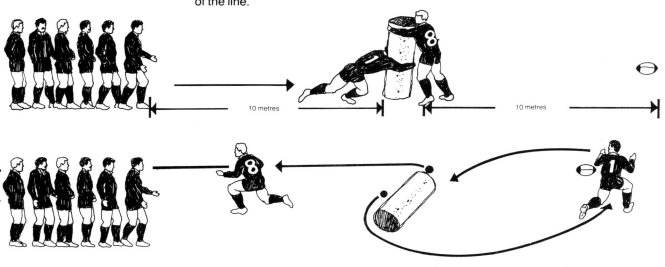

10 metres

10 metres

Kneeling tackling practice

221

Wilson Whineray on

Captaincy

- The captain must be a leader, a confident and knowledgeable player, an overall game strategist and sensitive communications expert.
- With the captain lies the responsibility of team analysis and motivation. He must ensure that each player capitalises on his particular strengths and knows his task generally as well as for specific matches.
- Strength of captaincy relies on the overall mutual respect and support between captain and coach, and between captain and players, particularly the key players.
- A captain develops strategies with his team, designing and practising them to everyone's satisfaction.

The qualities required

To be an effective captain it helps if you have confidence in yourself and in the way you are playing. For some captains the first real pressure is when they start to have problems holding their place in the team, and this could worry them to the point where they don't know which to put right first: either their own game (and survive), or their captaincy (letting their own game slip). And the two do not alway run parallel.

A captain should have a good knowledge of the game in basic terms. I don't think we can expect more from youngsters or third-graders or young senior players than is fair, but I do think that whatever the level they are playing they must have a good knowledge of the game applicable to that level.

You should also have a high level of understanding of what strengths you have in the team — in short, an honest assessment which you are able to make from discussions with the coach and with other senior players — so that you are not endeavouring to do things on the field with an inadequate resource.

You must have a good relationship with your senior players, the key players, the players who establish a team's identity. In every team there are three or four players who, together with the captain, really run the show. You must have a sound basic knowledge of the rules, and be able to pull people together. You can call this 'leadership' (or whatever term you like) but you must be able to relate to people, so that you can deal with problems and pool the energies of the team for a common purpose.

At top level — and it's moderately important because it worries you if you can't do it — you also have to be able to handle the off-the-field duties, which are more intense now than in my day. The media, after-match speeches, receptions, school visits, talking to people. I know of All Black captains who didn't want to captain the team because

of this — not because of worries on the field, but because of concern over the intensity of off-the-field responsibilities.

Preparation for the task

I don't think we prepare our captains very well for the responsibilities they face at higher levels in the game. I had no leadership training of any kind, had never even spoken to anyone who had formal training in this area. In business courses, particularly in the United States, a tremendous amount of time is spent in the study of leadership. But in New Zealand we pluck out a relatively inexperienced young man, appoint him captain and expect him to have some knowledge of handling people under very critical and tense and emotional circumstances. We could do a lot better, when people are appointed to be captain or likely to become captain, to encourage them to spend some time meeting people in the community, in the business or academic or military worlds (experts on leadership training), to expose the fellow to the many aspects of leadership. Whether the coach nominates the captain or the team elects a captain, both ways have their merits and attractions — though I think captains should be appointed. This happens in all walks of life; someone in authority makes a decision and, hopefully, takes into account how the team is going to regard the appointment.

Handling the team

One important thing, however you do it, is to get the team fixed on a common approach to winning the game or the series or the tour. To recognise where they fit into the overall pattern. What part is a Colin Meads to play in the team pattern? Where does Mac Herewini fit in?

Generally I have found that people like to know what is expected of them. 'What role am I expected to play, so that when I'm judged afterwards I know how I've performed in relation to the task given me at the start.' This is what they think. A fellow who is anxious to retain his place in the All Blacks wants to know what's expected of him from the start. If he's a full-back he's required to catch every ball, kick accurately, join the backline on attack, not miss a tackle on defence, and so on. If he does that during the game, when he comes off and has his shower he'll think 'Yes, I'm happy. I did everything that was required of me.' Perhaps too many of our teams go on to the field when the players do not know what their prime tasks are and where they fit into the whole strategy.

Motivating the team

Behavioural scientists will tell you that you can't really motivate anyone, all you can do is set the parameters for people to motivate themselves. The technique is to say to yourself, 'What conditions must be set to stir the players to perform well?' Stature is important to most players: the prestige of being in a winning team rather than a losing one,

Phil Bennett and Sid Going lead on to the field. Lions v North Auckland, 1977.
Peter Bush

Acclaimed by fellow players, commentators and spectators as a conscientious rugby footballer, a skilful ball handler and an inspirational and dedicated captain. Generally he played as a front-row forward. Played for Auckland Grammar School 1st XV 1950, 51; senior club rugby for Wakaia, Southland 1952; Wairarapa 1953 (Martinborough); Mid-Canterbury 1954 (Rakaia); Manawatu 1955 (University); Canterbury 1956, 57 (Lincoln College); Waikato 1958 (City); Auckland 1959-63, 65, 66 (Grammar); also South Island 1957; North Island 1958, 59, 61-63, 65; NZ Trials 1957-63, 65; NZ Under-23 1958 (as captain); NZ Colts 1955; NZ Universities 1956, 57. Represented NZ 1957-65. During his All Black career he captained the team in 68 of his 77 appearances; first appointed as captain at the age of 23 in 1958 against the Wallabies. In his 30 Test matches as captain of the NZ team he sustained only five losses. Coached Auckland Grammar Club 1970-73 and Onslow in Wellington 1974. Named New Zealand Sportsman of the Year 1965. Honoured with the OBE in 1961.

the stature which comes with being a leading player whose advice is sought by other players. You've got to set conditions in the team where players say, 'Too right I'm going to play well. I know exactly what I'm required to do; I know where we are focusing our attention as a team. If we play well I will get a trip to Britain, we'll have wonderful times together, we're going to be the best team in the world — that's what I want and I'll give it all I've got.' That is the essence of it.

I've seen a lot of captains criticising their team at half-time, and this, I think, is no way to motivate the team. It might be a part of a leadership style — where you've got to hop into people — but belting a person verbally is not far removed from belting a person physically, and this has never been an effective way to motivate people. Perhaps sometimes it might be effective . . . But goodness me, the fact a person wants to play in an international is the biggest motivation of the lot, he *wants* to be there. How does he get there? He plays better than anyone else. How does he stay there? By keeping on playing better than anyone else. So you have him eager right from the start. Criticism, in my view, should always be in private — unless it is fairly mild and absolutely fair.

The captain's playing position

In modern rugby I don't think you can get too far away from the forwards (perhaps half-back, maybe at first five-eighth), but the game tends to be won or lost up front, and if you get too far away you can't influence the prime struggle that goes on for much of the game. The position of tight forward has many advantages, in that you can feel how the struggle is going. You start to feel you're getting on top, when you can feel the thing going forward, or the ball coming back more cleanly or more often — or conversely, you're in trouble, and you know you're not getting on top of it.

I think that a loose forward is possibly better still, in that you have closer liaison with your backs and with your forwards, because you're 'hitched' on to your forwards (so to speak). Half-backs? There have been some great half-back captains over the years who were directly involved. All I know is that if it is a tight forward — which was my position most of the time — you can function only through a very good relationship with one of the backs, who works with you and makes sure that if you want something done from set pieces, you can rely on them to see that the instructions are carried out. I had great help from Connor and Laidlaw and Briscoe and Urbahn.

The preparation of a team is something much bigger than the involvement of just the coach and the captain and vice-captain. I think it really needs the whole team if possible; but if you can't have that, at least the coming together of your key players. Looking back to the era I played through, it was the support of seven or eight or ten really outstanding players and very solid people who set the platform for the successes that came our way.

Relationship between coach and captain

The relationship between a captain and a coach has to be very close indeed, otherwise it's going to fracture. The coach can only do so much. I used to envy cricket captains because at drinks or between overs they could talk to their senior players. In rugby it all happens quickly once the whistle blows; you don't really get a chance till half-time, apart from the off-injury, to talk to your key players, and talk to the backs and see how they are finding things. Half-time is the first real opportunity, then you're into it again; so really all your preparation has to be complete before you take the field.

To a fair extent all the options and tactical variations must be considered in advance. A captain can say, 'Well, we will go more deeply into *this* part of the way we practised and less on *that*', but the coach can do nothing, the coach has to trust the captain from the moment they go on to the field, to get the feel of things and follow through. Again, the demanding coach who is totally autocratic isn't going to last long in today's world of coaching — perhaps the team will win some games in the short-term, the team will be so motivated and keyed-up (and scared really) that they'll play beyond themselves for a time. But I don't believe that modern youth will put up with that for long — it's not the way to build teams.

I don't think a coach is much good who goes and says at half-time, 'You've got to get stuck in!' What does 'stuck in' mean? I don't know. What do I have to do? Better far to say, 'Tight forwards are going to have to drive more often for the next ten minutes or so. Line-out forwards are going to have to get the ball in their hands.' Commit people; give them specific instructions. Just to shout at people and say 'Get stuck in!' is no good at all. I believe that if you have a team of players who are all agreed to a certain approach to the game, and are prepared to commit themselves to it, then even if what you want to do is 'the wrong thing', if they commit themselves to it and do it with enthusiasm, often 'the wrong thing' can be the right thing. What you need is clear understanding on what each player is expected to do, understanding on their part of the total game you're trying to play, and enough enthusiasm to commit themselves whichever way it's going to go. You can either use that approach, or you can get them on the field and say 'We'll bloody-well get stuck in', and get mud on your knees as you charge at them — and you'll win a lot of games that way too. Often, of course, you do a bit of both. I think most fellows get the message, whether it's four-letter words you use or straight English — but in my experience it's almost always the latter.

Again, as I said earlier, you must recognise the strengths you've got in the team. Obviously if you have an Otago or Southland type of forward pack, you would go on to the field with a different approach than you would with a North Auckland team. The players have different attitudes and skills and neither would play the other's game really well.

The captain talks to his team, (Australia 1962). From left to right, Wilson Whineray, John Le Lievre, Kevin Barry, Nev McEwan, Stan Meads, John Creighton, Waka Nathan and Colin Meads.
Sydney Morning Herald

Delegating authority

Generally speaking, one of the key players in the teams I played in was the half-back — Connor, Laidlaw, Briscoe or Roger Urbahn, very reliable and experienced players. Contrary to what many people think, you don't go on the field as a captain issuing an instruction from every scrum and every line-out, giving a stream of directions. You train and practise a certain approach. You say, 'We will play it this way and see how things go for twenty minutes or so', and away you go. Then you might come in and say, 'We've got fair control up front — free the game up for the next four or five good balls' (and if this didn't happen you'd be angry). Ten minutes later, depending on how things were going, you might wish to change again. You do it in blocks. You take a block of the game, for ten minutes or a quarter of an hour. You might say to your five-eighth — if they are coming up too quick — 'we'll kick a bit to get their backs back again'. There's no point in kicking one, you have to kick six or eight to ram it back, so it's a block that would take ten minutes to do.

These blocks are then laid down by the coach only to the extent that in your training and talking you'd talk about the *what ifs?* This is the game we are going to start with, we're going to do this, that and the other. *What if* our forwards don't get on top? Well, we'll run a lot more ball, we'll drop a loose forward off and take the punishment. *What if* our backs are getting cut to pieces in the field? Well, we'll stay on their blind side, go in deeper, do this and that.

So that, hopefully, most of the *what ifs* should be in the captain's and team's minds before you go on the field, so that when you say, 'I want the middle of the back line strengthened up — full-back deep, loose forward off', they've all done it in practice. We mightn't have expected to use it, but the team knows what's expected of them. It's too late to start thinking on the field, 'My God, we're in real trouble now, what will we do?' By the time you were able to instruct the players, ten minutes would have gone. They're not listening. They can't even *hear* you — they're emotionally charged up. No, you have to work into a pattern that becomes almost a part of the players' behaviour, so that they react that way instinctively when under pressure. Some call it training, some discipline, some pattern.

Argentina's brilliant fly-half and Puma captain, Hugo Porta, running at speed.
Evening Post

A captain's view of other captains

I've played against, or with, some great captains. And what were the qualities that made them good? Well, this is a very personal thing. If you ask a dozen people, they'll give you a dozen different answers. Of the overseas captains, the one I would most like to have played with was John Thornett, the Australian captain. He went through a very good period, when the Australian teams consistently struggled to do well — they took a test or two off us from time to time, they drew a series in South Africa two-all, and went to Britain and had a good tour. I liked John's quiet approach on the field, the fact that his team always seemed to be in control of themselves. His knowledge of the game was profound; he played prop, lock and loose forward and played it well, and he was just a thoroughly agreeable and pleasant chap off the field, and that appealed to me. On the other hand, there were fellows like the French captain Moncla who was in New Zealand in 1961; he was a very verbal captain, constantly shouting instructions from the end of the line-out. I'm not sure that helps the team spirit when you are under pressure.

Captains cannot motivate players — they can only set the parameters for the players to motivate themselves, and the biggest motivation is to be on the winning side in an international match.
Peter Bush

Peter McDavitt on

Refereeing

- **An efficient referee should control each match appropriately, according to grade.**
- **The referee should have a complete knowledge of the handbook:** *Laws of the Game of Rugby Football.*
- **While not every law will be enforced at every match, the basic laws of knock-on, forward pass and off-side must be observed always.**
- **To control a match accurately the referee must position himself so as to monitor all movement.**
- **The referee must ensure that no unfair advantage results from a scrum; the grade of the match will determine the referee's decision.**
- **The referee must also ensure that line-outs are played without unfair advantage.**
- **Rucks and mauls must also be carefully controlled by the referee.**
- **A referee may sometimes have to act as a touch judge, ensuring that the ball is fairly kicked or correctly placed for a try.**

The function of a referee in any sport is to see that no individual or team will get an advantage over an opponent by using unfair tactics. What is unfair will depend on the level of the game and the skills of the players.

A referee will have different attitudes to school teams, to college teams, to lower-grade club teams, to senior club teams, to first-class teams and to international teams. At each level, some things will be unfair and others will not. So there will be a marked variation in what a referee looks for in each match. This is why there is a difference in what good referees appear to let pass one week and will take firm action on the next. The game and the players determine the referee's attitude and actions.

The Laws of the Game of Rugby Football have been written to cover every unfair eventuality on the field. A referee should know all of these laws. But it is not expected that all these unfair things will occur in any one match. So it is not necessary for a referee to feel that in every match every law in the book will be enforced. In each match, the referee must use only sufficient rules to see that unfairness does not occur.

Peter McDavitt watches the play at Athletic Park, Wellington. Australia v New Zealand 1972. Sid Going is about to receive the ball from lock Peter Whiting.
National Publicity Studios. Wellington

Member of the Rugby Referees' Association. Played for the Clifton Club 1948; Ardmore Training College 1949, 50, and New Plymouth HSOB 1951. From 1966 until 1977 appointed referee for 24 international matches as well as one inter-island and three Ranfurly Shield matches.

However, the basic laws of knock-on, forward pass and off-side, must be enforced in every match, from social rugby through to internationals. The breaking of those three laws can give a team a very unfair advantage. Unfair play by one team leads to frustration in the opponents. And frustration can be difficult to control. Player frustration can make trouble spots, and when there are trouble spots, a referee has increased his difficulties in the game and lessened his own enjoyment of it.

All referees should understand what players are trying to do during a match. They should know what coaches expect each player to do in each position and at each phase of the game. By understanding what players are trying to do, the referee can then use a selected group of laws to see that no unfair advantage has been gained. The following suggestions make up the kind of guidelines a referee would follow in each phase of the game in order to observe the most commonly used unfair tactics in the game.

No attempt is made here to state all of the laws that are in the game. These can be elicited from the current issue of the handbook, *Laws of the Game of Rugby Football*.

Forward pass

A forward pass happens when a player passes the ball towards the opponent's dead-ball line. For instance, if a player is standing on the half-way line, or any of the lines going across the field, it is a forward pass if the ball ends up in front of this line. It might be blown forward. If the ball were caught behind the line, or even on the line, it is not forward. If the referee is in doubt, he should let play carry on.

It is important for the referee to be in a position to see if all passes are forward. The best position is slightly in front of the ball-carrier so that the ball-receiver can be seen distinctly. From this position, the referee can get a clear view to see if the receiver knocks the ball on, or is obstructed before catching the ball.

Note that it is also an offence for a player to pass the ball forward in-goal.

Knock-on

A knock-on occurs if a player knocks the ball forward with his hand or arm. If the ball goes forward from any other part of the body, such as chest or head, it is not a knock-on.

Again, the best position to see this from is on an angle in front of the ball-catcher.

The referee must be in a position to be sure that the ball has gone forward, but from the hand or arms, not from head or chest.

Off-side in general play

(General play is running and passing. It does not include scrums, rucks, mauls and line-outs.) A player is off-side if he is in front of the ball when it was last played by another player in his own team. Usually this takes place after the ball has been kicked. There is no penalty, though, if the off-side player takes no part in the play.

To position himself to see an off-side player play the ball, the referee must move forward to the ball, with players who are on-side. Thus, any players who are in front of him are in an off-side position. He can then see if the off-side players play the ball, obstruct an opponent, or remain within 10 metres of an opponent who is waiting to play the ball.

Scoring a try

The object of the game is to 'score as many points as possible', and one way of scoring points is to score tries.

The first player to ground the ball in the opponents' in-goal scores a try; the goal line is part of the in-goal area, so a try can be scored on the goal line. But the dead-ball lines and touch-in-goal lines are not part of the in-goal area.

To score a try, the ball-carrier must bring the ball into contact with the ground with hands or arms. If the ball is lying on the ground in in-goal, a try can be scored by a player placing hands or arms on it, or by falling on the ball and grounding it with the body from the waist upwards.

The best place for the referee to see most tries from is in front of the scorer. This usually gives a clear view of the ball and of who is holding the ball.

It is said that one of New Zealand's greatest try scorers, Kel Tremain, always knew where the referee was when play was close to the goal line. When he was scoring, Kel always turned so that the referee had a clear view of the ball. The referee could then see that Kel was the player who was holding the ball and had brought it in contact with the ground.

When tries are not given, many referees (and coaches) say, 'too many hands on the ball'. But there is now no such law. This was indeed a very old law. Perhaps if referees could remember the definition of a try, then far more tries would be given.

The referee must decide who is holding the ball (and a tackler is rarely holding the ball). Then, the referee must decide if the ball-holder brings the ball into contact with the ground. A defender getting a hand on the ball is usually not sufficient for the referee to say that a try has been prevented, or that 'there are too many hands on the ball'.

Positional play by the referee

From this position the referee can get a clear view to see if the pass is forward or if the player receiving the ball is interfered with.

This is also the best position to see a knock-on.

The perfect position for a referee to observe a try. J. P. ('Red') Murphy watches Kel Tremain score, Springboks v All Blacks, 1965.
Evening Post

Scrums

The scrum is a means of re-starting play after a minor infringement, such as a knock-on or a forward pass. The referee's job is to see that neither team gets an unfair advantage from the scrum. An 'unfair advantage' means different things at different grades. So the grade of the match will dictate how the referee will look at a scrum.

In all rugby, the scrum should be stationary and square on the field, when the ball is put in. For schoolboy rugby, off-side is critical. If off-side players are allowed to hinder the half-back, then the backs will never be able to learn to run with the ball. At this level, a crooked put-in is of little importance.

At secondary school and in lower-grade rugby, the put-in of the ball becomes important. Front rows and hookers are learning their skills, so must learn them correctly. Off-side must be strictly enforced too, so that backs can learn to run.

The put-in of the ball in senior and first-class level becomes less important. Now it is the positioning of feet and bodies of the front row players, and their binding, which is important. Controlling the players is of first concern to the referee, and the referee must see that physical strength is not used in an unfair way.

Scrum law is complex, and a good referee only enforces the many scrum laws to see that one team does not get an unfair advantage over the other one. As stated earlier, 'unfair advantage' depends on the level of the game and the ability of the players.

The referee's position at a scrum

Referee

Half-back putting the ball in

Unfair things that a referee should look for are:

- One team pushing just before the half-back puts the ball in
- Defending hookers unbinding their left arm, to get nearer the ball when it comes in
- Tight-head props packing on an angle (boring) to split a hooker from his own loose-head prop
- Half-backs who move to their right as they put the ball in, in order to shield their action and the hooker's action from the referee
- Front rows that collapse when their scrum is being pushed back
- The loose-head prop who grabs the opposition's tight-head prop's jersey with the left hand under the chest, instead of over the back. In this way, he can exert unfair pressure downwards and sideways.

Opposing half-back

Referee

Half-back putting the ball in

Off-side from a kick

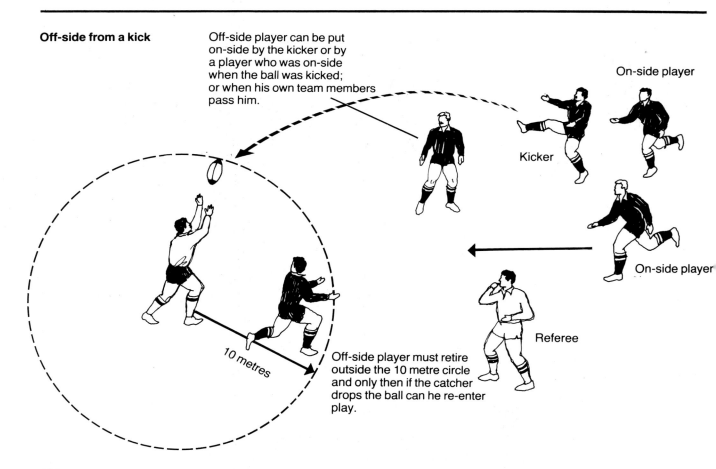

Off-side player can be put on-side by the kicker or by a player who was on-side when the ball was kicked; or when his own team members pass him.

On-side player

Kicker

On-side player

Referee

10 metres

Off-side player must retire outside the 10 metre circle and only then if the catcher drops the ball can he re-enter play.

Line-outs

The line-out is a means of starting play after the ball has gone out of play over the touch line. There will probably be 60 to 80 line-outs in any one match. Line-outs are complicated because usually there are 20 players involved. So line-outs are very difficult to referee.

The referee can stand in any position but five in particular are recommended.
(All give the referee a certain viewpoint and advantage in that viewpoint.)
1. On either side at the end of the line-out
2. On either side at the front of the line-out
3. At the end of the line of touch

The three key persons in the line-out, for the referee, are the jumper, the loose forward at the back, and the loose forward at the front. It is difficult to observe all three players at once, so the referee positions himself to try to see two sets of these players at each line-out.

It is the referee's function to see that neither team gains an unfair advantage over the other. So, the common things that a referee looks for are:
● Ball must land along the middle line of the line-out.
● Jumpers must be free to jump without interference. Most interference comes from the jumping opponent, or the player behind. This interference can be holding by shorts or jersey, holding down by hand on elbow or on shoulder, pushing or elbowing out of line, or inside arm pulled away from reaching upwards.
● Half-backs and five-eighths must be free of the attentions of the off-side loose forwards from the back and front of the line-out.

The referee's position at a line-out —
at the back of the line-out to one side

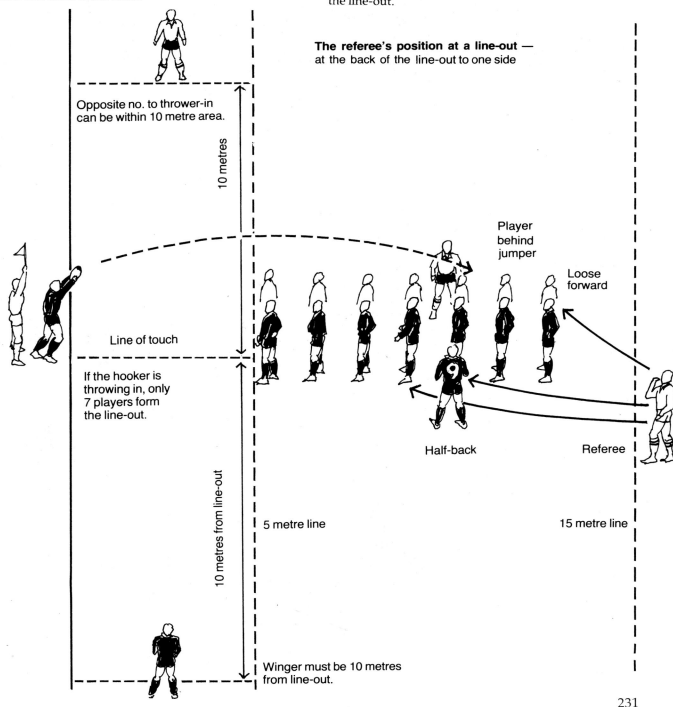

Opposite no. to thrower-in can be within 10 metre area.

10 metres

Line of touch

If the hooker is throwing in, only 7 players form the line-out.

10 metres from line-out

5 metre line

Player behind jumper

Loose forward

Half-back

Referee

15 metre line

Winger must be 10 metres from line-out.

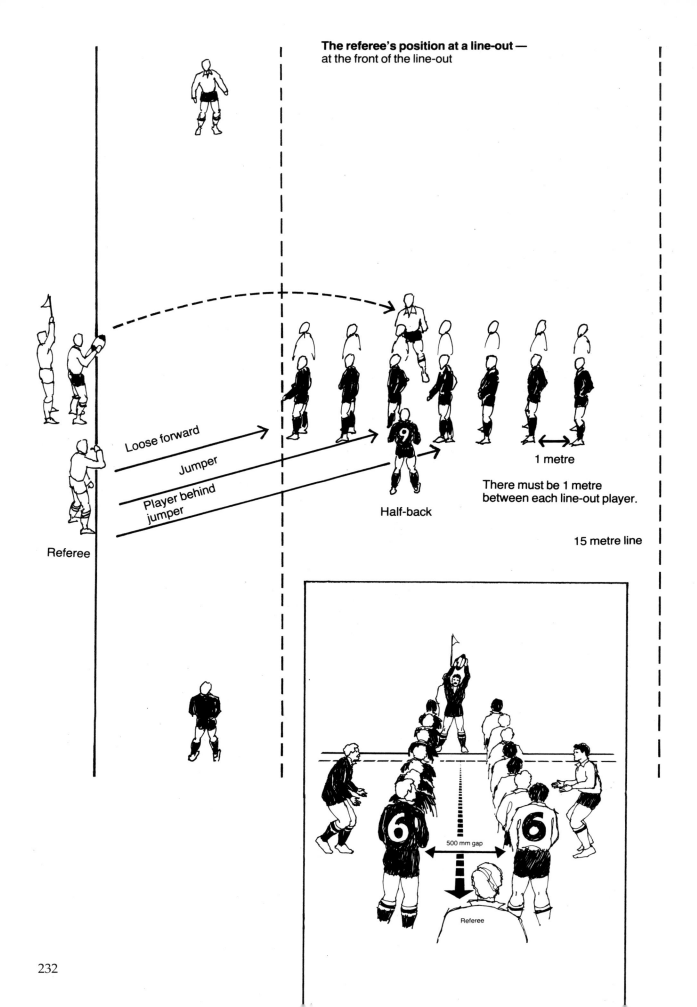

The referee's position at a line-out —
at the front of the line-out

Loose forward

Jumper

Player behind
jumper

Referee

Half-back

1 metre

There must be 1 metre
between each line-out player.

15 metre line

500 mm gap

Referee

Rucks

Rucks were a New Zealand innovation of the 1920s. At that time, the law stated that after a player had been tackled, the ball had to be played by a foot before it could be picked up. So eight players driving forward and playing the ball with the foot backwards was a good way of getting possession of the ball. It still is, even though it is not required now to play the ball with the foot after a tackle.

The key things that a referee must look for in rucks are:

- The tackled player must release the ball *immediately* and move away from it. Players who remain lying close to the ball are unfair players because they are stopping their opponents from getting to the ball quickly. This is frustrating for such players.

- Any player who is on the ground, but is not tackled, must play the ball immediately or get away from the ball immediately.

- If the referee allows a player to remain lying on the ground, then the referee must think that the player is not interfering with play. Opponents then have no right to 'ruck this player back', 'heel him back' or 'kick him off it'. Using any part of the boot on a player must result in a penalty kick and ordering off.

- Off-side around rucks is frustrating to players, particularly when they are looking for quick ball.

- All players who are in front of their off-side line, must be bound to other players who are in the ruck.

- At a ruck, the referee must take up a position so that he can see the ball.

The referee's position at a ruck or maul —— Two possible positions

The referee must be able to see the ball or any off-side players

Off-side line

Line of sight

Referee

Half-back

Optional referee position

Mauls

Mauling is a new technique for most New Zealand players, and it is a technique that few have mastered adequately.

- Unfair play and frustration is caused by off-side players who prevent opponents from tunnelling the ball back to their half-back.
- Referees should position themselves so that they have a clear view of the ball and so can observe any off-side players.

Touch judging

Many players, coaches and referees have to act as touch judges. The laws that the touch judges need to know are in the handbook, *Laws of the Game of Rugby Football*, though they do not state where the critical decisions are to be made. Here are three places where the touch judge must be 100 per cent correct:

- A touch judge should always know if a defender kicked the ball from inside or outside his own 22 metre line.
- A touch judge must always be about 2 metres past the corner post when an attacker dives for a try. Corner post decisions are best made when the touch judge can watch the player diving towards him.
- At a kick at goal. A touch judge must always be certain that the ball has crossed the cross-bar. 'Poster' decisions mean no goal.

The referee's position at a goal kick

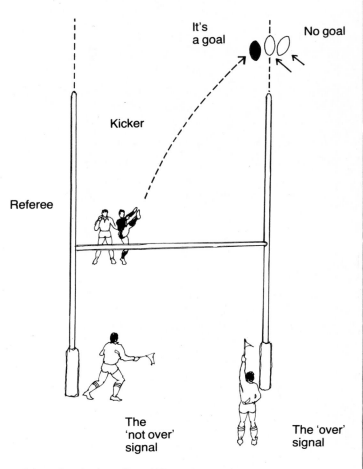

International referee Dave Miller at the Third Test, Lions v All Blacks, 1977.
Scott A. G. M. Crawford

Tom Johnson on

Mini Rugby

- **Fifteen-a-side rugby for young children in New Zealand has seen the development of some bad features, over-competitiveness, over-zealous coaches and parents.**
- **Mini-rugby is a scaling down of the number of players, the field size and other complications, thus enabling young players to run with the ball, to develop skills, and to find greater enjoyment in the game.**
- **In the United Kingdom mini-rugby has had widespread acceptance and a rapid expansion in the game's popularity — particularly among youngsters.**
- **Practice sessions should be carefully planned, with systematic coaching and plenty of variety in the skills to be tackled and the methods used.**
- **When coaching youngsters be generous with praise and encouragement.**

In recent years the growth of rugby has been explosive and widespread throughout the world, with people in countries in the communist bloc, in Asia and in North and South America taking to the game in rapidly increasing numbers. Significantly also in the United Kingdom mini-rugby in the past decade has extended the game's popularity amongst children — although surprisingly in New Zealand it has taken time for the concept to be accepted, possibly because of our traditional conservative approach to rugby, whereby anything that deviated from the 15-a-side game, as far as our diehards were concerned, wasn't rugby at all.

Why it is popular

Mini-rugby has been developed to simplify what can be for children a complicated game, with its numerous laws to be understood and a wide variety of individual skills to be developed. Rugby when played by young children on a 15-a-side basis offers few opportunities for the participants to run with the ball and enjoy themselves.

It seems ludicrous that for many years we expected 7-year-olds and 8-year-olds to play on large fields and to understand complicated laws. The mini game is designed to simplify rugby by scaling down all the important aspects of the major game. It enables youngsters to cope with the complexities of say, scrummaging, in a manner where the game will not become boring through lack of involvement. By providing smaller fields for playing, with fewer participants per team, each child gets an opportunity to run, handle the ball and generally be involved in purposeful activity which will develop individual skills and provide maximum opportunity for the basic understanding of rugby and enjoyment of the contest.

It is easy to see why mini-rugby has enjoyed such tremendous success in the United Kingdom, where coaching organisers such as Ray Williams and Don Rutherford have been instrumental in promoting the concept. Some 20 years ago, visiting British Lions players in this country were critical of the New Zealand obsessions with rugby, highlighted by young children playing 15-a-side games at such an early age. Much of the Lions' criticism was directed at supposedly fanatical coaching, but I believe they failed to recognise that much of the coaching was really non-existent — the so-called coach each week organised the team, shouted words of encouragement from the sideline (probably over-enthusiastically), and achieved little else for the development of the individual's rugby skills. It seems strange that even our teachers failed to recognise the need to break rugby down to its simplest elements for young children to get maximum enjoyment out of participation — particularly when at schools, in playgrounds and at home, aspiring young All Blacks playing under the pseudonyms of their current heroes in 3-a-side or 4-a-side matches, refereed by joint consensus, could play for hours running, swerving, tackling and kicking the ball.

Today there are some excellent publications and films which graphically illustrate for the aspiring coach the best methods of coaching and teaching young players a better understanding of rugby football. Examples of these are the Rugby Football Union's *Better Rugby* series, booklets by the Scottish Rugby Union, booklets available from the New Zealand Education Department and the publications of Ray Williams. Rugby at its best is an exhilarating game, and to motivate young children the coach must not only understand the principles of the game, but also have an understanding of the needs and aspirations of young players. It can be a frightening experience for a keen parent to take on the rugby coaching of children and be suddenly confronted with 15 or 20 youngsters, one football and a prospect of having to provide regular coaching sessions for a season. Unfortunately many coaches revert to their own rugby days, perhaps two or three decades earlier, and the result for the children is a boring session with a minimum of purposeful activity.

Coaching young children

The coach should plan each session thoroughly, so that individual skills are covered and the right progression carried through into unit skills and team skills. Coaching aids such as tackle bags and an adequate number of footballs should be available at all coaching sessions.

Mini-rugby, by scaling down the complexities of the game, allows children to run with the ball and enjoy themselves.
Tom Johnson

Particular interest is the encouragement and development of young rugby players. Has played for Counties 1957; Waikato 1958; Hawke's Bay 1959-63, 65-68; Auckland 1964; North Island 1962, 63. Has played 116 first-class matches. Selected for All Black Trials 1959, 62, 63. Chairman Hawke's Bay Rugby Union 1972. NZ Rugby Union Councillor 1973-81. Assistant coach Hawke's Bay Reps 1969. Currently a NZRFU administrator.

By using the grid system in a designated area, team members can be split up into twos, threes or fours to practise their individual skills such as tackling, passing and catching under match conditions. This allows the coach time to observe faults, make corrections and generally instruct all the players. More importantly, by introducing games such as shuttle relays, rugby rounders, end ball, corner ball and a wide variety of many skills activities, the players will enjoy each session. There are no limits to the number of games activities that can be introduced, and the innovative and imaginative coach who analyses players' weaknesses and then produces game situations to overcome the problems will give the players a sense of satisfaction and self-fulfilment as they improve their skills and those of their team.

Above all, enjoyment is the key factor for the young rugby player, and to achieve this a mini-rugby coach must provide meaningful sessions every time.

Areas of the standard-size rugby field that can be used for mini-rugby matches

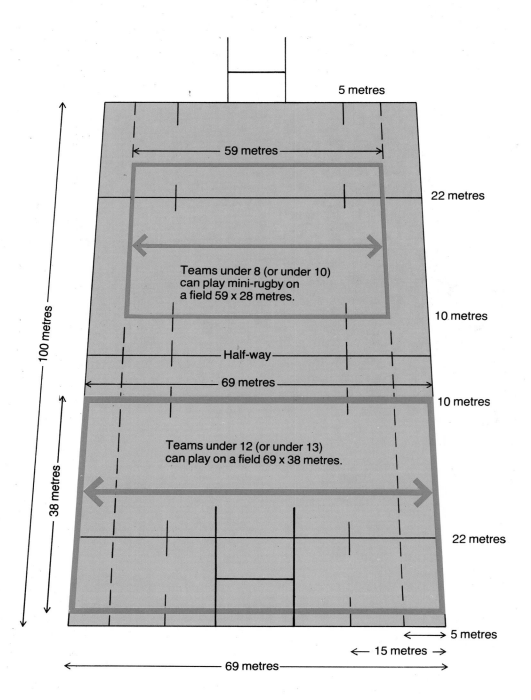

Teams under 8 (or under 10) can play mini-rugby on a field 59 x 28 metres.

Teams under 12 (or under 13) can play on a field 69 x 38 metres.

The mini-rugby scrum — the direction of each forward's shove is shown by arrows

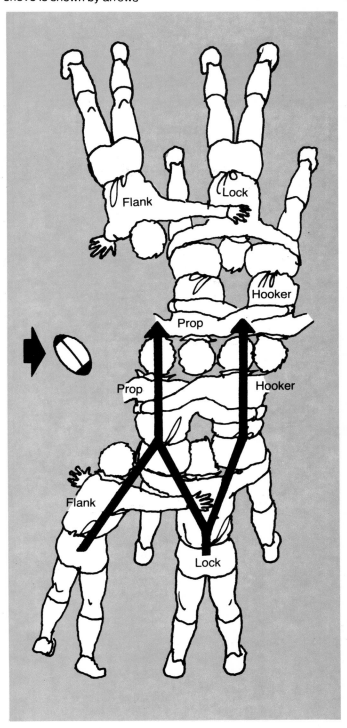

Dimensions of a smaller goal post suitable for mini-rugby

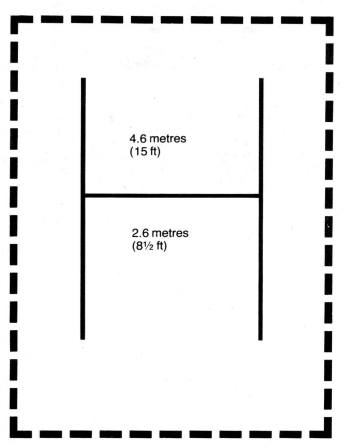

4.6 metres
(15 ft)

2.6 metres
(8½ ft)

Hamish Fletcher on

A Coaching Programme

Planning a training programme that covers all the basic skills of rugby can be a time-consuming task for an inexperienced (or experienced) coach. So many skills have to be learned by a player. But what are they, and how can they all be covered in one season?

The following programme sets out the skills in order of difficulty. For the young person taking up the game, usually at mini-rugby level, the early part of the programme is straightforward and basic: the youngster is taught to run, pass, catch, kick and tackle by the simplest methods. The age, experience and progress of the player will largely determine when the coach should introduce the skills.

For youngsters playing mini-rugby, the typical training session would include about 15 minutes teaching the skills, some drilling of the new skills, followed by games or a practice match. Two or three skills are covered in each of the 34 sessions in this programme, so a team which practises a couple of times a week can complete the programme in the rugby season.

Willing parents or teachers, who may not have had a wide knowledge of rugby, can be co-opted to help a coach who is handling a large squad of, say, 15 to 20 players.

Some coaching hints

- When introducing a new skill, commence at walking pace.
- As the players' confidence increases, speed up the techniques used.
- Make use of visual aids.
- Skills should be practised regularly, for no more than 10 minutes at a time, at all training sessions during the season.
- Vary the training sessions with different drills and games.
- Use incentives and be generous with praise.

In naming the skills introduced in this programme, every attempt has been made to conform with modern practice. Most of the skills are described elsewhere in this book .

Flick pass The standard pass across the body used by forwards and backs. It allows the player to 'back up' or 'double around'.

Short, soft pass Used in close situations — for example, hand-to-hand and scissors passing.

Smuggle pass Moving the ball in a maul situation.

Stab kicking sliding This is a kicking technique used mainly by full-backs and half-backs to avoid kicking out on the full. The ball is kicked hard and slides out at ground level.

Peripheral pass A pass received at eye level. It enables the ball-receiver to see a wide area of the field.

Option pass A receiver running on to the ball has a degree of choice of when he will take the ball.

Reverse pass The fast reverse pass by a half-back to achieve distance. Or the reverse pass used by a player who is close to a supporting team-mate; this pass is soft and very controlled.

Skip pass A pass to cut out a player, for example a pass from the first five-eighth to centre three-quarter cutting out the second five-eighth.

A programme for teaching individual rugby skills

(Fifteen minutes per session)

Session	Main skill	Sub-skill
1	Running	Swerving
	Tackling	Side-on tackle
	Scrum	Half-back, ball into scrum
2	Passing	Flick
	Passing	Catching
	Kicking	Punt kick
3	Kicking	Place kick, torpedo
	Throwing in	Two-handed
4	Kicking	Punt kick up-and-under
	Catching	A high ball
	Scrum	Body position and grip
5	Running	Fending
	Tackling	Rear tackle
6	Passing	Standing (half-back)
	Passing	Catching
7	Running	Side-stepping
	Passing	Dive (half-back)
8	Running	Change of pace
	Tackling	Frontal tackle
	Kicking	Spiral, also with left foot
9	Passing	Swing
	Kicking	Grubber kick
10	Tackling	Smother tackle
	Kicking	Place kick straight up-and-down
11	Running	Dummy
	Kicking	Pop kick, also with left foot
12	Maul	Ripping a ball clear
	Jumping	For line-out height
13	Kicking	Stab, sliding ball
	Running	Push-off
14	Kicking	Drop kick
	Kicking	Dribbling
15	Running	Bumping
	Kicking	Place kick round the corner
16	Passing	Soft, peripheral
	Tackling	Side-on tackle

Played for Athletic, Levin 1936-40; life member of that club. Represented Horowhenua seniors 1939-40; member and selector of the Horowhenua Rugby Union 1943-45. Selector-coach Rongotai 1947-55; Onslow College 1955-67; Wellington secondary schools 1971-74. Under-18 selector Regional team Wellington RFU 1972-74. Selector-coach for the Centurion Colts 1969-74.

17	Catching	A rolling ball
	Rush-stopping	Falling on a ball
18	Catching	Taking a mark
	Kicking	Punt kick low into wind
19	Running	Swerve, (winger) in and out
	Passing	Swing, with a dummy
20	Kicking	Drop kick with left foot
	Tackling	Frontal tackle
21	Kicking	Punt kick up-and-under
	Catching	A mark
	Kicking	Centre kick
22	Running	Side-step, in/out, pass
	Passing	Swing
23	Passing	Reverse (half-back)
	Tackling	Rear tackle
24	Running	Change of pace, then pass
	Tackling	Smother tackles
	Kicking	Place kick straight up-and-down
25	Throwing in	Overarm
	Kicking	Drop kick, grubber
26	Kicking	Into a space
	Passing	Reverse (for a back)
27	Running	Ball held out in two hands
	Passing	Smuggle pass in a maul
28	Throwing in	Spiral
	Passing	Swing, lobbed
	Kicking	Dropout
29	Kicking	Place kick, torpedo
	Kicking	For a kick-off
30	Scrums and rucks	Body position
		Feet positions
		Grip
31	Kicking	Tap kick, for free kick
	Throwing in	Spiral
32	Passing	Scissors
	Running	Breaking a tackle
33	Passing	Pivot (half-back)
	Passing	Standing spiral (half-back)
		Overhead
		Skip pass
34	Jumping	Line-out, guided ball
	Rucks	In close-quarter situations controlling and moving the ball with the feet

Passing: Australian scrum-half and Wallaby captain John Hipwell passing.   Col Whelan

The skills

	Session No.
Running	
Swerving	1, 19
Change of pace	8, 24
Side-stepping	7, 22
Dummy	11
Fending	5
Push-off	13
Bumping	15
Breaking a tackle	32
Ball held out in two hands	27
Passing	
Flick	2, 28
Swing	9, 19, 22, 28
Short, soft, peripheral	16
Lobbed, option	28
Scissors	32
Smuggle	27
Overhead	33
Skip	33
Half-back passing	
Standing	6
Standing spiral (half-back)	33
Dive, spiral	7
Pivot	33
Reverse	23, 26
Catching	
A pass	2, 6
A high ball	4
Taking a mark	18, 21
A rolling ball	17
Kicking	
Punting, spiral	2, 8
Punting, up-and-under	4, 21
Punting, low into wind	18
Punting, centre	21
Punting, into a space	26
Punting, tap for a free kick	31
Punting, pop, to retrieve	11
Grubber	9, 25
Stab, sliding	13
Dribbling	14
Drop kick	14
Drop kick, left foot	20
Place kick, straight up-and-down	10, 24
Place kick, torpedo	3, 29
Place kick, round the corner	15
Place kick, kick-off	29
Kicking, dropout	28
Tackling	
Side-on tackle	1, 16
Rear tackle	5, 23
Frontal tackle	8, 20
Smother tackles	10, 24

Skills from set play

	Session No.
Line-out	
Throwing in, two-handed	3
Throwing in, overarm	25
Throwing in, spiral	28, 31
Jumping	12, 34
Scrum	
Half-back putting ball in	1
Forwards' body position	4, 30
Forwards' hand grip	4, 30
Forwards' feet position	30
Ruck	
In close-quarter situations, controlling and moving the ball with the feet	34
Maul	
Ripping a ball clear	12
Turning a man in a tackle	12
Rush-stopping	
Falling on a ball	17

Kicking: M. A. Van Den Berg, Western Province, at South Africa v New Zealand First Test, Athletic Park, Wellington, 1937.

Evening Post

Catching: taking a mark. North Island v South Island match.
Evening Post

Scott A. G. M. Crawford on

Skills from other Sports

- **Today's rugby player looks for total involvement in the game, and to achieve this a wide range of skills is required.**
- **From basketball: additional ball-handling, passing and jumping skills, the philosophy of retaining possession of the ball, and the use of peripheral vision.**
- **From gridiron: aggressive running and tackling, pin-point accuracy in kicking and torpedo passing, and a thorough understanding of the ploys involved.**
- **From soccer: the grid system in practices, ball control during dribbling, and a greater use of planned moves for the free kick.**
- **From baseball, rugby league and wrestling: many elements of skills useful to a rugby player.**
- **A rugby coach with forethought and planning will select the most appropriate elements from other sports and use these methods and skills in coaching to provide increased skill and greater success and enjoyment for the players.**

In many ways rugby is a unique sporting activity. It is a contact-collision pursuit with a reliance on three major properties of movement: running, kicking, and catching/handling. The body can be used offensively and defensively, and increasingly every forward must be able to play like a three-quarter and vice versa. The traditional stereotyped notions of forwards and backs has been transformed into the training, conditioning, preparing and educating of 15 players to have the complete repertoire of skills so that 'intelligent action' rather than sheer brawn can win matches.

Contemporary training often has neglected the contribution that certain aspects of other sports can make to rugby coaching. Exciting innovations, techniques, strategies, research, training practices, philosophies, and other facets of play are found in many sports. Basketball, gridiron and soccer in particular are of major benefit, but useful tips can also come from less likely sources.

Basketball

In the early 1960s Scotland was fortunate to have in Pringle Fisher not only a lively and speedy flanker but also a great jumper at the back of the line-out. I remember vividly his soaring jumps on the Murrayfield ground either to take the ball confidently in his two hands or to tap the ball down accurately to a supporting forward or a fast-moving half-back. He was also an international basketball representative.

More recently the All Blacks have made use of basketball matches as both warm-up activity and as the lead-in to skill practice session.

What can we learn from basketball? Let us look at some basketball techniques: rebounding, and the pro pass, that is, the two-handed overhead pass — a basic basketball concept (peripheral vision at all times); the incidence of 'turnovers' in basketball (that is, when your team loses possession of the ball before they have made a possible scoring basket), and the operation of 'zone defence'.

Rebounding

Rebounding in basketball occurs when the defensive player takes off the ground, goes high and 'clears the boards' before setting an offensive play pattern in motion. The *Rothmans (N.Z.) Basketball Manual* advises:

- Be aggressive underneath the basketball board.
- Don't be afraid to use your weight (legally).
- Take up as much room as possible, keeping your elbows out and up and your tail out.
- Time your jump, leaping as high as you can with both hands fully extended.
- Leap into or towards the ball, not straight up.
- Grab the ball authoritatively and bring it down under the chin as quickly as possible.
- Keep elbows out and tail protruding.

Indeed, basketball is a non-contact sport, but these five points, with suitable modifications, are in fact prescriptions for props, locks or back-row players in a line-out. The rugby game does create real problems for the jumper — the player is not jumping in isolation, and is buffeted, and bumped and has to fight rival jumpers for possession of the ball. Moreover if a jumper over-stresses the leap towards the ball (not straight up), he may be penalised for barging.

Nevertheless these are valuable points: be aggressive, keep the 'tail' out, both hands fully extending, and grab the ball authoritatively.

Indoor practice sessions should include 'rebounding' exercises for forwards. In one exercise a forward stands under a basketball board and the ball (a rugby ball) is 'torpedoed' against the board. The player must then leap high to snatch the ball. To make the exercise more challenging, passive or static 'opponents' can be introduced, then active 'opponents'. Experiment also with an *accurate* one-handed tap-down pass. Such drills can improve a jumper's explosive vertical lift.

The great Russian high jumper Brumel could accomplish a Sargent jump of more than 1 metre. A Sargent jump is one of the oldest yet most useful physical education tests. An athlete chalks his fingertips and, standing parallel to a high

Lion Terry Cobner dribbles the ball through, soccer-style, in the Third Test, Lions v New Zealand, 1977. Cobner's first school sport was soccer. Being able to dribble the ball fast and in a controlled fashion is a useful skill for the rugby player.
Scott A. G. M. Crawford

For many years Scott Crawford has been involved with physical education. He has played and coached rugby in Scotland, England, the West Indies and the United States. He is a senior lecturer in Sports Studies at the School of Physical Education at Otago University. Currently he is researching New Zealand sports history — his particular interest.

wall, reaches up and rubs the fingertips on the wall. He then jumps as high as he can and makes a second fingertip mark at the peak of the jump. A measurement is then made (from first chalk mark to second) to find the effective height of the leap. Coaches should make use of rebounding drill *and* the Sargent test to train mechanically effective jumpers. There is little point in having a 2 metre (6 ft 6 in) lock if his vertical lift-off is minimal.

The pro basketball pass

After rebounding, a good basketballer covers the caught ball with maximum protection and screening. Again this also is required in rugby. A successful jumper forms his wedge, is supported by other forwards to consolidate the V formation and then releases the good ball back on cue for the half-back — Gordon Brown often did this for the 1977 Lions in New Zealand. In rugby the usual pass is the swing or 'arm flick' pass — generally the quickest and safest method of transferring the ball. When the flanker takes the ball and bursts round the tail of the line-out there is some support but also much opposition traffic. One saving technique is the pro basketball pass whereby the momentum of the movement is continued with a two-handed overhead pass. The ball-carrier raises the ball high, commits the tacklers and passes the ball down to the supporting player who is driving through. This isn't an ideal pass — the ball is away from the body and therefore vulnerable. However, the great French teams of the 1960s popularised the wheel from the back of the line and much of their passing was of this variety. Paradoxically the pass that Bruce Robertson gave Stu Wilson to score a try for New Zealand in the Second Test against France in 1977 was a modified 'pro basketball pass'. The capacity of rugby players to pass in this way depends very much on the level of their ball-handling skills — skills that can be acquired if coaches are using basketball games to complement their rugby coaching.

Peripheral vision

There is a tendency in rugby for players to have 'channel vision' — they look straight ahead and move accordingly. With peripheral vision an athlete attempts to achieve a field of vision encompassing 180 degrees. He scans constantly so that he knows what is going on in front of him *and* to the left *and* to the right. The former Canterbury half-back, Lyn Davis, is a classic example of a player who exercised peripheral vision all the time. Such vision is of paramount importance on attack so that you, as ball-carrier, know and are aware of the available support. Often a good movement is wasted when the player with the ball has been downed despite sure support on the player's 'blind' side?

'Turnovers'

In basketball ball possession is of tremendous importance. In rugby league the same applies. A 'turnover' yields ball possession without a shot being made on the basket. Basketball coaches and players, however, are so highly skilled and 'turnover'-conscious that such losses of ball possession are rare. This explains why, in most top-level matches, the score is so close. In the controversial U.S.S.R./U.S.A. basketball Olympic final at Munich in 1972 Russia won 51-50. The results stay close because possession equals scores. In rugby, obviously, so much more can go wrong after gaining possession of the ball, but coaches should be much more concerned about what is done with the ball. When the Rumanians toured New Zealand in 1975 they played enterprising and attractive rugby, but they also kicked away a prodigious amount of ball possession. In basketball, having the ball should end up with points on the board. Rugby coaches take note.

Zone defence

'Zone defence' means that instead of a man-to-man defence system, certain players accept responsibility for covering certain zones of the playing area.

Rugby has a long history of being a 'one man on one man' sport. Virtually every coaching book emphasises taking out 'your' man. In other words, centre marks centre, and winger marks winger. But if a winger who can run 100 metres in 11 seconds is being marked by a winger who can run 100 metres in 12 seconds, in a one-to-one situation, the faster winger will win every time. To some extent this accounts for the incredible try-scoring performances of the Irishman A.J.F. O'Reilly on the Lions tour of South Africa in 1955. Of more relevance to modern rugby is the excursion into the three-quarter line by the full-back; both Scotland's Andy Irvine and Otago's Bevan Wilson have been successful exponents of this. Whose responsiblity is it to tackle this player?

The 1977 Lions who toured New Zealand failed to use Andy Irvine, the 'Flying Scotsman' successfully in this role in the test matches, but his scoring feats during matches against some of the regional and provincial teams showed that their coaches had not been able to devise a system of 'zone defence'. The message is clear: coaches need to look carefully at this aspect of rugby. If the opposition wins the ball from broken play on your own 22 metre line it is unlikely that the traditional man-to-man defence will always keep the line intact.

Gridiron

The two games of rugby and U.S. gridiron football are for some wholly incompatible. U.S. football has two units, one defensive, the other offensive; it has many of the plays called by the touch line coach, and it has a squad of referees. However, in five respects our rugby teaching/coaching could be greatly improved by drawing on the experiences of U.S. football: tackling, explosive running, short-distance speed, the torpedo pass and running.

Tackling

In rugby the tackler is still considered a defensive player: the ball-carrier as the stronger position. The aim of the tackler is to stop the attacker. It is not unusual in school teaching situations to see the tackler looking nervous and apprehensive while the ball-carrier is 'raring to go'.

The American game of gridiron refutes this one-sided notion. The ball-carrier is there to be hit and the tackler is taught repeatedly in drills that he must launch himself at the runner. The tackler has two hands to attack the runner, while the runner has the ball to protect. Not only does the tackler train to drive 'through' the opponent, but he also scores points if he can break the ball loose. In other words, the tackle is a chance to stop the opposition and if this collision is forceful enough the ball will break loose and be possessed by the fastest back-up player to the breakdown.

Players of the U.S. game have a useful training in variations on a heavy padded sledge, which is easily transported, with a suspended contraption like a punch bag. Their coach can take up position on the sledge and watch the players as they accelerate in and tackle the surrogate target. Perhaps it is time rugby considered the tackle as an opportunity to gain possession.

Explosive running

Rugby and U.S. football are running games. Frequently in U.S. football, however, the running back with the ball in the first few metres is a desperate attempt to gain the advantage line. The swerve, feint and side-step may beat one opponent but will reduce the ball-carrier's chance of gaining distance, and the heavy press of opponents may mean that the ball-carrier does not reach the advantage line unless the player is an explosive runner, with such an exaggerted knee-lift that even a committed tackler can be run over. In practice sessions drills should be at sprinting speed over tractor tyres and low hurdles. The driving thighs are conditioned to prepare themselves for crashing through a weak or poorly conceived tackle. The gridiron player realises that in broken-play running, an assortment of skills must be deployed, including the swerve, side-step and dummy, but the player also has that ability to break a tackle by swift and direct running.

Short-distance speed

The U.S. football coach, like the rugby coach, wants an athlete who can kick far and accurately, or pass with precision, or tackle tenaciously. Yet the final criterion for players, even for defensive players, is their speed over 36 metres (40 yards). This distance is arbitrary, the emphasis being upon speed over the short distance — speed for forwards as well as for backs.

In rugby coaching, particularly at school level, physical education teachers often promote running repetitions over the distance of the pitch — stamina inducing but not designed to create that burst of match-winning speed. In top-level U.S. football, while height over 2 metres (6 ft 6 in) is a bonus and 'forwards' like to weigh more than 115 kg (18 st), *the* area of evaluation is the player's speed over 36 metres. In our rugby teaching, are we looking for height, strength, stamina or speed?

The torpedo pass

Perhaps the greatest contribution that U.S. football can make to rugby is the torpedo pass. The torpedo pass can be construed as a negative manoeuvre, as it is lateral and does not in itself advance the play. Nevertheless it has numerous advantages. For example, the line-out area is one of congestion — with often twenty players, including scrum-halves and wings. Why is the ball always returned to this busy section at the line-out throw-in?

A long throw to the centre of the pitch would be statistically unsuspected, and the offensive players would be operating with room to spare. Its essence is effective teaching of the torpedo pass at an early age.

The torpedo pass has other merits. Expertly executed, it will mean that the hooker can throw to a team-mate with precision instead of the optimistic, speculative lob which too often passes for a line-out throw-in. In the hands of the imaginative player, particularly after the 'run' penalty or in broken play, it can change dramatically the direction of attack.

The emphasis on running

In U.S. football the idea of the game is to advance the ball, and there are three opportunities to move the ball forward every 10 metres. If the ball is not moved 10 metres the last resort is to kick the ball deep into the opponents' territory. Naturally, from this the opponents have possession and they now try to move the ball upfield in running or throwing plays. Therefore, to kick is to admit that every other course has been tried and has failed.

By all means capitalise on a superb kicker — otherwise run the ball at the opposition. In U.S. football, the cry is 'run, run, run' — and then kick.

In essence, then, rugby and U.S. football may be worlds apart, but in the areas of the tackle, player speed, the torpedo pass, and emphasis on 'run it, not kick it', perhaps one game can benefit the other.

Scientific study of the game

The extensive scientific study of gridiron in the U.S.A. may result in a game that is less intuitive and less dependent on initiative and instinct, but there is no question that the Americans have made lasting contributions to the improvement of their national pastime.

When the 1977 Lions toured New Zealand considerable amazement was expressed at the round-the-corner or soccer-style of kicking used by Andy Irvine. Diehards shook their heads and swore that Bob Scott or Don Clarke never had to resort to such 'impractical' ways. And, of course, Scott and Clarke were outstanding kickers. As a youngster in a Scottish village in 1959 I still remember the chagrin of picking up a London newspaper and seeing the headline 'Clarke 18 — British Lions 17'. But the point is that Irvine consistently kicked points, often from an awkward angle and off heavy and muddy playing surfaces.

A valuable article on the technique of an adopted soccer-style kick appeared in the American publication *Athletic Journal* in 1977. Author George Colfer made the following points in his definitive study. (Colfer is discussing the procedures used by star U.S. college kicker, Tony Franklin.)

Angle of Tilt on the Placed Ball: While most place kickers tilt the top of the ball back from the kick at an angle of about 12 to 15 degress, Franklin has the ball mounted straight up with no angle of tilt at all. He feels this increased his contact surface with the ball and increases the initial velocity of the kick. The lacing of the ball is pointed straight ahead in the direction of the kick.

Steps in Approach: The approach consists of a short stutter step backwards with the left foot and a full step with the right foot; the left foot then takes a full step and is firmly planted a few centimetres behind the ball. The entire approach is a one-half step backwards and three steps into the kick. The stutter step appears to aid Tony in achieving body momentum.

Path of Approach: The path of approach to the ball is curvilinear. The angle to the approach is dependent on place on the field of play. However, the steps remain the same and the ball is kicked in a straight line direction. The kicking leg travels about 245 degrees from flexion of the lower leg to follow-through.

Position of Foot at Contact: The kicking foot is in a plantarflexed position. The position of the foot remains constant throughout the kick.

Point of Contact on the Foot: Contact is initially made on the anterio-medial aspect of the first metatarsal which upon initial contact offers greater impact of the kicking foot and depresses the ball allowing increased foot surface contact with the ball. This in turn appears to increase initial velocity as well as accuracy of the kick.

Body Position at Contact: At contact, there is a distinct backward lean of the upper torso, while the lower torso is past the centre of body gravity. Using the hips as the vertical midline of the body, the angle of the upper and lower torso is about 25 degrees behind and forward of this point. This is known as bilateral symmetry and is important as a balance factor in obtaining full power on the kick as well as equalizing the gravity point of the body.

Angle of Projection: Franklin launches the ball at 29-30 degrees. Other soccer-style kickers might launch the ball between 25-30 degrees.

Follow-through: An important factor is the position of the head. It is kept down until the kicking leg is lowered. It is a most important coaching point that the kicker keep his head down until the maximum height of the kicking leg is reached during the follow-through.

You may think this is excessive discussion about kicking a ball. But this systematic research can enable kickers to develop precision kicking and consistently kick goals instead of missing them.

Soccer

Two aspects (among many) of the soccer player's training can be advantageous in rugby: the training grid, and individual fitness/conditioning prescriptions.

The training grid

A full-sized rugby field is marked out with a grid to give eight working areas, each approximately 22 x 28 metres. Each area provides adequate space for four players to work in, thus accommodating players in eight groups. When I coached in the Bahamas we marked out such a grid with large, empty milk-shake cups — easily seen, but not dangerous if a player fell on them.

Within each area of the grid the four players practise a skill under pressure — doing things correctly and quickly in a small area. For example, the four players in area A would practise passing.

Areas of the grid can be combined for work with larger groups. For example, a game of mini-rugby can be played on areas A, B, C and D by players from A and B versus players from C and D.

Again with the emphasis of doing things correctly and quickly in a small area, larger groups can use one 22 x 28 metre area for drills. In one such drill four players stand within the grid area each holding a tackling bag made of jute material containing 30 kg (80 lb) of sawdust. Each tackler's aim is to sprint to the first tackling bag, knock it down, sprint to the second bag, knock it down, then the third, and the fouth, in the shortest possible time. Later the practice is made more realistic by having the 'tackling bags' move about.

This next example draws on a training device of 1974-80 All Black selector Eric Watson. Here the forward pack practises rucking. Four tackling bags are placed on the ground, each with a ball beyond it. Three players act as an opposition front row, standing by the first tackling bag and facing away from the forward pack being coached. On a whistle blast the pack sprints to the first tackling bag and drives the ball back over the tackling bag to a half-back who spins the ball out. The three players who provided an opposition's 'resistance' then sprint to the second bag and set up a second three-man target. The pack then races over and rucks the ball back, then to the third bag, and so on.

These examples of tackling and of rucking in just two of the 22 x 28 metre areas give some idea of the possible scope of training in an eight-area grid. The slogan again — *skill under pressure*.

The training grid — the field is divided into eight areas for practising different skills

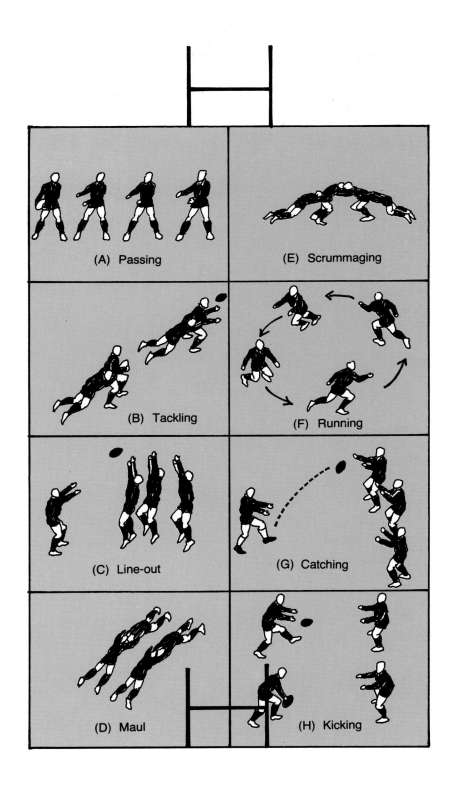

(A) Passing

(E) Scrummaging

(B) Tackling

(F) Running

(C) Line-out

(G) Catching

(D) Maul

(H) Kicking

Fundamentals of training — tackling practice for the NZ All Blacks.
Peter Bush

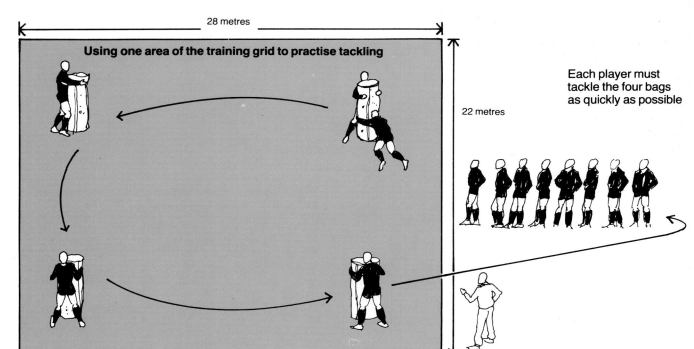

Using one area of the training grid to practise tackling

28 metres

22 metres

Each player must tackle the four bags as quickly as possible

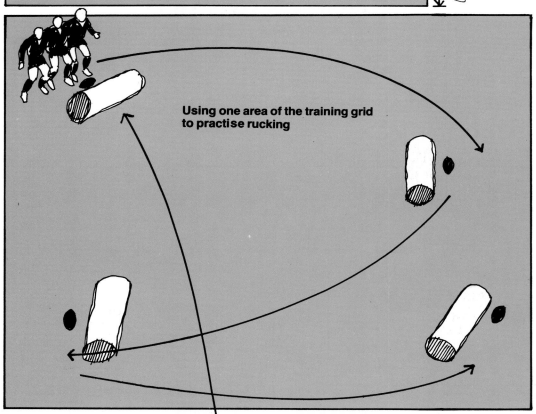

Using one area of the training grid to practise rucking

Forward packs practise rucking over the tackling bags and against a three-man 'opposition' target.

The 'rugby-base' game — practising skills on a baseball diamond with a rugby ball

Only two passes
may be used:
the torpedo pass,
and the 'sweep-spin'
half-back clearing
pass

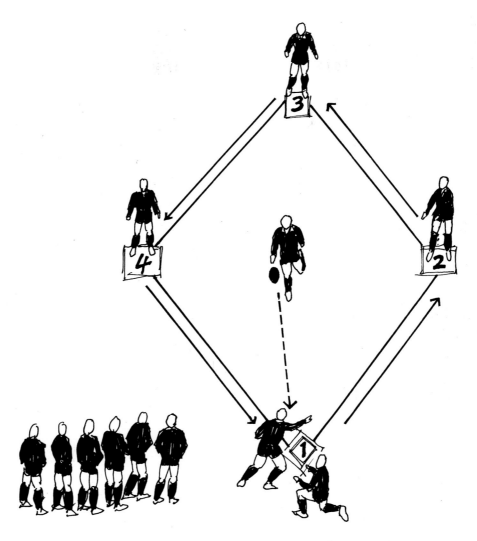

Performance analysis with video

For too long rugby coaches have tried to create fit rugby fifteens by a training philosophy of 'Let's all get stuck in, lads'. Prop forwards are not long-distance runners like New Zealander John Walker, and to attempt to train them accordingly is madness.

Two English researchers in 1976 used video to record and then analyse the work-rate of players in different positional roles in professional soccer match play. As could be expected, they found considerable difference in how far and fast various players moved. Similar work-rate difference must surely also show up in rugby. From video-analyses of rugby games a coach would know, firstly, what a player has to do, and therefore, secondly, how to scientifically condition the player for the special demands of that role.

Video, used for many years in the U.S.A. with gridiron, is now being used in soccer, and more recently, in rugby, but much more remains to be done. In an interview in 1977 Scottish rugby coach Bill Dickinson, an acknowledged rugby exponent, discussed some of his research:

> In a four-year ongoing study of rugby, in the broadest possible terms the game breaks itself up into somewhere around 120-150 pieces of activity. These pieces of activity

vary in duration from about 5 seconds, some under 10 seconds, some under 15 seconds, a good few about 20 seconds and a very small number over 30 to 40/45/50 seconds . . .

It places (as we are looking at this from the fitness point of view) a big stress on anaerobic work. We are going to be dealing with activity of high intensity over periods of 5-8 seconds. If we start to look at some individual positions we would find that a full-back runs about 2¼ miles [3.5 kilometres] in an international football game. Of which he does about 1100 yards [1000 metres] at full-speed. A scrum-half half-back runs about 4 miles [6 kilometres] of which he does one mile [1.6 kilometres] at full speed . . . and a prop forward runs about 4 miles too, and he does about a mile at full speed. If you look at a prop forward in a club game, he runs just over 3 miles [4.5 kilometres] but he very often doesn't do 200 metres at full speed . . .

If you start to look at the game (before we had the limitations on kicking), the ball was in play on an average of 14 minutes and in some games as little as 11 minutes. That was in the days of the 'war of attrition' down the touch line. . . On an average now the actual 'playing time' is 27-28 minutes. . . a different ball-game. And, it requires

251

certainly different physical levels. There are now about 40 scrums in a game and coming on for 60 line-outs. And, about 70 mauls and rucks. That would be so because the game is more fluid. It is not going to be tied to the touchline. Now, many of the stoppages are going to be 'temporary arrested stoppages' in the middle of the field in what is known as second phase-play. Now, all this gives us a fair picture of what we have to concentrate on. Line-outs are vitally important — so are scrums, so are rucks and mauls . . . these possession phases of the game require a lot of attention.

Obviously too if you start to look at physical requirements you start to wonder why you are running 5 or 6 miles [7-8 kilometres] or (as coach) sending someone out for a 40 minute jog. What comes out of this is that there is an endurance factor in the game. But that endurance factor wants to be achieved with the minimal expenditure of time on distance running. We need something of high quality work because we want to produce runs of short duration time after time, after time. We have to build up lactic acid tolerance somewhere . . . Even long scrums only last about 30 seconds . . .

. . . in such a situation . . . men must be able to harness their resources very quickly and explosively. They must be a cohesive unit because the mis-timing of the first shove and that is the scrummage finished. It also indicates the tremendous demands that are placed particularly on the front five who have all this power work to do. They are often the second wave in the ruck and maul, where they have to drive over the top or dig out the ball from the maul with their arms and shoulders, and yet they also have this movement across the field from line-out to line-out and then back and covering . . . With so many line-outs (looking at the skill phases) it is vitally important that the throwing and catching and support play is of high value.

From all of this you are now starting to look at the game either from a playing point-of-view and seeing where specific emphases can be placed, or you are looking at it from a fitness point-of-view. This tends to make practices and training programmes pertinent to the particular group that you are operating with . . . For example, not so long ago some of us at a coaching conference in Scotland were advocating the two-handed catch in the line-out. Then when we started to examine international match films we found it 'raised the roof' if you got one caught ball! This is not the inability of the individual to catch the ball, it is because other people don't let you catch it! So it becomes expedient to deflect the ball.

Looking at rugby in this way has given me information which certainly at international level allows me to switch on a piece of film and say, "There it is lads — you make your comments."

Pre-arranged moves after penalties

One other aspect of soccer worth mentioning is the free kick in a potential scoring situation. In rugby the law changes have made the tap penalty much more common, and coaches should drill players so that the team has at least three pre-arranged moves that can be implemented. In soccer the free kick can be a complicated manoeuvre, with dummy moves, decoys, floating personnel, and short passes leading up to the attacking shot. Such set-ups require intense concentration, discipline and practice. The same should apply in the preparation for each run penalty in rugby. Both the Wallabies and the Irish Universities players during tours of New Zealand in 1978 showed imagination and flair in 'run' tap penalties.

Drawing on other sports

The innovative coach should examine any sport that can benefit rugby play. Wrestling, for instance, can benefit mauling, the emphasis being on wrestling the ball free from the opposition.

U.S.A. Amateur wrestling coach Dave Long, who toured New Zealand in July 1978, considers gridiron and rugby to be similar. He observes that almost 50 per cent of his wrestlers play gridiron and feels that the strength, skills and mental-set (a combination of aggression, discipline and intelligence) derived from wrestling have a positive influence on gridiron. If rugby players had opportunities for acquiring wrestling expertise he feels they would know how to break the ball loose, quickly and more effectively in the maul situation. In gridiron often the good hard-hitting tackler (in the head-on tackle) moves body and arms quickly to get 'in and under' the offensive players' fend or shoulder charge. This, he says, is exactly what has to happen in wrestling.

Dave Long also focuses on 'mental conditioning'. He stresses that near the end of a work-out when athletes are exhausted and irritated — in essence, at 'breaking point' — he teaches the athletes 'fair play', an element Dave Long considers as important as winning. Whatever the extent of crowd harassment or provocation or even deliberate fouling, 'stay cool'. Wrestle legally at all times, respect the decision of the official, never question any decision, and at the end of a contest always shake hands with your opponent.

It may be heretical to assert that we can learn something from rugby league, but particularly the notion of the two-man tackle (accepting that our team is operating an effective zone defence) should be considered. A heavy prop running strongly with a few metres to go takes some stopping.

What of the basic strategies of even seven-a-side rugby? Here the tactic (at least the style of play traditionally seen at the Middlesex Sevens Tournament) is to repeatedly move the ball laterally until an overlap strike is 'on'. Most coaches would be scornful of such a style of play. But if the opponents are massive and strong scrummagers but neither fast nor mobile, then such lateral movements while not advancing the ball territorially would tax the stamina of the opposition. A mobile and intelligent All Black pack was responsible for winning the Second Test against the French in 1977.

Using the configuration of a baseball diamond and the location of bases can provide an effective warm-up activity for rugby players as well as giving them a chance to consolidate skills. We can use the basic rules of baseball but adapt the playing implements.

The hooker in team A acts as pitcher and, using a torpedo pass (good practice for the hooker), 'fires' the ball at team B's first player who stands at home base. The team B player 'bats' the ball with a clenched fist into the playing area of the diamond, and then has to sprint to attempt to reach the second base before being tagged by a member of team A. Players in team A are allowed to use only two passes: the torpedo pass or the 'sweep-spin' half-back clearing pass.

A game like this provides enjoyment and light relief from rugby drills. But (and here is the big bonus of such a 'rugby-base' game) the players are getting practice in using two skills under pressure: accurate and fast passing, and quick acceleration over a short distance.

Equipment

I played rugby for four years in the U.S.A on hard pitches frozen by winter winds and two years in the West Indies on hard pitches baked by scorching heat. By using sponge volleyball knee guards and elbow guards, I was able to avoid irritating and painful knee and arm abrasions.

In the 1978 World Cup the goalkeepers wore very sophisticated gloves, which are ultra-sensitive and have a pimpled rubber surface that helps to make the ball cling to the fingertips. A possibility for rugby half-backs, especially in wet weather.

Watching Gerald Davies play firmly has convinced me that rugby is the best game in the world. Nevertheless, by drawing on the happenings, resources and techniques of many other sports, the game of rugby can certainly be improved.

At half time Wallaby captain Tony Shaw tells the Wallabies what is expected of them. Wallabies v All Blacks, Eden Park 1978. In this game Wallaby Greg Cornelsen scored a memorable record four tries.

Peter Bush

253

Dr William Treadwell on

Sports Medicine

For many years medical officers who had been appointed as Honorary Medical Officers for individual rugby clubs could do little to assist injured players. This situation resulted from lack of facilities and often the doctor's inadequate knowledge of soft tissue injuries. Generally the player was advised to rest or cease playing for a period of time, or if the injury was a severe one, to stop playing altogether. A major injury to a shoulder, knee or ankle could mean that a player would be out of action for the whole of the season. Often the player called to see the doctor some days or even weeks after the injury occurred because he could not afford the treatment — he was dependent on reimbursement from various insurance schemes or other funding. Frequently he stopped his medical treatment prematurely, before he was completely recovered and was left with residual or chronic problems.

Some years ago, however, doctors, physiotherapists, physical educationists and other people interested in the treatment of rugby players, and especially the preventative aspect of sports medicine, started to share their knowledge and take an interest in the whole well-being of the player. No longer were they treating just the acute injury, but were giving advice on pre-season build up, the psychology of physiology of pre-match build up and the methods of preventing injury. The players therefore no longer had to fear the consequences of injury.

The growth of Sports Medicine

Sports medicine started to expand in New Zealand, local regional groups developed and the parent body, the NZ Federation of Sports Medicine, was formed in 1965 and has continued to grow. Now there are many people associated with the overall care of the rugby player. Rugby clubs, and especially the coaches, have begun to realise how much the application of sports medicine principles can affect a game and maintain the well-being of players.

Time and motion studies have been carried out and applied to the principles of training, particularly in pre-season training. Other progress has been made through the use of better footwear, understanding of the application of strapping and the necessary techniques to be used. First aid was improved; for example, the use of ice, or cryotherapy, to control swelling, and compression and elevation immediately a player left the field with a soft tissue injury.

Rugby players, referees, and St John Ambulance personnel have been made much more aware of the need for special care in many situations, for example, when there is the possibility that the player has injured his spinal cord, special care is needed when moving the player off the field.

The Accident Compensation Act

On 1 April 1974 the Accident Compensation Act came into effect in New Zealand and it has given some impetus to Sports Medicine. From 1.4.74 the Act has enabled any injured person to see a doctor or physiotherapist without fear of the expense of the treatment, and be examined and later treated with the best methods available. If treatment requires the use of radiology, or physiotherapy or any ancillary method to cure or to treat the injury, then this is to be freely available. Rugby players, therefore, can continue treatment without financial barriers and thus make a complete recovery.

Injuries — treatment and prevention

Sports Medicine now has accepted a responsibility towards rugby players and other contact sports. It conducts surveys on rugby players to determine the most common forms of injury and how best these can be treated or, if possible, prevented. Injuries to the shoulder are fairly common in rugby, and there have been changes in the principles applied to their treatment, particularly with the more minor dislocations around the collar bone and the shoulder. In the past the player was immobilised for a period of several weeks, but now the patient is encouraged to have more active movement at an earlier stage. The emphasis is on increased mobility, so that the joint heals as a freely moving, well-functioning joint.

The more serious injuries such as head injuries with loss of consciousness require firm treatment and directives from Sports Medicine. It may be necessary to stop a player from returning to the game if he has had a serious head injury or recurrent head injuries — no sport is worth permanent brain damage.

Sports Medicine is refined to study injuries to the spinal cord and to determine whether there is any common causative pattern and if so, to make recommendations on how these injuries can be prevented.

It is a matter of concern however, that despite all this inquiry and study, some injuries appear to be on the increase, for example hamstring injuries and injuries to the calf muscle — and these injuries amongst players who appear to be fit or have been playing for some weeks. New treatments and investigations are thus required to meet all cases of injury, but even with this study rugby players still have to be made aware of simple needs such as an adequate warm-up, and also be made to understand the principles behind stretching the muscles and of keeping the body warm during an interval or break in play.

Sports Medicine must make the rugby player a party to any major health or fitness decision, and in addition must decide on the importance of diet in the training programme. There is more of a partnership therefore, between Sports Medicine and the rugby player and the rugby coach or administrator.

Dr Bill Treadwell helping Chris Laidlaw off the field. The decision about leaving the field can only be made by the captain. In this match against the Springboks, Laidlaw captained NZ Universities. He opted to play on, drop-kicked a goal and collapsed.
Ray Pigney/NZ Newspapers

Wayne Cottrell being taken off the field, South Africa 1970.
Ray Pigney/NZ Newspapers

Selected bibliography

Physical fitness and sports medicine

Corrigan, Brian, & Morton, Alan. *Get Fit the Champions' Way.* Souvenir Press, 1968

Doherty, J. K. *Modern Training for Running.* Prentice-Hall, 1964

Kirkley, G., & Goodbody, J. *The Manual of Weight Training.* Stanley Paul, 1970

Knapp, B. *Skill in Sport.* Routledge & Kegan Paul, 1963

Lindsey, Ruth, & Tolson, Homer. *Concepts in Physical Education.* Wm C. Brown, 1974

Lydiard, Arthur. *Run to the Top.* A. H. & A. W. Reed, 1962

Lydiard, Arthur, with Gilmour, Garth. *Run the Lydiard Way.* Hodder & Stoughton, 1978

Stokes, Peter. *Rugby and Sports Medicine.* Alistair Taylor, 1973

Thomas, Vaughan. *Exercise Physiology.* Crosby, Woodward & Staples, 1975

Watson, Bill. *Agility Fitness.* Stanley Paul, 1963

Coaching

Allen, Fred, with McLean, T. P. *Fred Allen on Rugby.* Cassell, 1970

Craven, Danie. *On Rugby.* R. Beerman, 1952

———— *Rugby Handbook.* 1969

van Heerden, Izak. *Tactical and Attacking Rugby.* Herbert Jenkins, 1967

Higham, E. S. & Higham, W. G. *High Speed Rugby.* Heinemann, 1960

Jarden, Ron. *Rugby on Attack.* Whitcombe & Tombs, 1961

New Zealand Rugby Football Union. *National Junior Coaching School 1972.* N.Z. Rugby Football Union, 1972

Reason, John (ed.). *The Lions Speak.* Rugby Books, 1972

Rugby Football Union. *The Manual of Rugby Union Football* (U.K.). Rugby Football Union, 1952

Rutherford, Don. *Rugby for Coach and Player.* Barker, 1971

Saxton, C. K. *The ABC of Rugby.* N.Z. Rugby Football Union, 1973

Scott, Bob, with McLean, T. P. *On Rugby.* Kaye, 1955

Wallace, Jim. *The Rugby Game.* A. H. & A. W. Reed, 1976

Williams, Gerwyn. *Tackle Rugger This Way.* Stanley Paul, 1957

———— *Modern Rugby.* A. H. & A. W. Reed, 1964

Williams, Ray. *Skilful Rugby.* Souvenir Press, 1976

Rugby history, major tours and players

Booth, Pat, & Clarke, D. B. *The Boot: Don Clarke's Story.* A. H. & A. W. Reed, 1966

Chester, R. H., & McMillan, N. A. C. *Men in Black.* Moa Publications, 1978

———— *The Encyclopedia of New Zealand Rugby.* Moa Publications, 1981

Craven, D. H. *Springboks Down the Years.* A. H. & A. W. Reed, 1954

———— *Springbok Story.* A. H. & A. W. Reed, 1956

Donoghue, Paul. *Rugby versus Rommel.* 2NZEF Rugby Reunion, 1961

Jenkins, Vivian. *Lions Rampant.* Cassell, 1956

———— *Lions Down Under.* Cassell, 1960

Howitt, R. J. *New Zealand Rugby Greats.* Moa Publications, 1975

———— *Grant Batty.* Rugby Press, 1977

Knox, Ray (ed.) *New Zealand's Heritage.* Paul Hamlyn Limited, 1971

Lalanne, Denis. *The All Blacks Juggernaut in South Africa.* Tafelberg-Vitgeivers, 1960

———— *The Great Flight of the French XV.* A. H. & A. W. Reed, 1960

———— *La Melee Fantastique.* A. H. & A. W. Reed, 1962

McCarthy, Winston. *Broadcasting with the Kiwis.* Sporting Publications & A. H. & A. W. Reed, 1947

———— *Fifty Years of the All Blacks.* Phoenix, 1954

———— *Haka! The All Blacks Story.* Pelham Books, 1968

McLean, T. P. *Bob Stuart's All Blacks.* A. H. & A. W. Reed, 1954

———— *The Battle for the Rugby Crown.* A. H. & A. W. Reed, 1956

———— *Kings of Rugby.* A. H. & A. W. Reed, 1959

———— *Great Days in New Zealand Rugby.* A. H. & A. W. Reed, 1959

———— *Beaten by the 'Boks.* A. H. & A. W. Reed, 1960

———— *Cock of the Rugby Roost.* A. H. & A. W. Reed, 1961

———— *Willie Away.* A. H. & A. W. Reed, 1964

———— *The 'Bok Busters.* A. H. & A. W. Reed, 1965

———— *The Lion Tamers.* A. H. & A. W. Reed, 1966

———— *All Black Magic.* A. H. & A. W. Reed, 1968

———— *All Black Power.* A. H. & A. W. Reed, 1968

———— *Red Dragons of Rugby.* A. H. & A. W. Reed, 1969

———— *Battling the 'Boks.* A. H. & A. W. Reed, 1970

———— *They Missed the Bus.* A. H. & A. W. Reed, 1973

———— *All Blacks Return.* A. H. & A. W. Reed, 1974

McLean, T. P. With Nepia, George. *I, George Nepia.* A. H. & A. W. Reed, 1963

McLean, T. P. with Scott, Bob. *The Bob Scott Story.* A. H. & A. W. Reed, 1956

Nicholls, M. F. *With the All Blacks in Springbokland 1928.* Wright & Carman, 1936

Oliver, C. J., & Tindill, E. W. *The Tour of the Third All Blacks 1935.* Wright & Carman, 1936

Owen, O. L. *The History of the Rugby Football Union.* Playfair, 1955

Parker, A. C. *Now is the Hour.* Sporting Publications, 1965

Price, Maxwell. *Springboks in the Lions Den.* A. H. & A. W. Reed, 1961

Reyburn, Wallace. *The World of Rugby.* Elek-Lothian, 1967

———— *A History of Rugby.* Garker/Hicks Smith, 1971

Slatter, Gordon. *On the Ball.* Whitcombe & Tombs, 1970

Stent, R. K. *The Fourth Springboks, 1951-52.* Longmans, 1952

Swan, Arthur C. *History of New Zealand Rugby Football,* Vol. 1, 1870-1945. Whitcombe & Tombs, 1958

———— *History of New Zealand Rugby Football,* Vol. 2, 1946-57. Whitcombe & Tombs, 1958

Sweet, Reginald. *The Kiwis Conquer.* Howard Timmins, 1956

Veysey, Alex. *Colin Meads, All Black.* Collins, 1974

———— *Fergie.* Whitcoulls, 1976